Ben Ando has been a BB
In a broadcast career spannin
also worked for ITN, Channel
numerous high-profile crime stories,
killer Levi Bellfield and mass rapist Delro _rant. He has also
covered major national and international events, such as the
war in Kosovo, 9/11, the Space Shuttle *Columbia* disaster, and
the death and funeral of the Princess of Wales.

Nick Kinsella is a former Detective Chief Superintendent
and Assistant Director of the National Criminal Intelligence
Service, who served as a police officer for thirty years, gaining
a first-class law degree from Sheffield University in 1995. In
2006 he founded the United Kingdom Human Trafficking
Centre, and, a year later, a UK-based fund to support victims
of human trafficking. He now works as a trainer and specialist
consultant, advising governments and other bodies around the
world on policy, law and strategy to combat the trafficking of
human beings. He is a recipient of the Queen's Police Medal
and a trustee of the United Nations Global Voluntary Trust
Fund for Victims of Human Trafficking.

Beyond The Call Of Duty

Ben Ando and Nick Kinsella

Constable • London

Constable & Robinson Ltd
55–56 Russell Square
London WC1B 4HP
www.constablerobinson.com

First published in the UK by Constable,
an imprint of Constable & Robinson Ltd, 2013

A copy of the British Library Cataloguing in Publication
Data is available from the British Library

ISBN 978-1-4721-0832-6 (paperback)
ISBN 978-1-4721-0835-7 (ebook)

Printed and bound in the UK

3 5 7 9 10 8 6 4 2

To all serving police officers throughout the
United Kingdom

A small donation from the sale of this book will support the
work of the Police Dependants' Trust

www.pdtrust.org

CONTENTS

FOREWORD
by Sir Hugh Orde

Police officers move towards danger while others walk away. This is, quite simply, 'what we do'.

All those who take the office of constable, whatever subsequent rank they attain, attest to a sense of duty, a commitment to serve communities, a willingness to protect life and property, to keep the peace in full knowledge of the dangers they may face. And every day, police officers up and down the country will routinely put themselves between vulnerable and innocent members of the community and those who seek to do them harm. The overwhelming majority of those interactions will end peacefully, be over in a matter of minutes and subject to little thought thereafter.

Acts of bravery do not always have happy endings, of course, and it's just a fact of the job that our officers, regrettably, will sometime face tragedy in the course of their work. But the stories so vividly told here show that commitment and sense of duty, the willingness to step into harm's way, the instinct to protect, are alive and well in policing.

Within the huge complexity of policing, the situations police officers and staff face range from the exceptional to the commonplace. The link between police and communities is the bedrock of our policing model. With 132,000 (and falling) police officers in England and Wales serving a population of 56 million (and rising), it can be no other way. British policing is built on the notion of the police officer as citizen in uniform, routinely unarmed and making minimal interference with citizens' rights. It is only with the trust, confidence and support of our public that we are able to do the job, prevent and detect crime, and keep the public safe.

Over seven years I had the unique experience of leading the Police Service of Northern Ireland, an organisation full of people who are incredibly proud of the critical service they deliver to the people of Northern Ireland. The situation they face there is unique, but the values they live by and embody through their work are shared across the police family.

During my time there, tragically, Constable Stephen Carroll lost his life, answering an ordinary message for help from a member of the public, on 9 March 2009. Stevie was a Territorial Support Group officer engaged in community policing the night he was murdered. He was working with the local community team who were responding to an urgent call, protecting both his colleagues and the local people when he was shot.

Stephen was one of many officers who die in service, doing the job they love. Constables Fiona Bone and Nicola Hughes, and Constable Ian Dibell – killed intervening to protect the public, despite being off duty – are just three recent examples. I know that none of them will be forgotten by their colleagues.

There were also many acts of daily courage that illustrate

commitment. I recall an officer, resolutely determined to deliver a community service in an area traditionally hostile to the police, who told me he entered a different shop on his beat every single day. His greetings were unacknowledged when he began, but over a period of years he moved to a place where everybody knew his name and gave a response.

The best policing is like this: doing things differently, taking risks, going that extra mile, using discretion – all qualities that are part of the job. Failures can be for many reasons, ranging from complete incompetence through to the unexpected, unpredictable and unknowable. When we get it wrong, we should recognise the facts quickly: we should encourage and be willing to listen and learn from those who wish to engage in policing debate

But we also recognise that successful policing involves accepting risk. It requires individual officers to take responsibility for the actions they make on behalf of the public. The Service will always attract exceptional people who want to do good work – and acts of extraordinary courage will remain a key part of this unique and special profession. These people should be supported, and it is right that their acts of courage are recognised and celebrated.

INTRODUCTION

The phone rang at home. 'It's me, Dad. I'm fine but I'm on my way home. I'll be there in a few minutes. Can you open the back door? I'm a bit wet and need to get a shower and a dry uniform.'

My son Joe, a frontline police officer in Sheffield, had left for work a little over an hour earlier. He'd been in the police for five years at that time, but, like many young people nowadays, was still living at home.

'Is it blood again?' I asked. Only months before his uniform had been soaked in blood when he gave essential first aid to a man who'd been shot in the stomach at point blank range.

'No, not this time,' he said. 'I'll explain when I get in.' Even though his mother had been married to a police officer for over thirty years she never really got used to phone calls like these. No one does. The relaxation of the evening had been shattered and replaced by anxiety until Joe walked through the garden gate.

Within an hour he was showered, changed and back at work. I learnt later about his attempt to save a drowning man – another example of how police intervene on a daily basis to try to save lives. No fuss, no fanfare, just 'get on with the job'. A job where uncommon valour is a common virtue.

Many months later at an award ceremony we heard the full story of Joe's actions that evening. He was one among many officers being recognised for their actions and bravery. The hall was full of proud family and friends – no press, no pomp. Joe, like the other officers honoured, felt he had just been doing his job. That day inspired this book.

A month or two later I sat down in a café in London for a meeting with Ben Ando, a journalist colleague. Over coffee, I mentioned Joe's experience and in an era of cutbacks and criticism how so few of these stories get the recognition they deserve.

Within moments, this book was born.

We sought from the outset to make the book different. We didn't want a series of police reports or a blandly positive account that recorded the glory but glossed over hardship, doubts or procedural failings. We wanted to hear the voices of the officers directly involved: their motivations, their feelings, and their struggles. A police constable's starting pay is not especially high and so clearly there is something more than financial reward that drives people to become police officers, to chose a profession where they might well be expected to put their own life on the line for a stranger. There are examples in this book of those who left far better paid jobs to join the service. What is it that drives them? While writing this book we have heard repeatedly from officers of their desire to put something back into society, to 'make a real difference' – what many used to call a sense of duty.

We wanted to record the detail of the incidents they attended but also, uniquely, the impact on them and their families, the human cost. To achieve that it was important to secure the support of the major police staff associations in England, Wales, Scotland and Northern Ireland. We record here our grateful thanks for the cooperation given by the Association of Chief

INTRODUCTION

Police Officers both in England and Wales (ACPO), and in Scotland (ACPOS), and the Superintendents' Association and the Police Federation in both jurisdictions. We are also grateful to the many staff officers, awards coordinators and PR personnel who assisted us in collating the candidate stories and arranging the many interviews. Our particular thanks also go to the president of ACPO, Sir Hugh Orde, for agreeing to write the Foreword.

Our thanks, too, to our publishers, Constable & Robinson, for offering to donate a proportion of the profits from this book to the Police Dependants' Trust. This charity was selected after all the officers featured in this book were asked to choose from a shortlist.

What is brave? When does an individual step beyond the call of duty? These were questions that Ben and I set out to answer. *Beyond the Call of Duty* details through real events the reality and diversity of modern day policing in the UK and the toll it takes both professionally and personally on police officers and their families. Over the course of a year, we have travelled the length and breadth of Britain to talk to the officers involved. We have met them in police stations, cafés, at their homes, and on one occasion on board the royal yacht *Britannia*. Some of the interviews were carried out at the scene of the incident, to give us a better understanding of the events that took place. Wherever the venue, the stories were always humbling.

Beyond the Call of Duty tells the stories in the officers' own words. It reveals, in vivid detail, the raw courage of those who put themselves at risk to save others and the physical and mental strength required to prevail against overwhelming odds in horrendous conditions. We asked them to tell us what they said, what they were thinking, how they were feeling. Without exception we found them candid, open and forthright.

As well as revealing the innermost thoughts and motivations of those at the heart of incredible, and in some cases notorious, events, the book lifts the lid on what it's really like to be at the sharp end of policing. There are accounts of amazing courage and bravery: the two officers who braved gunfire and a hail of petrol bombs to rescue a grievously wounded colleague or the lone policewoman who faced up to a knife killer.

There are stories, too, of the physical and mental determination of those who've recovered from a life threatening injury to return to active duty, or the strength of those who've learned to cope with traumatic experiences that most will never face.

Not every story we have heard could be told in this book. For reasons of space many remarkable stories have had to be omitted, and we would like to thank all our interviewees, whether their story is included or not.

Without doubt, too, there will be feats of heroism, tenacity or endurance that we did not hear about and many, many more officers with stories that are worthy of inclusion in a collection such as this.

We believe the stories recorded offer a snapshot of the range and risks of UK police work in the twenty-first century and reflect the culture of bravery and public service within it that is rarely reported.

Over the course of the past year we have heard stories of incredible power and amazing diversity but all shared a common factor: those involved went 'beyond the call of duty'.

Nick Kinsella and Ben Ando
May 2013

1

FALLING THROUGH WARM TREACLE

*'I had my baton out, but I think it was more
for confidence than anything. Note to self: don't go
to a gunfight armed with a baton!'*

PC LUKMAAN MULLA QGM

The dark figure was at the top of the stairs for less than a second before he raised the gun. Standing below, PC Dave Lomas could see the dull sheen of the sawn-off single barrel, the wooden hand stock, and the passive, emotionless look in the face of Stephen Hensby – known all around Rawtenstall, Lancashire, as the Crusty Man.

Without closing an eye to aim and without any warning, Hensby pulled the trigger. The bang seemed to fill Dave Lomas's world, and an instant later it was as if a searingly hot, supersonic wind passed straight through him.

It felt like someone had taken an orbital sander and pressed it to his right cheek just for a split second. Dave staggered backwards and then ducked into an alcove to the side of the staircase.

'Bleeding hellfire!' he thought. 'Hensby's got a shotgun cartridge, emptied the pellets out and filled it full of sand.

1

The dirty bastard!' Then, as Dave pressed himself against the wall, a second shot rang out. Dust flew into the air and the carpet seemed to jump in the spot where, just a second ago, he'd been standing.

The noise was deafening, and Dave was slightly dazed, but through it he could hear the voice of his colleague, PC Lukmaan Mulla: 'Dave! Get out! Get out!'

'Yeah,' thought Dave, 'I think I better had.' The front door, already hanging off its hinges from where they'd smashed their way in, was just a short distance away. Dave took a step towards it. But, as soon as he took that step, he realised he was in trouble. It felt as though his body wasn't working anymore. He managed a step with his left foot, then another with his right. He was through the door, but his energy seemed to be draining away from the scalp downwards. Dave was a big man – well over six feet tall and at least seventeen stone – and a keen bodybuilder. In front of him was the path up to the parked police car – and safety – yet he knew he would never make it that far.

As his senses began to grow hazy, Dave turned to the right, to the side of the small end-of-terrace house. His shoulders slumped, and then his arms fell to his sides. The only parts of him that were still working were his lower legs. He knew he would soon be unable to stand, but he did not know why as he could not feel any pain. As he reached the corner, he felt himself toppling forward, unable to stop himself. He took one, perhaps two more steps before dropping to his knees, then falling back.

Dave blacked out briefly before hitting the floor but came to within seconds and realised he was lying on his back. It was becoming difficult to breathe – it felt as if a hand was pressed fast against his mouth, stopping the air. It took every ounce of his energy just to suck in a single breath. He seemed to be able to see every second of his future laid out in front of him. 'I only have the strength for another seven, maybe eight breaths,' he thought. 'Then that's it.'

Everything felt surreal. He could hear gunshots going off, and screams and shouts. He could hear his own personal radio squawking as Lukmaan Mulla tried to call in to control:

'Assistance, assistance. Dave's been shot!'

The communications officer couldn't understand: 'Dave's where?'

'No, Dave's been shot!'

'Dave's hot?'

'NO! HE'S BEEN SHOT!'

'He's where? What's happening? We can't understand what you're saying . . .'

Then Dave heard another voice come on the line, much closer. He recognised it as belonging to Sergeant Paul Leigh. Leigh wasn't part of Dave's team; he'd simply answered a request that Dave had put out a short while ago and brought an enforcer device that he had in his car to break down the door.

Sergeant Leigh spoke calmly and slowly: 'Clear comms, clear comms. This is the situation. 3856 has been shot in the head. He is down. We are receiving gunfire from a building at Hardman Avenue. We need an ambulance! We need police armed response units now!'

Dave felt something cool and soft being pressed up against the side of his head. He didn't know it at the time, but it was Paul Leigh's jacket. Paul and Lukmaan had run from the building when the first shots rang out, but returned when they realised Dave had been hit.

There was more gunfire, more loud bangs, and then something else – the crash of breaking glass and the smell of petrol.

Someone seemed to be starting a small war, yet as Dave lay on the ground the noise and fury seemed to be oddly distant.

He listened absently to shouts over the radio as he fought to inhale. By now, he was on what he thought would be his last few breaths. He was surprised he was still conscious; but everything was becoming very simple. An hour at least: that was how long it would take for a negotiator to get there. And it would take an hour to put into place any kind of rescue plan. And Dave knew he didn't have an hour. He wasn't even sure if he could last another minute. He became acutely aware of how hard his body was working just to keep him alive. Each second he could sense his heart pumping, its valves opening and closing, his skin perspiring, his muscles moving, his lungs breathing. And it could not continue much longer.

'This is it,' he thought. 'This is how it ends.' And suddenly, it didn't seem like a big deal. 'God, it's quick, this life. It's kind of sad, really.'

By any sort of measure he'd lived quite a good life, hadn't he? He'd soared among the clouds alone in a hang-glider, 5000 ft above Pendle Hill. He'd dived to the bottom of oceans, and jumped from a plane over Florida in a 14,000-ft skydive. Dave felt he'd done more, at the age of 35, than most people manage in three or four lifetimes. But it didn't seem enough.

As the world retreated, he found himself looking up at a dot of blue sky. It was all he could see; his peripheral vision was failing; the outer edges of his field of view turning black. Odd, almost trivial thoughts crossed his mind: 'I haven't tidied my house up – there are pots that need washing on the drainer. Who's going to look after my cat, Pudding? But then, it's not going to matter in a minute.'

The blue spot above continued to slowly recede. It felt to Dave as though he was falling gently backwards through warm treacle. Everything was becoming more and more distant – the bangs, the radio, shouting, the smell of petrol. They all seemed less and less important. As Dave fell backwards and as darkness engulfed him, his overriding feeling was a soft glow of comfort . . .

The woman looked anxiously out of the side window of the farmhouse. There he was again: the Crusty Man. Why was he coming here now, constantly walking past her house? Looking in! Leering! And making those horrid threats about the animals!

She turned to gaze at her husband. His cancer seemed to be in remission now, but she knew it would be some time before he'd be able to work on the farm again. And he was relying on her to help him along the road to recovery.

Outside the window, in the lane below, the Crusty Man was still there. She was sure he couldn't see inside the house, yet he seemed to be staring straight at her. Though they were on the edge of the town, not up on the high fell, she felt isolated. She had become afraid of making the rounds of the outbuildings and sheds, especially after dark, although she knew the animals needed tending.

She shuddered, and decided to call the police again. This time she would make them listen!

'Look, I used to be on friendly terms with him. I used to let him ride his dirt bike up the path and occasionally we'd chat. I thought he was an oddball, but he didn't scare me. Not then, anyway.'

PC Dave Lomas looked at the woman. It was a glorious

July day and they were sitting outside her old farmhouse on the southern edge of Rawtenstall, bordering the northern slope of Whinberry Naze, well known locally for its annual fell race. She was obviously frightened. 'What did you say his name was again?'

'Hensby. Stephen Hensby. He lives down in one of the council houses on Hardman Avenue – just down the hill from here. Everyone round here calls him the Crusty Man because that's how he looks. Crusty. And he knows it – he writes it on walls and things. He's not got a job. He used to live with his mam but she died. He's never married or anything – I think he's a bit of a loner.'

'Well, fair enough,' started Dave. 'I'll record this visit, put it in our log and . . .'

'No!' she interrupted. 'Look, I have had this from six different bobbies and he has been warned before to leave me alone. Now he's threatening to burn down my barn with my horses and my breeding dogs in it. And I believe he'll do it.'

Dave thought again. The woman clearly believed she was in danger. He looked across at her husband. He looked poorly. The stress of caring for him and keeping the farm going must be a lot, thought Dave. These are genuine victims, in need of his help. He made a decision.

'OK,' said Dave, 'I'm going to take a proper statement from both of you, and then I'm going to arrest Stephen Hensby.'

After he'd taken the statements, Dave drove down the hill to the address the woman had given him. Hardman Avenue was a U-shaped street on a hillside, and the home he wanted to visit was on the end of a block of terraced houses on the inside of a bend. It was an unprepossessing house in grey pebble-dash, with a small, sloping front garden and a row of shallow steps leading down to the front door.

Dave knocked. No answer. To the right was a window. The curtains were open and he peered inside. The room was a mess. The only sign of life was an elderly Rottweiler dog, which showed little interest as Dave tapped on the window. There was no sign of Hensby.

Dave sighed. He phoned the woman, and explained that because the man wasn't in there was little he could do. He promised that he would return after the weekend and arrest him then. He also said that if she had any more trouble she should dial 999 straightaway.

As Dave came on duty at 8 a.m. the following Monday at Haslingden police station, he explained the situation to his colleague Lukmaan Mulla.

'Listen, Luke, I've picked up this job doing cover work in Rawtenstall. I don't want to let it fester; I have got statements and I want to go and arrest this guy today.'

Dave liked Lukmaan – they'd often worked together. Physically, they were almost opposites: Dave was heavily into body-building and spent hours in the gym while Lukmaan had the build of a lightweight boxer, wiry and quick. Lukmaan was born and brought up in Preston, and had gone to St Andrews University to read Economics. But after graduating he decided to not to become a banker or an accountant because, as he explained to colleagues, he 'didn't fancy making rich people richer'. He joined Lancashire police in 2003, shortly after graduating, and had been identified as a potential high flyer, qualifying for the force's High Performance Development Scheme. It earmarked him for fast promotion – but in July

2005 he was still a police constable, having only just finished his two-year probationary period.

'OK,' said Lukmaan. 'Let's go and do that first then.'

The pair took their marked panda car and drove across to Rawtenstall police station. There they agreed to give another officer, Matt Walton, a ride back towards Bury. He was coming off duty after a night shift and hadn't been able to get a lift home.

After completing the usual checks to identify whether Stephen Hensby had any outstanding warrants or a criminal record, and finding nothing, they drove the short distance to Hardman Avenue. It was a beautiful clear day. Because Matt Walton wasn't in uniform, Dave suggested he stay in the car while he and Lukmaan went to make the arrest.

They walked down the steps to the front door but, before knocking, Dave decided to have a quick look through the living room window. The dog was still there but now, sitting in an armchair, they could see the figure of a man. He looked unkempt, with a full beard and straggly hair. Dave estimated he was in his mid-50s. This, he thought, was Stephen Hensby. He certainly fitted the name Crusty Man.

Dave tapped on the window and the man looked round, startled. He didn't seem used to visitors, and certainly wasn't pleased to see the police. He got up and walked round to the front door, opening it on a chain.

'Are you Stephen Hensby?'

'Yeah.'

'Can you open the door and let us come in for a chat?'

'No,' came the reply, and the door was shut in their faces. Dave and Lukmaan looked at each other. Dave banged on the door.

'Stephen, you have to let us in. There has been an allegation made and you need to come with us.'

'Fuck off!'

Dave was starting to get irritated now. This was supposed to be a routine job – Hensby would be taken to the station, interviewed about the woman's accusations and then either released, cautioned or charged. Either way, there would be some kind of resolution. But now it was getting complicated.

Dave tried again: 'Look, Stephen, if you don't open the door I am going to have to break it down.' In response, all Dave could hear was incoherent shouting.

And now he had a problem. Because the officers knew Hensby was in there, and because he was wanted for an arrestable offence, they had the legal power to force entry under the Police and Criminal Evidence Act. Unfortunately, they hadn't brought their 'enforcer' – the steel cylinder with handles that police officers use to ram doors.

Dave didn't want to leave and come back later, because he'd made promises to the woman. He was also worried that if they did leave, Hensby would go straight up to the farm and cause more distress.

Lukmaan put out a call on the radio, asking for the enforcer. There didn't seem to be one at Rawtenstall police station, but soon another voice came on the line.

'This is Sergeant Paul Leigh. I've got one in the back of my car. I'll bring it over.'

'Cheers, Sarge!' replied Lukmaan. 'Nice one!'

Within five minutes, a blue Renault Laguna pulled up behind the marked police car already parked on Hardman Avenue. Paul Leigh was working in a unit that tackled prolific criminals – usually burglars – and had got into the habit of keeping an enforcer in his car because he needed it so often.

Paul was originally from Rochdale but after working briefly as a carpenter and a prison officer had joined the Metropolitan Police in London in the mid-1990s. After stints in Brixton and Clapham he'd transferred back to Lancashire when his family was young. Despite his northern roots he was much teased by the others for sounding like a southerner.

Lukmaan walked up to the car and Paul gestured towards the boot. 'It's unlocked – help yourself. Let me have it back when you're done and I'll be on my way.'

Paul was in plain clothes – jeans, t-shirt and lightweight jacket – and he watched Lukmaan carry the heavy steel cylinder down the path. The other officer he could see, Dave Lomas, was still talking at the door. Paul decided to get out and wander down the steps. Like many police officers, he couldn't resist sticking his nose in.

Dave was giving Hensby one last chance to see sense. 'Come on, Stephen, there's a door hammer here and we're going to break your door down. It doesn't have to be like this.'

There was no response from inside the house, so Dave shrugged. Although considerably heavier than Lukmaan, he wasn't trained in what the police describe as Method-of-Entry techniques whereas the younger officer was. If wielded properly, the enforcer device – a metal rod with a diameter of around four inches and a thick circular metal head – can deliver several tons of force at the point of impact. If used wrongly, though, it can cause considerably more damage to the luckless police officer's hands than the door.

Lukmaan sized up the job. It was a relatively modern uPVC coated wooden door. He knew these were considered among the hardest to break – the plastic was flexible enough to absorb much of the energy of each blow without shattering, yet the wooden core was strong, and prevented the door being bent out of shape. Here goes, thought Lukmaan, and raised the enforcer behind him.

Bang! Bang! Bang! Bang! Bang! The standard technique was to give the door five hard strikes and then pause. There was no sign of the door giving in. Lukmaan tried again. Five more bangs. The door flexed in its frame but did not give way. He heard Hensby's mocking voice from behind the door: 'You haven't had your Weetabix this morning, have you, lad?'

Lukmaan tried again, giving the door another dozen or more strikes, but he was tiring. And apart from one of the window panes cracking the door was showing no signs of giving way.

Gasping a little, he handed Dave the enforcer. 'You have a go!'

Dave took the device and swung it at the door. On the second strike, it burst open. The officers smiled at each other. 'It was good of you to weaken it for me,' laughed Dave.

They looked inside the house. There was a small hallway, and directly in front of them a flight of stairs straight up. To the right was the door to the living room, to the left a small alcove, and a door off to the kitchen. A makeshift curtain was drawn across the bottom of the staircase.

'Stephen,' shouted Dave, 'it's the police. We're coming in.'

The dog was barking, but it was too old to be any kind of deterrent. Lukmaan took it by the collar and shut it in the living room before wandering back into the hallway. There was no sign of Hensby.

'There's a barricade on the stairs!' Hearing this, Lukmaan turned round to see Dave had pulled back the curtain.

A few feet outside the front door Paul, peering over Dave's shoulder, could also see the barricade. It looked like a metal bed-frame fixed across the staircase, a couple of steps up. Dave took a step forward, and at that moment looked up to see the shadowy figure at the top of the stairs . . .

Lukmaan and Paul heard the bang and ran instinctively. As Paul moved back he saw Dave reel around, his face covered in blood.

'Dave's been shot! Dave's been shot!' Lukmaan shouted into his radio as they sprinted back up the path towards the police car. Ducking out of sight of the house they watched, horrified, as Dave emerged from the building dripping with blood and lurched round to the side of the house, where he slumped to the ground.

That's it, thought Paul. He's dead.

But what if he was still alive? Paul decided that, despite the danger, he had to go back. He ran down the drive, barely daring to look inside the front door, skirted around the edge of the building and reached Dave. The stricken officer was lying on the ground by the glass panelled kitchen door at the side of the house. There was no response. He was deathly still; his eyes were closed; his face was covered in blood. Paul felt sure he was dead.

Paul didn't have his personal radio but Dave's was still clipped to the front of his body armour. Both it and the armour were riddled with pellets, but amazingly the radio still seemed to be working. Trying to remember his training, trying to remain calm and not get too excitable, and trying to speak despite his horribly dry mouth, Paul flicked the transmitter:

'Clear comms, clear comms. This is the situation. 3856 has been shot in the head. He is down. We are receiving gunfire from a building at Hardman Avenue. We need an ambulance! We need police armed response units now!'

Paul took off his jacket, a lightweight black cagoule. He remembered his basic first-aid training and knew he had to prevent loss of blood. The problem was the whole of Dave's face and neck seemed to be bleeding. In the end he simply wrapped his jacket round Dave's head. Paul wasn't sure what else he could do, and he felt horribly exposed by the side of the house. He knew they'd both be sitting ducks if the gunman came to the kitchen door, or walked round the corner from the front. And he still wasn't sure if Dave was alive. Paul realised it had gone quiet, and in that moment suddenly remembered his own children, his own responsibilities, and that he wasn't wearing any body armour. What was he doing here?

Paul was jolted out of his reverie by the sound of more gunfire. Hensby was firing out of the upstairs front window towards Lukmaan, who'd broken from cover to get the first-aid kit from the police car. Hensby fired again and again, blasting out the side windows of both the marked panda car and the blue Laguna, showering the pavement with glass and just missing Lukmaan as he grabbed the medical pack from the car boot and sprinted back behind the hedge.

Paradoxically, the gunfire gave Paul some comfort: he reasoned that as long as Hensby was firing at parked cars up in front of the house, he wasn't shooting at Dave or himself down by the kitchen door. But the relief was short-lived – moments later, Paul heard another crash – this time behind him – and saw flames licking up the side of a shed a few feet away near the back of the house. Hensby was now throwing home-made petrol bombs out of the rear window. 'Heck,' thought Paul, 'this doesn't happen in a small town like Rawtenstall!'

The radio was squawking with messages confirming that various armed response cars were on their way – though one was delayed because it had stuck in third gear. The closest was based at Accrington. Paul knew that was barely seven miles away, but it suddenly seemed a huge distance when he was in the sights of a man with a gun,

Then Paul became aware of the sound of music, 'Da-da, da-da, da-daaaa, da-diddly-da, da-daa'. It was the Mexican Hat Dance, the ringtone of his mobile phone. He realised he'd forgotten to take out of his jacket pocket – and there was no chance of retrieving it now. The caller rang off, but over the coming hours the phone kept ringing intermittently, an incongruous musical accompaniment to the terrifying sounds of petrol bombs and gunfire.

Paul could see that Dave was still bleeding, and became aware that he was breathing. At least, he thought, that means he is still alive, that blood is still pumping around his system. But he knew he needed the first-aid kit. He decided to leave Dave and ran back to Lukmaan.

'Luke, give me the first aid kit and your body armour,' said Paul. Lukmaan was certainly not about to take off his body armour, but Paul was right: Dave needed help.

'It's OK,' he replied. 'I'll take it.' And with that, crouching low, he ran back down to the side of the house.

Although Paul had done his best with the jacket, Lukmaan was shocked at how much Dave was still bleeding. The blood was almost spurting out of small circular wounds in his face and neck. Lukmaan even tried putting his finger in one of the holes to halt the flow. Dave was struggling to inhale too; Lukmaan shuddered at the rasping sound as his colleague fought for breath. He crouched down and patched up Dave as best he could, just trying to keep him alive and hoping he might regain consciousness.

Every now and again Hensby was letting off a shotgun blast and Lukmaan could see more petrol bombs being thrown out of the back of the house. He pulled out his baton, though he wasn't sure what good it would do if Hensby decided to confront them. 'Note to self,' he thought ruefully: 'Don't bring a baton to a gunfight!'

Enveloped in soft, gentle blackness, Dave could still see the tiny point of blue above him getting smaller and smaller. But his feeling of comfort started to disappear. He suddenly thought of his mother – oh no, this would be terrible for her. And what about his finances? What would happen to them? At that point, a brownish blob came into his view, and he heard a voice saying, 'Dude, dude, wake up!'

'It's Luke,' thought Dave. 'I can tell him where my financial papers are! I can pass messages for my mum to him!'

Suddenly, Dave felt he was trying to wake up from the deepest sleep he had ever known. He was trying to swim back through the treacle, slowly clawing himself up towards the dot of blue. He managed to get in a big, deep, rasping breath, and with that, he felt his systems start to kick back in. He could see that it was Lukmaan bending over him.

'I'm glad you're here, mate,' he said. 'I don't really want to die alone.'

'What do you mean, die?' replied Lukmaan. 'You're fine!'

Dave realised he could breathe again, and as he did, his surroundings came sharply back into focus. He could see the kitchen door, the gable roof, the window. He remembered the stairs, the barricade, the gunman . . . he looked back at Lukmaan.

'Dude, get out of here – bugger off! He's going to come through the door and finish the job!'

'No,' replied Lukmaan, 'we're fine. You're fine.'

Dave thought, 'Right, in that case I'm going to get up.' He rolled forward to sit up, but as he did it felt as if every nerve-ending in his body fired at once. He felt a crunching sensation, and the soft comfortable feeling he had disappeared in a split second to be replaced by searing agony across his body – a pain he'd never felt in his life before. It was as if a plane had crashed on him. Even his hair hurt. He fell back and gasped, 'I'm not all right, I'm fucked up!'

'I know, dude,' replied Lukmaan gently. 'Just stay where you are!'

Dave began to despair. He felt like a turtle lying on its back. He couldn't feel his right arm, or anything down his right side. Would he even live? If he did live, would he be paralysed? What would life be like as a cripple? Overwhelmed by a crushing wave of self-pity, he began sobbing to himself.

Lukmaan was worried. He knew Dave was badly hurt. Despite his best efforts, his injured partner was still losing blood and lapsing in and out of consciousness. And there was the ever-present danger that Hensby would return. He wondered about trying to make a dash for it, perhaps carrying Dave to safety. But Dave was huge – seventeen stone – and he, Lukmaan, was barely eleven stone. There was no way he could lift Dave and carry him up the steps, or make it over the hedge.

Lukmaan strained to hear inside the house. Could he protect Dave, or himself for that matter, if Hensby appeared at the back door? Could he knock the gun away with a baton? Get in the first blow, and disarm or disable Hensby before he could fire a lethal shot? What chance did he have? Suddenly Lukmaan tensed: he was sure he could hear the gunman moving around in the kitchen, close to the back door. But the sounds moved away, and Hensby did not find the two vulnerable policemen, one close to losing his life, the other desperately trying to save it.

In the office at Accrington police station used by the firearms unit, Wendy Bower filled the kettle. A brew and a catch-up on the computer with latest police reports was the traditional way of starting a shift.

But as she picked up her mug, the phone rang: 'Code 1 to Rawtenstall – an officer has been shot in the head!'

Without pausing, Wendy put down her untouched cup of tea and shouted out to her partner that day, Kevin Jones. They ran out of the office and down the corridor to the back of the police station where their armed response car was parked. Normal procedure was to go over to the loading bay to prepare their equipment and weapons, but there was no time for that. Wendy climbed in and switched on the engine and Kevin scrambled into the passenger seat.

Both had served as military police and then joined Lancashire Constabulary on the same day in 1997, though oddly they'd never met during their time in the army. For Wendy, moving to the firearms unit was a natural progression, as she was comfortable around weapons and enjoyed the operational side of policing. Kevin also wanted to take advantage of his military experience with guns, and working as an armed officer was one of the goals he'd set himself when applying for the police.

As Wendy checked the address they'd been given against the map, Kevin grabbed their weapons from the long, coffin-like gun-safe in the back of the car and dropped them into the passenger-side footwell.

Each armed response vehicle (ARV) carries a variety of weapons. They vary from force to force, but in 2005 Lancashire's firearms officers were issued with Glock pistols and Heckler and Koch G36 assault rifles. The ARV cars also carried baton guns and 'taser' non-lethal electric shock weapons, which at the time were only issued to firearms officers.

With its lights flashing and sirens screaming, Wendy steered the Ford Galaxy out of the car park and accelerated towards Rawtenstall. Frequently swearing at, cursing or scolding the clumsy or inattentive driving of other motorists, she drove faster and harder than she had ever driven before. As the car lurched from side to side, Kevin scrabbled around checking, loading and racking the four guns – a rifle and a handgun for each of them – while the radio continued to relay information.

He held out little hope for the injured officer – people who get shot in the head do not usually survive – but if someone was on the streets with a firearm it was their job to contain the situation and protect other members of the public.

They pulled into Hardman Avenue and drew up to the police cordon and rendezvous point. As Wendy turned off the engine, the car almost seemed to sigh with relief. When they got out, they could hear the engine making a 'tinking' noise and smell the burning clutch. While they were pulling on their body armour and helmets, a second ARV arrived with officers Phil Bayliss and Peter Corser.

Wendy and the other firearms officers went to speak to a nearby inspector who was in command. Standard procedure was to wait for three ARV units to attend – this would provide sufficient officers to cover all four sides of the building, while leaving two free to attempt any rescue.

Unfortunately, as Paul Leigh already knew, that third car was stuck in third gear and wouldn't reach them for some time. And time was a luxury they didn't have.

The team assessed the situation: There was an officer down, one or two officers with him, and the gunman still in his house and armed. They had to act quickly. Phil Bayliss took the role of team leader, and the inspector, acknowledging their expertise, told them to deploy as they saw fit. They decided to take a single paramedic up to the property with them in one of the cars, and while Phil and Pete provided cover Wendy and Kevin would go and recover the injured man.

The gun cops walked back to their cars. They trained regularly, and every seven weeks all firearms officers had to pass a qualification shoot to retain their place on the team. The tests aren't just about hitting targets: the officers are judged on tactics and temperament. Those who fail are removed from firearms duties immediately. It may seem brutal but it's designed to ensure that those who are permitted to carry lethal weapons are at the peak of performance.

During the training, officers take part in numerous scenarios to practise techniques and tactics. They're given a choice as to what weapons they will take with them, and in the detached atmosphere of the simulation Wendy would often opt for just a lightweight Glock rather than the heavier long-barrelled G36 rifle. She chuckled remembering this because here, when it was for real, she wanted every single weapon she could possibly carry, along with the clear Perspex ballistic shield.

As she made her way up towards the bend in the road that was next to the siege property, Wendy saw a man in jeans and a t-shirt. She wondered what a member of the public was doing there and ordered him, brusquely, to get out of the way. She didn't realise the man was Paul Leigh, who wasn't wearing a jacket because it was still wrapped around Dave Lomas's neck.

The firearms officers approached the house and took up their positions. Their training is often deliberately sparse on details, to encourage them to think on their feet and make decisions in fast-moving or changing circumstances. With barely a word being said, Phil and Pete took up positions covering the front and side of the property. When covering a building, firearms officers use a simple target indication system. The front is always referred to as white face, the back is black, the left green and the right red face. Pete trained his G36 on white face while Phil covered green face.

Everyone and everything was in position. Now it was time for Wendy and Kevin to go and rescue Dave Lomas.

To avoid making themselves an obvious target, Wendy and Kevin approached from the side. There was a small wooden gate leading to a second path up to the house. Wendy tried pushing against it, but it wouldn't open. This wasn't supposed to happen. She tried again, harder. The gate still wouldn't budge. There was nothing for it. Wendy aimed her boot at the gate and lashed out – it smashed, with a cracking splintering sound, and the armed officers moved through.

The smashing gate was answered by another bang – Hensby

firing again from the upstairs window – but Wendy had no idea where the pellets went. She and Kevin moved forward with their ballistic shields held up in front of them facing the threat.

Over by the kitchen door, Dave heard the loud banging. 'Bloody hell!' he said to Lukmaan. 'He's shooting again!'

'Dude, dude, it's all right,' replied Lukmaan, gripping Dave's arm reassuringly. 'It's ARV – they're coming for us. They're breaking the fence down.'

Dave closed his eyes, and when he opened them there was a helmeted figure bending over him. Because of the balaclava, all he could see were the eyes.

Wendy could see Dave was barely conscious. 'Dave, we're going to get you up,' she said, 'and I want you to just keep looking at me, Dave, just keep looking at me.'

At five foot eight, Wendy wasn't short but she could see Dave was considerably taller and much, much heavier. Even with Lukmaan's help, there was no way she could carry him and keep hold of her gun. Even though it meant she now had no quick way to defend herself, she slung her rifle behind. She would just have to trust her colleagues to provide covering fire should Hensby suddenly appear at the door with his gun.

She reached down and grabbed Dave's collar. On the other side, Lukmaan reached under Dave's arm and together they pulled the big man to his feet. Wendy began walking backwards, her right hand supporting his shoulder, her left reaching around him and using the ballistic shield to provide some protection.

Dave did not know the ballistic shield was there and he didn't know who, exactly, was holding him up. He could see from her clear grey eyes that she was a woman, and he knew she'd had to drop her rifle down to support him. Brave girl,

21

he thought, here protecting me. He glanced at the faces of the other three officers – they were all staring fixedly at a point over his head – presumably at the window Hensby had been shooting from.

But Dave had barely any control over his body and was terrified he was going to fall. If he did, everyone would be exposed. 'I can't let these people down,' he thought. His legs were weak and he had no sensation on his right side. Could he control them? Would they fail him? He clamped his knees together and turned his toes inwards. 'My colleagues have got my top half,' he thought. 'All I have to do is keep moving the bottom of my legs. I'm not going to fall,' he kept repeating to himself, 'I'm not going to fall. I'm not going to mess up this poor girl's chance of getting me out of this.'

Step by agonising step, he moved forward, his eyes locked on those of the firearms officer facing him as she slowly moved backwards, all the time saying: 'Just keep looking at me, just keep walking. That's great, Dave. Just keep looking at me and just keep walking.'

After what seemed like forever, they reached the police car with the paramedic inside. Dave was unceremoniously bundled into the one of the two single back seats positioned either side of the gun safe. The second his backside hit the seat, he felt the last of his energy ebb away, and he flopped like a rag doll. He still had no sensation in his right side, and he became aware that his right arm was hanging out of the door. He became terrified that the door would be slammed on his arm, crushing it, but one of the officers pushed it in and the car drove off. A paramedic wearing a borrowed firearms helmet was in the front passenger seat and he turned to Dave to start assessing him.

The vehicle drove down the hill to the cordon. Dave could see colleagues peering at him in the car and then recoiling with shocked looks on their faces. I must look bad, he thought. Things were still hazy, and every now and then Dave still kept hearing the annoying Mexican ringtone of the phone that was somewhere near his head. He was led from the car to an ambulance, then laid down and strapped to a trolley. Again, his right arm dropped down and he became preoccupied that it would get trapped beneath the trolley wheels; again, one of those around him lifted it back.

The ambulance made off, but it did not travel very far before stopping. As Dave was lifted out he realised he was at the cricket ground at New Hall Hey – a short distance away he saw the yellow tail boom of a helicopter and recognised the North West Air Ambulance. As he was strapped in, Dave could hear the pilot reporting in: 'Helimed Zero Eight, casualty on board. Now preparing to lift . . .'

The North West Air Ambulance team operate two Euro-copter EC-135 helicopters – one based in Blackpool, the other in Manchester. Lancashire and Cumbria are served by the Blackpool aircraft, with the call sign Helimed Zero Eight. Flying at 150 mph, the ambulances can reach any location in the North-West within ten minutes.

To Dave it seemed they were only airborne for a moment or two before they landed again and he was rushed into the casualty unit at the Royal Preston Hospital. Doctors and nurses crowded round, and as the battle to save his life continued. As Dave blacked out, he thought he could just hear a phone ringing one more time, 'Da–da, da–da, da–daaa, da–diddly–da, da–daaa'.

*

Back at the house, the siege was on.

The firearms officers had surrounded the building, but there was no sign of Stephen Hensby making a break for it although every now and then the muzzle of a gun emerged from an upstairs window. Over the coming hours more firearms officers arrived, along with negotiators and senior commanders. But Hensby ignored all attempts to open up a dialogue or give him the chance to surrender peacefully.

During late afternoon, the decision was taken to conduct what's known as a 'limited entry' on the kitchen door. This simply meant a team of officers breaking it down, but not actually going inside the house. The tactic was designed mainly to make contact or provoke the occupant into coming out. Because Hensby had no hostage, and all escape routes were cut off, there was no need to actively enter the house. The firearms team would always prefer to deal with a suspect outside, on their terms, rather than inside, on his.

Wendy was asked to be a part of the limited entry team, because she already knew the layout around the kitchen door, while Phil Bayliss would use the enforcer to break open the door.

However, before they could go in there was one more problem: the story had made national headlines and a news helicopter was hovering overhead relaying pictures that were being shown live on Sky TV. The firearms team knew this ruled out a covert approach, so they asked for the helicopter to be moved away. Sure enough, a short time later it flew off and the live picture feed was halted.

The team approached from the side of the house, first scaling a seven-foot wall and then crossing a narrow stretch of ground to the kitchen door. The officers linked their ballistic shields together to form a protective barrier. At the door, the shields parted to allow Phil access. First he knocked, but as expected there was no reply. So he brought up the enforcer and began to pound the door – yet just like its counterpart at the front several hours earlier, the uPVC kitchen door showed no sign of breaking. Suddenly, after the fifth strike, there was the sound of gunfire. Two shots – one after the other.

'Shots fired, shots fired, get out, withdraw,' came the command over the radio, and Wendy, Phil and the rest of the team moved back quickly but carefully.

The firearms team resumed their positions of containment, as the commanders decided on the next move. It was getting dark and the decision was taken to do nothing more that night.

Shortly after daybreak the following morning, with no movement or activity being observed inside, armed officers entered the house. After breaking through the barricade on the stairs they climbed up and found Stephen Hensby dead in a bedroom. He had shot his elderly dog, and then himself. He left no note.

⊱⋅⋆⋅⊰

Stephen Hensby's inquest the following year heard that he had a deep-seated fear of authority, and was worried that he might be evicted for falling behind with his rent payments. He had died from a single gunshot wound to the head. The coroner recorded a verdict of suicide.

Dave Lomas suffered a collapsed lung and still has sixty shotgun pellets inside his body – including four in his heart and one behind his right eye. A nerve in his shoulder was destroyed, leaving him in almost constant pain. He attended a police convalescent centre in Scotland and later saw a counsellor who used sophisticated neuro-psychological techniques to help him deal with flashbacks.

Although he returned to active duty, he gave up flying, and a previously strong interest in faith and spirituality has gone. He has lost any ambitions for promotion. Dave believes that a part of the man he was remained on the floor that day.

Because so many pellets were able to enter Dave's body through the gap between the chest and shoulder plates, police body armour vests were redesigned to offer increased protection against a shot or blow from above.

Lukmaan Mulla and Paul Leigh were both awarded the Queen's Medal for Gallantry, for staying with their wounded colleague and administering first aid despite being unarmed and directly in the line of fire.

Paul Leigh no longer has the Mexican Hat Dance as his ringtone.

2

REACH FROM THE SKIES

*'We're not a search and rescue helicopter. We're
a police helicopter. But sometimes, unfortunately,
we're all that's available.'*

IAN WORTHINGTON, FORMER SERGEANT

The call was logged as incident 143, timed at 0750 on 2 July
2007. On the computer screen in the Derbyshire police control room it read, simply:

> Call Type: Concern for safety

> Informant: Member of the public

> Location: Raynesway, Derby

> Message: am running down a path at the side of the
river, there's a woman floating in the river . . . she is conscious,
she's going past the bridge now . . .

An alert was sent, and police officers on duty near the
Raynesway road started making their way to the River
Derwent, which passes through Derby. At 0804, the inform-
ant called again:

> The lady is floating with the current, from Derby
towards Alvaston. I'm on the bridge. She's face up but I think
she slipped.

Already a command process was being implemented; the duty inspector was made aware and the fire service was informed.

By 0808, the first officers were on the scene. One – call sign DM131 – radioed in: 'We can see the lady, but we can't reach her. We cannot see any access point at present and are making our way down to the footpath now.'

In the control room, the duty inspector realised that if the woman was in the River Derwent, which was heavily swollen because of flooding, then even if anyone could clamber down to the riverside, they had little chance of rescuing her.

Sure enough, officers who did manage to reach the river bank reported that although they could see the woman they had no chance of getting close to her. And, more worryingly, she was being carried towards a large weir: if she reached it, she would almost certainly drown.

Another call came in – this time from the fire brigade; they were having trouble even finding the location. The inspector turned to the operator.

'Ask Oscar Hotel 88 if they can lift,' he said grimly. Oscar Hotel 88 was the call sign of the police helicopter. The inspector wasn't really sure what the chopper could do, and with time running out it seemed like the last throw of the dice . . .

Sergeant Ian Worthington had just arrived at the helipad next to Derbyshire police headquarters, just outside Ripley. The hangar was about the size of a tennis court – just large enough for one helicopter. It looked like a red-brick barn with a corrugated steel roof. Parked inside was their Eurocopter 135-T2, and workbenches and equipment racks lined the sides and back. At the front were a pair of large concertina doors that led out to the pad. Flanking the main hangar bay were several smaller rooms, including an operations centre, kitchen, conference room and locker area.

The North Midlands helicopter was operated jointly by Derbyshire and Nottinghamshire police and covered both counties. Officers to crew the aircraft were drawn from both forces, and when opportunities came up to join the team there was usually no shortage of applicants.

Ian booked on, changed into his dark blue flight suit and, as usual for a Monday morning, checked the computer for any jobs or requests that might have come in from either force.

He'd joined Nottinghamshire police as a cadet in 1972, and at one time or another had walked the beat in most of the county's towns. After a period as a traffic officer, and a promotion to sergeant in the mid-1980s, he became interested in aerial police work, and set up the police helicopter unit at Ripley.

Crime-fighting from the skies goes back to the 1920s, when the Metropolitan Police used an airship to keep an eye on the crowds at Epsom and Ascot races, but the advent of efficient and reliable helicopters in the 1980s saw a significant growth in police aviation. Fitted with high-resolution cameras and thermal imaging devices, police helicopters were ideal for urban crowd control and surveillance as well as tracking criminals on foot and in vehicles.

The EC-135 could carry four but normally flew with a crew of three: a civilian pilot and two police officers – one sitting in the front left seat, next to the pilot, operating the day and night cameras and recording equipment, the other sitting in the rear right position and taking care of navigation, map reading and radio communications.

Ian's regular colleague was off, so sitting in the back seat that day was PC Graham Fish, a Derbyshire officer who had joined the police in 1998. Before that, he'd spent seven years as ground crew in the RAF – most notably at RAF Staxton Wold, near Scarborough, which lays claim to being the world's oldest continuously operational radar station.

Graham was just getting changed. Like Ian, he wore a thermal shirt and leggings. These were both fire-resistant, as was the dark blue one-piece zippered flight suit that was a similar fabric and design to police riot gear, but with clear pockets in the front of the thigh for maps or other paperwork.

Pilot Eric Church was in the main part of the hangar checking the aircraft itself – Civil Aviation Authority (CAA) regulations require it to pass what's known as an A-check once every twenty-four hours – without that, the helicopter was not permitted to fly. This daily inspection ensures that the helicopter doesn't take to the air with any obvious problems. As Eric walked round he examined the rotor blades for visible damage, looked for any traces of leaking fuel or hydraulic fluid, and ran his hands over any hatches and panels to ensure they were flush and securely fastened.

He also stepped back to take an overall look at the helicopter and see that it was 'sitting right' on its skids. In the flying fraternity, there are apocryphal tales of pilots who've tried to take off with spanners in the engine inlets or missing tail rotors, because engineers had been at work and the pilot hadn't properly checked.

Eric had been flying helicopters since the early 1980s. He first piloted the Westland Scout – the army's version of the Wasp – before graduating to the Gazelle, then the Lynx. After a long army career, including tours in Afghanistan and Iraq as an electronic warfare officer in Apache helicopters, he had retired from the military at the age of 50 to become a commercial pilot. Eric had been with the police unit for four months. The Eurocopter was far more modern – and comfortable – than the military helicopters he had previously flown.

Suddenly, Ian ran out of the office.

'Graham, quick. We've got a job on: a woman floating down the Derwent right in the centre of Derby. They can't reach her because she's right out in the middle of the river. Can we get airborne straight away?' This last was shouted at Eric, who had ultimate responsibility for declaring whether the aircraft was fit to fly.

'Yes,' he replied. 'Last night's A-check is still valid as we haven't gone over twenty-four hours yet. I'll strap in and start the pre-flight checks and start-up if you wheel us out.'

Unsurprisingly, the need for a quick launch was not uncommon, and each crew-member knew what to do.

Most smaller helicopters have skids, not wheels, so manoeuvring them on the ground is awkward. The crew used a heli-lift, a wheeled frame that clamps around the skids and raises the vehicle off the ground by an inch or two so it can be moved around relatively easily. This made pulling the chopper out of the hangar a one-man job that could be completed in just two to three minutes.

After folding open the hangar doors, Ian grabbed the T-bar handle, disengaged the handbrake and pulled, using his weight to get the helicopter moving then steering it outside and onto the pad, around twenty-five yards away in front of the building.

Already sitting inside, Eric was checking the instrument panels, flicking switches and plugging in the intercom built into his helmet. One of the first readouts he looked at was the fuel level – it would be pointless taking off and discovering they only had ten minutes' flying time. Normally the helicopter is kept fully fuelled. This both ensures it's ready for an immediate take off should the need arise and also minimises the chances of condensation in the tank. Water in the fuel can cause engine damage or even failure, and while it's a hazard more usually associated with hotter countries it's possible in Britain, especially in the summer.

It's normal practice for a flight team to refuel the helicopter before they go off duty; however, CAA protocols insist that pilots must leave work at a certain time – to ensure they get enough rest. If the helicopter has worked late, it can mean there isn't time for refuelling before the flight crew is 'out of hours', so the incoming pilot always checks. Luckily, Eric noted, the tank was full. Depending on the weight of the crew, this would be enough for around one hour and forty-five minutes' flying time. Allowing for half an hour at the scene of any incident, this gave them a maximum effective range of around sixty miles.

Graham, the third crew-member, was thinking ahead to what equipment they might need. Like cars, helicopters have a boot at the back, and there was some water rescue equipment stored here. Although it is possible to reach into the boot from inside the cabin, it can be awkward. To Graham it made sense to extract anything that might be useful before lift-off. He opened the boot's clamshell doors, grabbed throw-lines and life jackets and put them on the floor next to him.

Ian had disconnected the heli-lift and moved it out of the

way, and Eric was ready for lift-off. As Ian climbed in next to him, Eric started the rotors turning and as they gathered speed the noise and vibration in the cabin began to build. The two police officers put on their helmets and plugged them in – so they could talk to each other and hear communications from the ground above the throbbing of the engines and rotors.

'Derby Control, this is Oscar Hotel lifting now. ETA is less than five minutes and we have got water rescue kit, life jackets and throw ropes, so if officers can stand by we will assess the situation when we arrive.' Graham's voice crackled through the intercom as he advised headquarters that they were getting airborne.

For an instant, the rotors' down-force was exactly equivalent to the helicopter's weight, and it seemed to pause on the pad, twitching, on the cusp of flight. Then the bonds of gravity were shuffled off, and the smooth, rounded form of the yellow and dark blue craft rose into the air, twisting and curving away.

In the control room, the call was logged. Timed from the moment Ian had taken the alert call, it had taken the helicopter eight minutes to get into the sky, and they should be at the scene very soon. In the meantime, more officers had managed to reach the bank, but all said the same thing: the river waters, surging and powerful thanks to the high rains and flooding there had been, were simply too dangerous for them to attempt any kind of rescue. The summer of 2007 was shaping up to be the wettest on record, with far heavier rainfall than usual in May and June.

Flying at 1000 feet over Derbyshire, heading due south,

the first priority for the helicopter crew was to get to the scene as quickly as possible. Although their Eurocopter, like all modern aircraft, was fitted with a GPS unit (similar to a car's sat-nav device) and digital mapping equipment, it is a requirement that all helicopter cops can read paper maps and are familiar with the terrain of the area they cover. The navigator is expected to be able to talk the pilot onto a target – be it a specific house number or a grid location – in real time, and this requires the skill to convert what is on the map to what can be seen out of the window.

Graham looked down at the ground for distinctive landmarks as they flew: the rectangular green block of Derby County football club's Pride Park stadium, and the huge white-roofed Rolls-Royce factory where engines for many of the world's civil jets – including the Airbus A380 super-jumbo – are manufactured.

Flying at 120 knots – around 140 mph – it did not take long for them to reach Derby. As they crossed Brian Clough Way – the bypass named after the charismatic and controversial football manager – the green-brown waters of the River Derwent came into view.

En route they'd been discussing their options and listening in to other police communications. In total they were monitoring four police radio frequencies, plus air traffic control and their own internal intercom. This meant that at any time they could have six different sets of audible information coming into their headsets.

They knew that both police officers and fire crews were on the river bank and could see the woman, but none of them could reach her.

Some of the firefighters had life jackets in their vehicles, but they weren't allowed to enter the water because of their strict health and safety rules. Eight years earlier, a firefighter had drowned in Manchester while trying to rescue a student from a lake. The fire brigade had been prosecuted under health and safety law. Though the jury had found it not guilty, there was a swift response from fire chiefs around Britain. Regulations around water were tightened up – and anyone breaching them was subject to disciplinary action or dismissal. And no one on the bank had any kind of throw lines. 'Well, we've got throw lines,' said Graham, 'but I'm not sure they'll be any use in these conditions.'

To deploy the throw lines, the helicopter would have to land as near to the riverbank as possible. A crew member would run to the edge and attempt to throw the weighted line across the river to a colleague on the other side. The line would then be held at the water's surface at an angle for the person in the water to grab hold of, and ideally they would be taken to the bank by the flow of the river. The crew had practised this, and knew it worked. But the riverbanks were very steep – making access awkward, and the ropes were only twenty-five yards long.

'Forget it,' said Ian. 'The river's just too wide right now.'

Graham agreed. There was no way of throwing one of their lines across the swollen Derwent.

More promising was a new piece of equipment called the C-Buoy. This lozenge shaped float was about two feet long, made from very light closed cell foam wrapped in a bright orange reflective fabric sheath, and fitted with grab ropes. If a victim was in difficulties it would keep them afloat until they could be reached. The C-buoy was hanging on a small hook in the back of the cabin.

'OK,' said Ian, 'the first thing we'll do is try the C-Buoy. But what if she can't reach it? What if it doesn't work? Could we jump in? Eric – if we have to – can you get us low enough for that?'

Eric hesitated slightly. He was new to the team, and while he was confident in his own flying skills he didn't want to put the two officers at undue risk. 'I can get you low enough, but are you sure?'

'Yes, if we have to,' replied Ian.

'Me too,' came Graham's voice from the back, and he passed Ian one of the life jackets that was in the footwell beside him.

'But let's hope it doesn't come to that!' said Ian, as he unbuckled his seat harness and passed the life jacket over his helmet and across his shoulders.

By now, they were flying in across the river. Looking through the Perspex canopy, they could see the surging, malevolent brown waters of the swollen river. There were several uniformed figures on the bank – police officers – and Ian trained the camera on the river's surface.

Through the viewfinder, Ian could see a new danger. Ahead were the heavy sluice gates of the weir, and he could see a large amount of debris – branches, twigs, pieces of wood and other rubbish – pushed up against it to a height of around six feet by the current. Ian was sure that when the woman reached the gates she'd be swept beneath this pile of detritus – making her far harder to reach even if she didn't drown.

'There she is – further up!' Ian heard Eric directing his gaze towards something in the water about fifty yards away. He adjusted his camera and zeroed in on the woman. She wasn't waving or shouting – just floating motionless face up in the middle of the river. He zoomed in for a closer look. She was elderly – in her early 70s – and appeared to be wearing a cardigan over her pyjamas. The baggy clothing bulged with pockets of trapped air, which were keeping her afloat. Ian looked at her face. It was pale but still had some colour. She was alive!

As the helicopter floated overhead, the woman gave no sign or response. Ian couldn't see whether her eyes were open or closed. He estimated that the current was taking her at a fast walking pace.

'OK,' said Graham. 'I'm going to try the C-buoy. Eric, can you get me into position? Practice had taught the team that deploying the C-buoy required accuracy. Ideally, it was thrown – but not dropped – straight down towards the water. Attempting to launch it sideways or at an angle was troublesome and likely to be inaccurate; because it's made of lightweight foam, the C-buoy is susceptible to wind and the downwash from the rotor blades.

Deploying it was Graham's duty, and he unclipped the float from its hook in the back of the cabin before opening his door and rotating his seat to face out. He looked down. They were hovering almost directly above the woman. He wanted to get it near enough for her to reach it easily, but obviously he didn't want to hit her.

Remembering their training and weighing up the conditions, Graham raised his arm and threw the C-buoy. It pitched down through the air and splashed into the water, right next to the woman. 'That's a pretty good shot,' Graham thought, as Ian turned and gave him the thumbs up.

But joy quickly turned to despondency – the woman did not react and made no attempt to grab the C-buoy. Because it was so light, it just sat on the water, and within a few seconds the downwash from the rotors caught it, whereupon it started to roll away faster and faster down river. Safety regulations prohibit anything being fixed to the helicopter, so there was no cord or tether. It was a one-shot attempt – and that shot had failed.

In the pilot's seat, Eric was concentrating hard. Ahead, near the weir itself, he could see electricity pylons and high tension cables stretching across the river. Contact with these would mean almost certain disaster for the helicopter. Luckily the wind wasn't too strong – about five knots – and was well within acceptable parameters for low level hovering. But time was running out.

The woman was just beneath him to the right – at the two'o'clock position, in the clock-face designation popular with pilots – and he noticed that the downwash was pushing her. He tried to angle the draft to steer her towards the bank, but the water started lapping over her face, and while it was pushing her a little it was also going up her nose and into her mouth. He realised the downwash was probably doing more harm than good, and backed off.

Ian looked at Graham. They weren't a search and rescue helicopter; they were a police helicopter. But unfortunately they were all that was available. 'I think we're going to have to go in,' he said. He glanced across at Eric. 'We're going to jump. How low can you get us?'

Eric had already been thinking about this. Over hard ground he could drop to a height of around two to three feet and hover, while his colleagues simply stepped out and jumped to the ground. It's a technique known as hover-deplaning, and they'd practised it numerous times.

Over the river it was different. Some helicopters are fitted with flotation pontoons to allow them to land on water, but this one wasn't. Eric knew that if it touched the surface it would probably flip over onto its roof and sink within seconds, while the rotors would be torn free and then disintegrate – sending deadly shards hurtling off at high speed in all directions. No, Eric didn't want tears and a wet helicopter.

Even hovering above the water presented some risks. UK police helicopters are twin-engined so they can fly at low levels over urban areas, while complying with CAA regulations designed to reduce the risk of casualties on the ground in the event of engine failure. But Eric also knew that if an engine failed, by the time he could react and increase power in the other one to compensate the helicopter would probably have dropped around thirty feet – and hitting the water from that height would be disastrous.

'I'll get in as low as I can,' he said reassuringly, and gently tilted the stick to bring the helicopter in.

Flying a helicopter is very different to flying an aeroplane. The centre stick is called the cyclic, and makes the vehicle go forward or backwards or from side to side. It's very sensitive, demanding a light touch. Beside the pilot's seat is a lever called the 'collective', which is controlled by the left hand. It looks a little like the handbrake of a car. This causes the helicopter to climb, descend or hover. On most helicopters, the blades rotate at a constant speed and the collective simply adjusts the pitch, or angle, of the rotor blades to achieve the desired result.

Finally, the pilot has pedal controls to steer the aircraft. Most helicopters have external tail rotors, but the Eurocopter EC-135 has a 'fenestrom', or ducted tail fan. While the design is more aerodynamic and efficient in forward flight, Eric knew from experience that it could be temperamental when hovering.

He dropped the aircraft as close to the surface of the water as he dared, while keeping the woman in view at all times. No more than thirty feet above the water surface, he was right at the very limit of what he felt was the minimum safe height. Aviation rules are strict: as the pilot in control of the vehicle, Eric is the captain; he has ultimate responsibility for the safety of the aircraft and the crew and makes the final decisions. Nonetheless, he could see his colleagues were determined to do all they could to save the woman, and he was equally determined to do all he could to help them.

'Eric, am I OK to go?' Graham, in the back seat, had already opened the door on his side of the helicopter and slid it back and out of the way. Eric signalled in agreement, and Graham stepped out onto the skid, holding onto the gutter rail above the windows.

Hovering at thirty feet, the drop to the water was about the same as jumping off the roof of a two-storey house. Looking down, Graham felt confident. He had decided to jump upstream of the woman, so he could swim down towards her. He inched along the skid towards the front of the helicopter and looked back through the canopy. Next to him, sitting inside, Eric steadied the controls and gave the thumbs up. 'This is it,' thought Graham, 'no turning back now!' Taking a deep breath, he stepped off the skid and fell towards the river below.

Because the water was dark, he had no idea how deep it was or what lay beneath the surface. What if soft, silty mud on the riverbed trapped his feet and gripped him in a deadly, cloying embrace? What if he struck a submerged trolley and became entangled, or wounded? All he could do was kick his legs and put his arms and elbows out in an effort to make as big a splash as possible and prevent himself going too deep.

It was shockingly cold, even in July. His feet and arms smacked against the hard, foamy water, but the speed of the drop plunged him deep beneath the surface. Graham looked up and saw what seemed to be a brown tunnel of light back towards the surface. He kicked off, and started swimming up the shaft of light. As he broke the surface, he looked up and saw the helicopter, then turned and swam towards the woman.

Above, Ian knew it was now his turn. After Graham had jumped, the sudden reduction in weight had caused the helicopter to climb, meaning that Ian had considerably further to fall. Sitting in the aircraft, looking through the windscreen, it hadn't looked that far. Now he was standing on the skid, the water seemed a very, very long way below. 'You prat,' thought Ian, 'what are you doing?' But Graham had made it, and Ian wouldn't leave him alone in the water.

Because he was that much higher, Ian lowered himself down and hung from the bottom of the skid, instead of jumping straight off, then let go. Like Graham, he was terrified of jumping into such dirty water with no real idea if there was anything beneath the surface, and as he dropped he was thinking, the longer I fall, the harder I'll hit and the deeper I'll go. Just before he hit, he held his nose.

The instant he struck the water, everything went black. When he opened his eyes and looked up, the water was not brown but green. The surface seemed a very long way off. Although he couldn't feel the bottom, it seemed to Ian that he had gone down a very long way. He kicked for the surface, but it felt as though he was still sinking. After what felt like an eternity, he stopped descending and slowly began to rise. Ian's lungs were bursting. The light was still a long way off; he wouldn't make it. He forced himself to hold on, but the water was bitterly cold. He kicked out frantically, and reached towards the surface. Just as he felt he could take no more, he burst through the surface and took a shuddering, euphoric lungful of air.

Above, in the helicopter, Eric breathed a huge sigh of relief that both his colleagues had surfaced safely.

On the riverbank, the officers looked at each other. 'I didn't think they were going to do that!' said one. He hit the transmit button on his radio. 'The lady is with two officers, but we can't get to the lady. Err . . . Two members of Oscar Hotel 88 are in the water with life jackets.'

Back at force control, the inspector and the communication operator looked at each other. That couldn't be right – could it?

By now, Graham had reached the woman. He saw immediately that she was still alive. The water was carrying them both along, and he wasn't sure how long they had before they reached the weir. Looking around, he saw a half-submerged tree that seemed to have fallen out from the bank. He put his arm around the woman's front and under her arm, then with the back of her head resting on his chest began swimming towards the tree using the traditional lifesaver stroke.

Ian had got his breath back and began looking around for Graham. He spotted the fallen tree and, seeing his colleague's intent, started swimming towards it himself.

By the time Ian reached the tree, Graham was already there. Although he was able to keep the woman's head above water, getting her to the branch had taken a huge amount of effort, and he did not have the energy to lift her out. Ian took over, climbing onto one of the boughs and then reaching down and pulling the woman up.

'Let me go, let me go, I want to die,' she said, over and over again, swearing at the officers.

They ignored her. Their rescue kits included shiny mylar space blankets that are useful for countering the effects of hypothermia, and Ian wrapped one of the blankets around her. Both officers were cold and shivering, so they could only imagine how the woman must be feeling. The blankets – based on materials developed by NASA for the US space programme during the 1960s – minimise heat loss through evaporation and provide a degree of protection from the wind. Ian wasn't sure how effective it was but it had to be better than nothing, and they had no idea how long they would be waiting on the tree.

Both men pulled off their helmets and hung them on overhanging branches to dry. They're similar to those used by military pilots, manufactured from carbon fibre bonded with high strength epoxy resin. They include retractable twin clear and tinted visors, microphones, earpieces and the associated electronics. Each is custom made, and costs around £1500. Ian and Graham watched the water dripping out. They were ruined.

In the air, Eric looked for somewhere to set the helicopter down. Riverbanks can be awkward, because if the ground is waterlogged the aircraft can sink in and become stuck – making it hard or impossible to take off again.

Though the tree Ian and Graham had climbed on was nearer the northern side, Ian landed about fifty yards from the southern bank, because that was where all the other police were. He ran down and gave them the throw lines from the helicopter, but it quickly became apparent they weren't long enough to reach the fallen tree, and the officers on the bank didn't know how to correctly tie them together.

As a precaution, Eric returned to the helicopter and began to reconfigure the cabin for emergency evacuation, in case the woman needed to be airlifted to hospital.

Across the river, Ian was sitting on a branch about the thickness of his leg. He asked the woman a little bit about herself. She told him that she had family, but that she spent her days in a nursing home in Derby. She had decided that she wanted to die, and just jumped in the water.

Ian was starting to warm up a little, but Graham seemed to be getting colder, shivering, standing on a submerged branch with his boots still in the water. As the minutes passed, it dawned on them both that the rescue wasn't actually over, and though they'd done the hard part there seemed no strategy or plan to get them back to warmth and safety.

For twenty minutes they waited. With no way of talking to the team of officers across the river, all they could do was watch and all they could see was a lot of head-scratching and radio chit-chat.

Luckily, some way down river, the fire brigade water rescue unit had managed to commandeer a small plastic boat from a unit at an industrial estate. When the tiny boat came into view, with four burly firefighters paddling furiously, Ian and Graham burst out laughing – both with relief and at the absurdity of the image. Graham began singing the *Hawaii Five-0* theme, 'ba–ba ba–ba baaaa–ba, ba–ba, ba–ba, baaaaaa . . .', much to the amusement of everyone bar the four men in the boat.

As it drew alongside, Graham helped the woman into the boat, and started to climb in himself.

'Sorry, lads,' said one of the firefighters, 'there's only room for one more.'

Ian knew his weight meant he wasn't feeling the cold as much as Graham, who was of a slimmer build and was still shivering visibly. 'You ride in the boat,' he said. 'I'll be fine. Besides, technically you've been in the water longer than me!'

Ian dropped back into the water and held onto the back of the boat as the firefighters began rowing it back to the other side of the river. Once they arrived, the fire brigade lifted the woman up the bank. By now, another helicopter – the air ambulance – had arrived, and the woman was airlifted to hospital.

Eric returned the seats to their normal positions, then laid down plastic sheeting to stop his soaking colleagues making the helicopter too wet. They lifted off and returned to their base.

❦

When Ian contacted the helmet manufacturers and told them the helmets were waterlogged, they told him how to dismantle and strip them down. He laid out the parts until they'd dried, then reassembled them. They were fine.

A little later, the team discovered that a senior fire officer had made a formal complaint about their actions. Sergeant Ian Worthington agreed that it had been dangerous, and possibly stupid, but said that he would never be able to sit in a helicopter and video someone drowning. He, Graham and Eric were later nominated for bravery awards.

The C-buoy was recovered several months later by a canoeist many miles down river. It was covered in green slime. In the meantime, the helicopter team had acquired a replacement – so now they have two.

Neither the woman nor any member of her family ever contacted the officers to say thank you, or even to acknowledge their efforts that day.

3

THE SHADOW IN THE DARK

*'I had this image in my head of this big black silhouette
of him coming to the door. When I was on my own
that's all I could see. When I was in the dark that's
all I could see. It was imprinted ...'*

PC JESS WOMERSLEY

Weronika Gospodarczyk had had enough. The holiday in
Poland had been a disaster. She had hoped that taking her
British boyfriend Colin back home to meet her family
would bring them all closer together. But her parents and
brother had hated Colin, and rather than trying to win them
round he'd been surly and defensive. Most of her friends
had disliked him too, so he'd simply accused them of being
racist.

Weronika had first met Colin Campbell in 2005 when she
was on a school exchange trip to Sheffield, but she'd thought
little of it when she went back to her home in Radom in
central Poland, around sixty km south-east of Warsaw. She
had long harboured a dream to live and study in England, and
had fallen in love with the warmth and character of South

Yorkshire. Three years later she returned to study for a degree in tourism management at Sheffield's Hallam University.

By chance, she'd run into Colin Campbell again on a night out with friends, and the two had started seeing each other. But, she sighed to herself, after a turbulent few months it was clear the relationship had run its course. She was tired of his fits of jealousy, tired of his outbursts and tired of the womanising she suspected he was indulging in behind her back. Every time she'd tried to end it before he'd self-harmed, and foolishly she'd allowed her kind nature to get the better of her. But this time, she told herself, she would not be swayed. There would be no more chances; it was time to make a clean break.

PC Jess Wormersley liked working with Gary Holland. He was easy-going and unlikely to flap in a crisis, and she felt their skills complemented each other well. Arriving for her night shift at Attercliffe police station, near the giant Meadowhall shopping centre, it cheered her to see they'd be patrolling together.

That night they were assigned to what was known as the Romeo car – the police response vehicle tasked with handling the most urgent emergencies. Each sector of the city had one. The Romeo cars were more powerful than standard panda cars and crewed only by taser-trained officers who'd also qualified as advanced drivers. Usually first to arrive at any given incident, those assigned to the Romeo cars were frequently at the front line of urban policing.

Jess was originally from Dorset, and had moved north when she married. Although she'd enjoyed her previous job working with deaf children, she saw the move as a chance for a career change, and joined South Yorkshire Police. By

September 2010 she'd been an officer for four years, and though occasionally teased about her soft West Country accent she was very much part of the team.

Like Jess, Gary Holland – known to all as 'Dutch' – was not a native Yorkshireman, having been born and raised in Mansfield, Nottinghamshire. He had completed his two-year probation just as Jess was making her application.

After a briefing about possible jobs that might be of concern, Gary grabbed the keys to their Romeo car – a Ford Mondeo – and they drove out into the night.

Two and a half miles away, Weronika and Colin were still arguing. She had a room in a shared house in Norfolk Park, a suburb close to the city centre that was popular with students. The house was on the end of a terrace, with two bedrooms upstairs, another downstairs, and a shared living room and kitchen.

The row had started that afternoon in the city centre, when she told him she wanted to split up, and had continued after they returned to her digs. Upstairs, in her room, he became increasingly resentful. Yes, he had been seeing other women, but Weronika was different. She was intelligent, beautiful, vivacious and fun-loving. In some ways, he couldn't believe she'd even got into a meaningful relationship with him. But now he couldn't bear to lose her – and she had no right to finish with him. It wasn't fair. Finally he went to brush his teeth.

In the bedroom, Weronika plugged her mobile phone into the charger, and it chimed as a text came through. Weronika picked it up and looked at the screen. The message was from one of her Polish college friends. As she started to read it,

Campbell came storming out of the bathroom – his face twisted with anger. She could see he still had toothpaste around his mouth as he shouted: 'You don't fucking listen to me! You're going to listen to me now!'

He snatched the phone, threw it away and then punched her, hard, in the face. For an instant Weronika was stunned, then she screamed and ran out onto the landing. Campbell followed, shouting and raving; he seemed to be getting more and more furious, beyond reason. In tears, Weronika fled downstairs. She could hear Campbell's footsteps and she shouted to the other tenants to help, to call the police.

She ran from the living room into the kitchen, then Campbell appeared in the doorway. He opened a drawer and pulled out a knife. Slowly, he raised it to his own face and drew the blade across the skin, cutting open his cheek. In the past, when he'd self-harmed during arguments, she'd felt sorry for him and had agreed to stay. But this time it was different. Terrified as she was, she knew there could be no reconciliation now.

She ran forward, and slammed the kitchen door closed. Once more, she screamed out for someone to call the police. Campbell began banging his fists against the thin internal door, shouting threats. Weronika pushed up against it with all her weight, but the door shuddered, and as Campbell maintained his assault she heard a cracking and splintering of wood. The door would not be enough to protect her. Campbell was too angry, and too strong. He was coming through . . .

In the Romeo car, Jess and Gary were parked by a roundabout, waiting. They'd heard reports of a stolen car in the area and knew it was, unwittingly, heading right towards them.

'This could be fun, Dutch,' said Jess. Sitting behind the wheel, Gary agreed. They were both trained pursuit drivers, and car chases were an important, and exciting, part of the job. They listened to the radio updates from other police cars already involved in the pursuit; sure enough, the offending car was getting closer and closer. Jess wound down her window, so they would hear it coming. As soon as they had it in sight, they would drop in behind and force it to stop.

Then over the radio they heard something new: a call to a suspected domestic incident – a fight between a boyfriend and girlfriend. Gary and Jess looked at each other: domestics can be very serious, but more often they're fairly trivial; arguments about what to watch on TV or whether the dinner has been properly cooked, or even a well-meaning neighbour who has mistaken the sound of shouting on a TV show for real events and has called the police.

Jess checked the time: it was 11.02 p.m. 'Look, we don't know how bad it is,' she said. 'Let's wait for this dodgy car.' Gary nodded, then looked up and down the road, willing the stolen car to come into view.

But barely two minutes later another update came over the radio: 'Caller says the offender has killed the girl. Caller says the male has a knife.' Jess looked at Gary. Suddenly this sounded much more serious. As the response car, they had to go.

'Romeo eight one Tango, we will attend,' she confirmed, and Gary switched on the blue lights and gunned the engine. While Jess was on the radio, he focused on the road: response driving requires skill, training and concentration. Gary positioned the vehicle in the centre of the carriageway, to 'own' the road. He wanted other cars not just to see him but to know immediately where he wanted to go, so they could get out of the way without delay or confusion.

As he approached the junction on Harborough Road, the lights turned green. Gary maintained speed, but suddenly another car appeared from the left – it must have jumped the lights. Jess caught her breath as Gary shouted out, 'Fuck!'

Seeing the police car, the other driver slammed on the brakes, but he was right in Gary's path. Hitting his own brakes, Gary just managed to swerve round – missing the other vehicle by inches.

As they passed, Jess looked at the two panicked occupants of the other car. That driver was a lucky man, she thought: not only had he avoided a nasty accident, but also a fine or penalty points – as she and Gary had no time to stop.

As the police car hurtled along city streets, Jess got back on the radio. Because the caller had mentioned a knife, she decided to ask for taser authority. Although in an emergency trained officers can make the decision to use their tasers on the spur of the moment, in circumstances like this they were expected to ask permission.

'Sierra two – this is Romeo eight one Tango. Can FIM be made aware and taser authority granted?'

Jess waited. Police regulations require an authorising officer – known as a Force Incident Manager or FIM – to use a particular form of words that itemise the reasons for granting permission. After what seemed like hours, but in reality was only a minute or two, the radio squawked into life:

'Taser authority requested as a contingency due to indications that the male armed with the knife has attacked his girlfriend and according to caller to the police she is fatally injured. Taser is a contingency due to the information passed to us indicating that the male is still in possession of the knife. Sierra two aware of the incident and potential seriousness of the incident . . .'

At the speeds they were travelling the crackly radio was hard to understand, and Jess was trying to map read at the same time.

'Please,' she interrupted, 'just tell me yes or no!'

There was a short pause, then: 'Yes – taser proportionate and justified at this time.'

They were close to their destination by now. Jess couldn't quite make out whether the address they wanted – Seabrook Road – was the first or second turn.

'Now – second right,' she ordered, and Gary swung the car into the junction. As they passed the street sign, her heart sank. 'Shit, it was the first one.' Gary drove to the end of the short street, turned right and then right again, and brought them back down into the right road.

Most police cars have spotter lights on the dashboard, and as Gary slowed the car Jess shined hers to the side to see if she could see the house numbers. Ahead, he could see group of figures in the street.

'I think it might be something to do with that crowd!' he said, and pulled up. The people were pointing at the house. Jess jumped out first. Although the street was reasonably well lit, the front of the building was obscured by a tree. Next to the front door there was a bay window. As Jess approached, a net curtain was pulled back and a man appeared. He looked Middle Eastern or Asian – and the caller had described the suspect as black or dark-skinned.

'Get out here now!' commanded Jess, but the man shook

his head. Jess moved closer. 'Get out here and open this door,' she said again.

The top window was open a little, and the man threw out something shiny towards Jess. She looked down: it was a pair of keys. She looked back at the man, who was very small and quite obviously terrified. Jess picked up the keys and moved to the front door. It was dark wood, with frosted glazing, and there was a light on inside the hall. As she put the key in the lock, a shadow fell across her and she looked up. A huge silhouette loomed up behind the door and Jess felt a sudden surge of primal fear. The figure reached for the handle behind the door.

'No,' thought Jess, 'you're not fucking coming out of there,' and she gripped the door handle with all her strength. After what seemed an age, the figure turned away and disappeared deeper into the building. Jess realised she was shaking a little, and felt a wave of relief as Gary appeared alongside her. As she turned the key, he pulled out his taser. She shook her head to get rid of the image of the dark shadow.

Jess pushed the door open and the two officers walked into the hallway. As they did so, a tall black man emerged from a door on one side. He moved towards them slowly, but appeared unaware of their presence as if disconnected from reality. He was wearing jeans and a dark shirt, and Jess noticed he was barefoot, with blood on his feet, and there was some kind of white foam around his mouth.

'Stop! Stand still! Police with taser!' shouted Gary. Jess jumped: Gary was usually fairly calm and she could hear the menace in his voice.

A red dot appeared on the man's chest. Gary had activated his taser's targeting beam. Police tasers have bright yellow plastic casings with a pistol grip and trigger. When fired, two metal barbs shoot out; these are designed to separate in the air and hit the subject a couple of inches apart. Once embedded in skin or clothing, they deliver a 50,000 volt shock – usually enough to incapacitate the target almost immediately. For optimum effect, officers are taught to aim for muscle mass – the chest, back or, if necessary, the buttocks.

The man paused, then slowly dropped to his knees. As Gary kept his taser raised, Jess put hers back in its holster and pushed the man forward to the ground, kneeling on the back of his legs.

'If you move you'll get 50,000 volts through you,' she snapped, and unclipped her handcuffs. As she reached for his arm, it slid from her grasp and she frowned: it was cold, wet and slippery. She realised it was covered in blood. Jess leant forward. 'Where is she?' she hissed.

'She was going to leave me,' he sobbed. 'She was going to leave me, man.'

Jess snapped on the handcuffs, then stood up and hammered on the closed door near the front of the house. The small Asian man opened the door. He stared at her, shaking visibly: Jess had never seen anyone so frightened. He slowly raised his hand, and pointed towards the doorway at the rear of the hall.

Leaving the man on the floor with Gary, Jess walked through the door into the unlit room. At first she could see nothing wrong. It was a communal living area with a coffee table, sofa and chairs. In the corner was a television. Normally they'd expect to find things out of place, but here nothing was in disarray.

Around the corner leading to the kitchen a light was on, and Jess turned towards it. As she did so, she saw the body against the wall – its feet towards the kitchen and its right hand pressed up against the wall.

She didn't notice that the woman was strikingly beautiful, or that she was wearing patterned pyjamas, or that she had had her nails done that day. What she noticed was the gaping hole in her neck, the vicious bruises on her face and the huge pool of blood.

'Get an ambulance NOW – female victim has been cut to the jugular!' she shouted into her radio, then knelt down. She reached for the woman's right hand to check for a pulse, and it was still warm. Jess could see blood oozing from her neck, and realised she needed to stop the flow. As she pressed down on the wound, she could feel the collar bone, tissues and blood vessels. The pool of blood around her feet was about half an inch deep. Jess looked around; the woman's chest was peppered with numerous stab marks and cuts, and blood was smeared down the wall where she had fallen.

Other officers were arriving, and Jess looked up as Rich Shirtliffe and Malcolm Sutherland came in. Both were already wearing latex gloves, and Rich passed a pair to Jess. She asked Malcolm to take over trying to stop any more blood loss from the neck, and prepared to administer CPR. Rich started pumping the woman's chest, but as he did so her head lolled to one side, causing the wound to open again. Jess shuddered: for a split second it looked as though her head was about to come off.

Jess pushed her plastic airway intubator pipe into the woman's mouth and knelt forward to give the kiss of life. With the first breath she felt a rush of air. The woman couldn't still be alive – could she?

'Game on here, mates, she's breathing, she's breathing!' said

Jess, elated. She blew again into the woman's mouth – again the rush of air. But the joy was short-lived. Jess quickly realised something wasn't right. She looked down, and realised to her horror that the draft she could feel was her own breath coming back at her through the woman's severed windpipe.

Then two paramedics arrived and took over. One fetched a defibrillator and tried to restart the heart, but there was no hope. The woman was dead.

Jess sat back. She had done all she could. The older paramedic looked at his watch. 'Time of death 23.22,' he said calmly. His colleague, a young woman, looked shell-shocked. Jess guessed she was relatively inexperienced – this might well be her first murder scene. The man seemed keen to get her out; besides, there was nothing more the paramedics could do.

Jess called in the time of death to her control room, then sighed and stood up. For the first time, she looked down at herself and became aware that her clothing was covered in blood. She took off the latex gloves she'd been given and took one of a small pile of wipes that the paramedics had left for the police. We need more of these, she thought.

Jess found herself oddly detached. She was thinking very clearly. As a police officer, she knew she still had a job to do. First, she pulled out her pocket book and drew a diagram of the layout of the lounge. On it she marked the position of various things – furniture, a broken door, the victim's body – and marked where things had been moved by herself or her colleagues. She knew this might be important when the case came to trial.

Then it occurred to her that she had not seen a weapon. Certainly there was no knife left in the body, and the man had had nothing in his hands when she'd seen him. She walked through the arch into the kitchen, stepping over the broken door. There were notes on the fridge written in a language Jess didn't understand, but in words heavy with consonants. A drawer had been left open, and there was a clear trail of blood spots from the victim and some blood on the handle. Inside there were various knives and utensils, but nothing she could see with blood on it.

'Come on, Rich,' she said to her colleague. 'Where's the knife? Let's find it.' Jess spent some more time looking around, but there was no sign of a murder weapon. Detectives and crime scene officers were arriving, and Jess realised there was nothing more she could do. She allowed herself to be led outside.

As she emerged from the house, Jess could see flashing lights and police tape everywhere. The scale of the job hit her, and she realised she was at the centre of what would become a huge investigation. Dutch was nowhere to be seen; he had probably gone with the suspect to a police station. Another colleague asked what it was like inside. Jess paused, and thought of the scene in the kitchen. 'Fucking awful, mate,' she replied, and suddenly, although she was not sobbing, she felt tears rolling down her face. She thought of the woman. She had been warm. Her skin was beautiful and smooth, her nails were immaculate baby pink, her hair shiny and blonde. Jess remembered how, for an instant, she had truly believed there might be a spark of that bright young life remaining. And she remembered the crushing sense of sadness when she realised there was not.

'Come on, let's get you back to the station,' said Jess's inspector. It was clear that she was in her own world. In the car, they teased Jess that she would need to get her clothes off and be given the utilitarian jogging bottoms and t-shirts intended for prisoners.

Back at the police station, Jess sensed the fascination among her colleagues. She could tell they were desperate to ask for all the details, but at the same time anxious not to probe too much.

She sat down at a computer to write her statement. As she leant forward, a spot of liquid hit the desk. She looked down: blood was smeared across the front of her jacket, and her torch and radio. Her trousers were sodden. Suddenly, she became aware of the foul, metallic smell, and began to retch and heave. Colleagues helped her to her feet and she went to change. She bagged up all her clothes and sealed them in paper evidence bags, ensuring they were marked with hazard tape to warn others about the contents.

As she walked back along the corridor, her station sergeant called her into a private office. 'All right, Jess, how are you doing? It's a terrible shame what happened to the woman, but you and Dutch did a great job tonight.' Jess found herself welling up. In public she kept a lid on her emotions, but here in the office it was different. She thought again about the woman with the beautiful blonde hair. She thought about the notes stuck on the fridge door – what had the woman been thinking or hoping when she wrote them? She thought about the wrong turn they'd taken driving to the scene – if they had got there thirty seconds earlier would they have been in time to save her? Jess leaned forward and let the tears come.

'Right, I think we need to get you home, OK?' the sergeant said. Jess nodded, and they walked down to the car park. Later, Jess would come to realise that this was the worst decision she could have made.

★

Jess sat down in her living room and sipped some tea. When her husband, Matt, came down, she tried to explain what had happened. She couldn't sleep, and Matt stayed up with her for most of the night before he had to leave for work. Jess started to doze, then was woken up by a call from her chief inspector. As they spoke, she felt the tears coming again. He told her about the counselling and occupational therapy that were available, and said she would be automatically referred. He described an experience of his own: being one of the first officers on the scene of the Hillsborough disaster, in which ninety-six football fans died in a crush before a match. For nearly thirteen years afterwards, he said, he had been unable to talk about it without crying. Jess was reassured.

Later that day, she received another call, from the officer in charge of the murder investigation. He wanted to check a couple of the points in her statement. Jess asked if they knew who the victim was. 'Oh yes,' he replied. 'Her name's Weronika – she's Polish.' She also learned that the murder weapons – two knives – had been found upstairs on the bed. There was also a length of towel, which the accused later claimed he planned to use to hang himself.

Jess sat back. Now she knew the name of the poor woman with the blonde hair and the baby pink nails. It struck a chord, as her brother's wife was Polish too.

As she'd come to the end of her run of night shifts, Jess was rostered off for the next four days. She knew her husband was doing his best to be supportive and was desperate to help her, but he couldn't imagine what she'd seen, what she'd been through. She texted Dutch, but he'd gone away for a long-planned holiday with his wife and young son, and couldn't really talk. Jess felt lonely and isolated, and she couldn't stop thinking about what had happened.

When she went back to work, her inspector took her into his office and handed her a coffee. 'Let's just have a quick chat – how's it going?' Jess found herself sobbing again. 'Well,' he sighed, 'it's obviously not going that well then!' Through the tears, Jess shook her head. She was told she could take as much time off work as she wanted, but Jess thought that had been her mistake before – leaving too soon. She felt that she wanted to be around other police officers: they would understand what she had gone through, and how to deal with that shock day by day. They would understand her feelings of helplessness, and her guilt that she could somehow have done more.

Eventually, Jess went to the senior investigating officer and asked to see all the information about the case, explaining that she thought it would help her process what had happened. He told her about the results of the post mortem examination, reassuring Jess that there was nothing she could have done to save Weronika. Jess asked to see photographs of the murder scene. Though she was in tears, seeing the pictures confirmed that it was as horrific as she remembered; that she hadn't made anything up; that she was still sane.

But Jess had another problem. She had become afraid of the dark. Every time she closed her eyes, imprinted in her mind was the image of a big black silhouette coming to the door. When she was on her own that was all she could see. When she was in the dark that was all she could see.

About a month after the murder, Jess was in the police station and went to her locker, which was past the shower area at the back of the changing rooms. Suddenly, the room was plunged into darkness and she froze, paralysed by fear. Who was that in the corner? What was that dark shape? Slowly, Jess reached for her phone and called a colleague, explaining where she was and asking for help. The instant the lights came on, she relaxed. There was no one there, obviously. The lighting in the changing area was controlled by a motion sensor, and a bag had been left in front of it. Because it couldn't detect Jess's presence, it had turned off the lights to save energy.

Jess was shaken. Privately, she was worried she'd lost the plot, and started to question her sanity. She had always seen herself as a sensible person – calm and collected – and to suddenly become nervous of things that she knew weren't there . . . that wasn't the Jess she knew.

Jess's anxiety had reached the point where she couldn't even walk alone in the dark to and from the police station car park, and a colleague had to accompany her. She was diagnosed with post traumatic stress and sent to a psychiatrist. Jess told him what had happened and described the dark figure that was haunting her thoughts. He tried a technique known as repetitive eye movement, which felt to Jess like a form of hypnosis. It worked in two stages. First, he helped her to make the dark figure in her mind smaller, so it felt as though it was further away. Then he asked her to actively think of the image but then imagine something humorous or non-threatening. Jess pictured a big red boxing glove knocking him out.

Over a period of weeks, the therapy started to work. Although Jess still had a problem with the dark she was able to function, to do her job, and she was reassured that her response was normal and could be managed. Her superior officers allowed her to adjust her shifts, so she was doing fewer nights, and ensured she was always double crewed. Where possible, at her request, they paired her up with Dutch. Jess trusted him implicitly, and felt the good working relationship they had was the best way of rebooting her confidence.

When Colin Campbell went on trial, Jess decided to go to court. Weronika's parents did not want to come over from Poland, but her brother attended. Jess sat in the public gallery. On one side were members of Weronika's family, on the other a woman whom she later learned was Campbell's sister. Directly in front of her, Campbell sat in the dock.

Jess listened as the barristers slowly and dispassionately read out the facts: Campbell had stabbed Weronika a total of forty-four times. At one point during the attack the knife had got stuck in her body, and Campbell had calmly gone to the kitchen, fetched another one and continued the attack. As the prosecutor relayed the words Campbell had said to Gary Holland – 'she said she was going to leave me' – Campbell looked directly at her. Jess stared back, wondering if he recognised her or not.

She'd expected Campbell's defence lawyers to enter a plea of diminished responsibility, but he confessed to murder. Campbell's own lawyer described him as a 'rather immature, pathetic and needy man'.

As she passed sentence, the trial judge, Mrs Justice Rafferty, spoke to Campbell directly, telling him: 'This was an attack, founded in resentment and jealousy, on a young woman you sought to possess.'

She then sentenced him to life imprisonment, and ordered that he serve at least fifteen years before he could be considered for parole. Jess looked at Weronika's family. For them, the sentence was a lifetime of regrets: of wondering what Weronika might have become, of never knowing the children she might have had. With good behaviour, mused Jess, Campbell would probably serve less time in prison than she would serve as a police officer.

Jess knew she shouldn't take it personally, but this did not feel like justice. Campbell wasn't even required to speak or explain himself during the hearing, but was allowed to sit there in what seemed to her like scornful silence. The sentence didn't seem nearly long enough.

༄

Jess Womersley largely managed to overcome her fear of darkness, and became a trainee investigator with the eventual aim of joining the CID as a detective.

Gary 'Dutch' Holland continues to be on the response team based at Attercliffe. He likes the unpredictability, and the work.

Colin Campbell can apply for parole in 2026.

4

JUST A FOOT IN A DRAIN

*'You either get heroic rescue because you have got a
survivor or you get tragic failure because you haven't
got a survivor. There is no middle ground.'*

PC RICHARD 'ROCKY' CLARK

It felt as though it would never stop raining. As Sergeant Phil
Young drove his Proton patrol car along Springfield Way
towards Anlaby, on the outskirts of Hull, he could barely
make out the road for the surface water washing across it.
Even on their fastest setting, the windscreen wipers seemed
powerless to interrupt the constant spattering of fat, heavy
raindrops that distorted Phil's view. He leant forward to see
more clearly.

The first floods had been ten days ago. Persistent rain
had raised water levels beyond any hope that city engineers
might have of the drainage system coping. Homes, businesses,
schools, whole streets had been indiscriminately filled with
filthy brown flood water. But then the rains had paused and
the flood waters had receded. Those whose homes were
spared had breathed a sigh of relief; those whose homes were
not had begun cleaning up.

Now, thought Phil, the rains were back, and it had not taken long for the waters to rise again. He peered ahead through the windscreen. What was that in the middle of the road? He slowed down, barely able to see, and barely able to believe what he was seeing.

A pillar of white water was gushing up from the centre of the road. Around the opening the ground had been forced up, and great chunks of tarmac – the size and shape of dustbin lids – were scattered around, lying where the force of the water had thrown them.

Phil parked half on the kerb and got out. On the other side of the gushing water he could see a long queue of cars. Some drivers were already turning round in the street to look for an alternative route. The severe flooding was already causing traffic chaos in this Monday morning rush hour, and the police switchboard was being inundated with calls from worried householders.

Phil sighed. He was supposed to be travelling to nearby Anlaby, to make an assessment of conditions there, but it was clear this road would have to be closed. For that, he would need cones and signs. He went back to his car, and picked up the radio handset.

Three miles away, at Cottingham police station in North Hull, PC Richard Clark had just come on duty. Richard – who was known to everyone as Rocky – had joined Humberside Police at the age of eighteen. He'd spent an entire career as a front line police constable. He was a member of the police diving club and also a keen mountaineer.

Hearing Phil's request for cones and signs, and having seen how deep the water was in some places, Rocky decided to take the police box van – a Ford Transit – as it had higher ground clearance. He fetched some cones from the yard store and threw them in the back. Jess Watts, a Police Community Support Officer (PCSO), went with him. They drove round to meet Phil and handed over the cones. Then Rocky had a thought.

'There are a couple of old people living in the houses on Tranby Lane,' he told Jess. 'It's just round the corner from here. I think we should go and check up on them.'

It didn't take them long to get there. Like many of the roads that morning, the entire surface was obscured by dirty brown flood water. Rocky knew that either side of the road, between the kerb and the front gardens of the houses, were open drains, but they were invisible beneath the water. As he drove up the hill, he focused on keeping the police van in the middle of the road. In the passenger seat, Jess was getting nervous.

Suddenly, Rocky realised the vehicle had stopped climbing the hill and had started drifting backwards.

'What's happening?' asked Jess, looking around.

'We're floating!' cried Rocky incredulously, looking out of the windows on either side. Although the hill wasn't steep, the van was picking up speed. He'd selected the van because he thought it was less likely to get bogged down – but he hadn't banked on becoming waterborne. He twisted the steering wheel from side to side but it made no difference. 'Crap,' he thought. 'I think we're going to crash.' But then the hill bottomed out and the water level fell. Rocky felt the wheels touch down and he recovered control of the vehicle.

'I think we'll turn round here and go back the way we

came!' he said, wondering if the day was going to get any stranger.

By now, Phil was on the move again. But communicating was becoming a problem. Not only was his own personal radio having problems with the wet; he was worried that the volume of calls to the police meant that their communications network was in danger of becoming overloaded. The radio system usually worked well, but when demand was high it struggled. He spoke to the duty officer at headquarters, and suggested bringing in extra operators and splitting the channels to double the capacity.

He'd also had to close another stretch of road; not because it was impassable but because the bow-waves from motorists driving too quickly, especially in 4x4s, were cresting front doorsteps and swamping the homes of people either side.

Phil had joined the Merchant Navy from school, and had spent nearly ten years sailing the world. But in his view the life of a sailor was not one for a family man, and at the age of twenty-nine he'd joined the police. A keen diver like his colleague Rocky, he had wanted to join the underwater search unit, but once he was promoted to sergeant there always seemed to be something else that needed doing.

Phil was continuing on his rounds when another message came through. 'Any units near Astral Close, there's a man with his foot stuck in a drain.' Phil frowned. It didn't sound too serious, but a trapped man was higher priority than some slow traffic. As the location was nearby, he began to make his way over.

Then, almost immediately, the radio crackled to life again:

'The water's up to the man's neck. Any units in vicinity Astral Close please attend.' Phil was taken aback and quickened his pace, trying to fathom how a man with his foot stuck in a drain could suddenly be up to his neck in flood water.

That morning, twenty-eight-year-old Michael Barnett had left home to go to work at the usual time. Michael had a job at an aquatic centre and fish farm nearby in Hessle. As he walked out into the pouring rain, his father, also called Michael, called out to him, warning him to steer clear of the storm drain next to his workplace.

The residents of Astral Close didn't like the storm drain. A horizontal, four-foot diameter concrete pipe, it took run-off water from the suburbs of Anlaby and the rising farmland beyond under the city centre and out into the Humber estuary. The end was protected by a large vertical box-grate, designed to allow water to flow round the sides even if debris blocked the front. But this didn't seem to be working: during the first floods the water had quickly backed up and left the street ankle deep.

The authorities seemed indifferent to the problem, so a group of residents decided to take action. A JCB digger was brought in, a chain was fixed to the grate and it was torn out. A short time later, the water level began to fall. The residents congratulated each other on their initiative.

What none of them knew was that the changing water level was nothing to do with the debris or the grate. Half a mile away, at the other end of the drain, was a tidal valve – a large metal flap – that closed twice a day to protect the town from any exceptionally high tides. The valve had opened shortly after they'd removed the grate. This coincidence gave the locals the wrong impression that removing the storm's safety grate had solved all their problems.

Once the first floods had receded, engineers were sent to inspect the box grate. It was damaged beyond repair and would need to be replaced. A new one would have to be ordered but, in the meantime, they couldn't leave the end of the concrete pipe at the side of the ditch exposed, as local children would surely climb in. As an interim measure they took a steel fence panel – of the sort usually found around the edges of park play areas – and placed it across the front of the open pipe, fixing it with wire, steel loops and reinforcing rods driven deep into the bed of the ditch.

On the morning of Monday 25 June 2007, the persistent heavy rainfall caused residents in Astral Close to look anxiously again at the ditch and the entrance to the drain. The surging waters seemed to be flowing freely, yet they could see the level rising. Should they remove the grate again? Would that save the street from flooding? The building where Michael Barnett worked was nearby. He was well known for his happy-go-lucky nature and willingness to help, and he offered to go in and see what was happening. Michael pulled on a set of chest-waders and climbed down into the surging water . . .

'Charlie Bravo nine five. We're responding and on our way.' Rocky had also heard the message about the man with his foot stuck in a drain, and it took him and Jess barely six minutes to reach Astral Close, though they'd had to use their blue lights and sirens as the roads were gridlocked. As Rocky climbed out of the van, a woman came running over.

'Where's your diving gear and your underwater cutting stuff?' she asked. Rocky was perplexed. This was a police van:

he had a couple of spare traffic cones and a broom in the back; why would he have cutting gear? He walked down towards the small group of people on the other side of a block of concrete garages. On a roof at the far end of one of the garages, Rocky could see a man with a rope. 'What's that idiot doing?' he thought to himself. As he rounded the corner, he struggled to make sense of the scene in front of him. There was a river of surging water, and in it the head of a man. Another man was in the water with him, holding on, while another was on the garage roof above, lowering a rope down. It was hardly the 'man with his foot in a drain' that he had been expecting.

Rocky immediately radioed through to control. 'This is a life threatening situation. The man's trapped up to his neck.'

'Watch out,' said someone as Rocky moved towards the water. 'It's six-foot deep there.' Rocky stood in the driving rain, wiping the water from his face, and assessed the scene. The dirty, fast-flowing water made it impossible to tell what was beneath the surface. He climbed carefully, feeling his way along the edge of the ditch, and then out onto what he'd been told was the top of the drain. The water here was only ankle deep. Standing on the curved top of the concrete tube at the side of the ditch, he could feel it shifting slightly. He knelt down. Michael was below him in the water, his body pressed against the vertical steel grate across the pipe's entrance by the force of the water. Rocky reached down and took his hands. They were face to face, Rocky on the top of the pipe, kneeling down, Michael trapped against the end and looking up.

'Don't worry, mate,' Rocky said. 'We'll get you out of there as quick as we can.'

He looked beyond Michael. Water was still surging down the ditch towards them and into the drain. He knew that flood water was largely raw sewage, and he could see pieces of excrement and used tampons flowing past, but he was more worried about the large branches and pieces of masonry that were also being carried by the torrent.

'Just hold on, Michael. Stay with me.'

It had taken Phil Young a little longer to get to Astral Close. When he parked his car and opened the door, the water was about a foot deep in the road. He was already soaked, and the rain showed no sign of stopping, or even abating.

As he arrived, his first impression was of boiling, surging water, and in the middle of it all the face of a man. Not his whole head, just his face: he was having to crane his neck back to keep out of the water. Rocky Clark was kneeling down, speaking to him. For a second, Phil struggled to comprehend how Rocky was kneeling and yet the other man was up to his ears.

A householder had brought out a child's snorkel. As Phil walked up, residents grabbed him and warned him about the deceptive depth of water in the ditch.

'His foot's stuck,' said someone. Phil tried to assess the scene. As a sergeant, it was up to him to take charge. Though he couldn't see below the surface of the water, the problem seemed to be that Michael's ankle had become lodged between two of the vertical steel bars. Phil started to wonder how they might force the bars apart to free the man's foot. But it wasn't just the bars: the sheer force of the water pressing him against the grate was just as big a problem.

Phil knew immediately that they needed reinforcements. His personal radio was totally waterlogged, so he borrowed Jess's.

'Charlie Delta three zero at Astral Close. We'll need police divers and fire brigade cutting equipment. This is an immediate priority.' Phil wanted the divers there with scuba gear, so that if the water continued to rise they would be able to help Michael breathe, and he felt that the heavy duty cutters used by firefighters in road accidents were all that would release Michael's foot.

Rocky knew the divers were on their way. A trained diver himself, he knew how underwater breathing apparatus worked, and started explaining it to Michael. At the rate the water was rising, the divers could only stop him from drowning if they got here quickly, Rocky thought, but the lesson gave Michael something to focus on and Rocky something to do.

At police headquarters, Ron Moughton and other on-duty members of the police diving unit were doing their best to help pump out parts of the building that were flooded. They were struggling with their radios too, but eventually someone managed to reach Ron on his mobile phone.

'Come on, lads,' he said. 'There's something down in Hessle. A lad with his foot stuck in a drain.' Even as he said it, he wondered why the divers were needed: it seemed a little excessive. Nonetheless, he told dive commander Dave Robinson, who ordered the team to deploy. Divers Mark Kelk, Ian Claxton and Simon Ravenscroft put one set of scuba gear in the unit's Land Rover and headed off, while Ron climbed into the thirty-five-foot lorry that carried the majority of their equipment and followed them down.

Rocky hadn't moved from his position on top of the pipe.

Michael was frightened, and Rocky was holding his hands and trying to reassure him.

'Stay calm, Michael. We're going to get you out.' Rocky was self reliant and used to making quick decisions and solving problems. He was familiar with the look of expectation on people's faces when the police arrived – that all their problems were about to be solved. He could see that look on Michael's face. But this was different. Rocky wanted to help Michael – he'd *promised* to help Michael – but at the moment he didn't have any answers. The flowing water was just so powerful.

Phil's main concern was the rising water level. He wasn't sure how long Michael would be able to breathe. There was a breeze-block wall along the edge of the ditch, and one of the local residents suggested knocking it down to give the water a run-off. Phil thought it was a good idea, and certainly worth a try. He asked people to fetch any sledgehammers they had. One man disagreed, and suggested using the winch on his pick-up truck to drag Michael out, but Phil thought that would do more harm than good. Another man was worried about an electrical junction box nearby, and Phil said they'd make sure it was undamaged. Once the sledgehammers arrived, the wall fell quickly and water surged out over the rubble. The effect was immediate, and the water level around Michael fell by around three inches.

Rocky focused again on Michael. His chin was above water, which was a good sign. The rain was still pouring down, but perhaps smashing down the wall had been enough to stop the waters rising further. Now though Michael was starting to shiver in the onrush of cold water. There was a new danger: not drowning but the cold.

When the police dive team arrived, Phil and Rocky relaxed a little. Most of them were Rocky's friends from the diving club. He'd kept talking to Michael, trying to reassure him and keep his spirits up.

One of the divers, Mark Kelk, put on a drysuit. The diving team decided to get him into the water as quickly as possible; there was no time to go through the procedures and checklists usually required when putting on breathing apparatus.

They fixed two tethered lifelines to Mark, and he climbed down into the water and moved round behind Michael. It was around an hour since the alarm had been raised, and Michael had been in the water considerably longer. The first priority was to try to warm him up. Mark put a coat around Michael to shield him from the water and to insulate him a little against the cold. Someone also fetched a silver thermal blanket. But each time something was put around Michael, it was very quickly ripped off and washed away by the force of the torrent.

'Can you move him at all?' asked Rocky. Mark stood behind Michael and reached around, trying to lift him. He used all his strength, but Michael was held fast against the grate.

'It's no good. He's jammed in solid,' he said, standing close behind Michael, to provide shelter and heat with his own body.

By now, more fire crews had arrived. Among them was their commander, 'Taff' Evans. He explained to Phil that he'd sent two of his vehicles upstream to start pumping water out of the ditch, in an effort to reduce the pressure and make a rescue possible. He also said that his crews were not equipped or trained to deal with such extreme water conditions, but he did have cutting gear, and ordered it to be brought up to the drain.

Dave Robinson was the dive commander. His problem, he said, was that the police divers were trained in underwater search techniques, not rescue. Their equipment – their suits, their masks, their breathing gear – was designed to help them go into water, not to help them get other people out.

Phil, Dave and Taff agreed that the divers would carry out all operations in the water, and the fire teams would do all they could to help from the sides.

One of the other divers, Ian Claxton, had put on breathing apparatus and was preparing to go in.

Dave Robinson briefed him. 'I want you to find out how he's trapped, and come back and tell us what we need to do. See if we can cut it. But watch yourself.'

A lifeline was fixed to Ian, and three firefighters took the end. He climbed down the side of the ditch and disappeared from view beneath the murky waters.

The visibility was zero. All Ian could see was dark, murky water. He moved towards the grate, feeling his way. The water pressure was intense: it was taking all his strength to inch forward. He could feel Michael's back, then his waist; and with a start he realised that not just Michael's foot but his entire leg – right up to the thigh – was pushed through the grate. He reached through the grate to try to feel the other side. The instant he did so, the water pressure pushed his whole body up against the grate, hard. He tried to twist around, but he couldn't move. One arm was now in the pipe, and his head and shoulder were pressed against the grate. As he turned his head, the force of the water ripped off his face mask, and he felt the cold water on his face and in his eyes.

He shut them tight, and instinctively clenched his teeth to grip his mouthpiece. Luckily it remained in place so he could breathe, even though he couldn't see. He tried to work his way out with his free arm and legs, but he couldn't get any leverage to pull clear. The force of the rushing water was too strong, and he was tiring rapidly. He tried again to get himself clear, but it was no good. Reluctantly, Ian reached for his lifeline and gave three firm tugs – the emergency signal. At the other end, the three firefighters began pulling. Eventually, with all their combined strength, he managed to get clear.

Breathing heavily, Ian waded to the side, quickly pulling his face mask back into place. He reported on Michael's position, and explained that it felt as if the waders the man was wearing had ballooned full of water. This explained why attempts to pull him back had all been futile. He said nothing about his own narrow escape, as he knew the dive commander wouldn't let him back in the water if he was told about it.

Up on the bank, Taff, Phil, Dave and the others were discussing other possibilities. For every idea, there seemed to be snags, problems or unknowns.

'What about driving a vehicle into the ditch to dam the flow?' 'Which vehicle will we use? Who'll drive it? What if the vehicle is swept down and crashes into him? It'll crush him, and probably kill any divers in the water too.'

'Could we attach a rope to the winch on our Land Rover and pull him out?'

'We could, but if his leg is badly trapped might we tear it off? If we sever an artery he'll bleed out in minutes.'

'Could we use the fire brigade's hydraulic cutter to free Michael?'

'You're welcome to try, but the divers aren't used to them

and they're big and heavy – hard for one man to control in such fast flowing water.'

The last seemed to be the only plan with even a remote chance of success, and Ian Claxton went back into the water with the heavy portable cutters. He tried time and again but the force of the water, the cutters' weight, debris around the grating and the complete lack of visibility made it impossible to use them.

Taff had called for a 'Hiab' truck with a jib – but it hadn't arrived. The fire brigade had one in Hull and one in Grimsby – where were they? And Phil had contacted the council earlier and asked them to send a lorry with sandbags that might be able to plug the ditch – if only to reduce the pressure for a minute or two and let them get Michael out. They'd also requested that a trauma surgeon come to the scene: as a last resort they might be able to amputate his foot to get him out.

The problem for Phil was that because of the problems with the waterlogged radios, he wasn't even sure if their messages were getting through. He'd been trying to keep his incident log up to date, but it was almost hopeless. In the driving rain the pages were sodden. Everyone who came up wanted to know the same things: What was happening? Why hadn't they rescued Michael? Why hadn't they got the right equipment? Phil understood their curiosity, but it was frustrating: he was supposed to be the ringmaster but he felt like the juggler. Someone had told him that Michael's father lived not far away. He sent off one of the police officers to go and fetch him, so he could see and talk to his son.

Rocky was still focused on Michael. He'd been in the water for over an hour and a half. Rocky noticed he'd stopped shivering; a text-book sign of the onset of hypothermia. The water wasn't especially cold, but it was so fast-flowing that it was simply stripping out Michael's body heat minute by minute, and this was starting to take its toll. Mark Kelk was shielding him as best he could, but it wasn't enough. Time was running out.

'Michael, Michael, stay with me,' he said, worried. Michael seemed drowsy; his skin was becoming very pale and his lips were turning blue.

'We need to do something quick,' Rocky called out to the side. 'I don't think he can hold on much longer.'

The senior officers looked at each other. A TV crew had arrived, and were setting up their camera to film. The story was becoming national news. They discussed the options again, all too aware of each minute ticking by. The heavy rain was continuing to hamper communications, but Taff finally got a message that there was a problem with the fire brigade's heavy cranes: one had broken down, and another was stuck in traffic that had been gridlocked by the floods. The senior officers tried to think of yet another plan.

'What if we can lift the bottom of the grate – break the seal, and raise Michael out of the way a bit? Maybe that will ease the pressure enough,' said Dave, the dive commander. No one had any better ideas.

One of the fire engines was fitted with an electric winch. They fixed it to the grate, but when they switched it on and it started to turn it immediately cut out, possibly overloaded.

The diving team's Land Rover was fitted with a similar device, so Phil went to fetch it and parked it next to the ditch, facing the drain. He then wound out the winch cable and passed it down into the water. One of the divers took the cable underwater and attached it to the grate, careful to avoid getting trapped.

Phil asked Rocky to climb off the drain and help hold the diver's tether with a couple of firefighters.

When everyone indicated they were ready, Phil switched on the winch. There was a whirring sound as the drum spun round and took up the slack, then the note changed as the cable went taut.

Phil kept the button pressed and the cable drew tighter and tighter. The Land Rover was wedged against the kerb, but the tension almost seemed to be lifting it off the ground.

Suddenly, there was a whooshing in the water. The grate had pulled away at its lower corner. As they watched in horror, it seemed as though an invisible hand had grabbed Michael and the diver behind him and pulled them both underwater. All he could see was bubbling on the surface, and the dirty water. Then, after a second or two, Michael's hands appeared, clutching at the air. Ron Moughton reacted instinctively. Although he wasn't tethered, he jumped in and grabbed hold of Michael, trying to pull him up.

Mark Kelk – the diver – still hadn't surfaced. He couldn't overcome the force of the water sucking him down towards the bottom of the grate. He wasn't wearing breathing apparatus and, unable to get clear of the filthy water, he was going to die. Then, suddenly, he felt a force pulling him back and up, and he burst into daylight. Those holding his tether pulled so hard he almost lifted clear out of the water.

Seeing what had happened, Phil quickly put the winch into reverse. The grate slammed back into place, and Ron was able to lift Michael's head back up above the surface.

Rocky climbed back round to the pipe, and reached for

Michael's hands. They were cold, cold. Mark Kelk got back in the water and put the coat around Michael again. Ron tried to place a breathing regulator in his mouth, but Michael was delirious and kept spitting it out. Ron tried explaining how the breathing apparatus worked, and trying to reassure him, but Michael refused to use it.

Suddenly Michael looked up towards Rocky, and stopped struggling. Rocky looked into Michael's eyes. The pupils had virtually disappeared. All he could see was blue – there was no black centre. Rocky held on to Michael's hands. He was still breathing, but his arms were limp and he had no expression on his face. At this point Michael was beyond fear and beyond pain. It was as though everything had stopped. Rocky had rescued drowning divers and had seen dead people before. He knew the look. He knew he was watching Michael Barnett's last few seconds of life.

Behind Michael, Mark Kelk was hugging Michael, trying to keep him going. But it was no use. Michael had stopped breathing.

Rocky stood up, walked off the top of the pipe and went for a smoke. He climbed up into the cab of the dive lorry to get away from everyone. His mind was spinning with raw, jagged emotions: anger, sadness, guilt, despair. The sour taste of failure. He had promised Michael he would save him, but he had not, and the last thing Michael would have seen was his face.

Back at the drain, the mood was sombre. Mark Kelk, who was still in the water, continued to support Michael's head.

A man came up to Phil and introduced himself as Herman Vixseboxse, a trauma consultant from Hull Royal Infirmary. He said he'd been told he may have to amputate a man's

81

foot, and had brought a special medical saw. Phil explained what had happened. The doctor checked Michael's pulse, and found nothing. He couldn't reach Michael's legs, and the filthy water made it impossible to see anyway. He said there was no real way he could amputate one or both of Michael's legs. Surgery had never, realistically, been an option.

Up on Astral Close, Phil wondered why Michael's father hadn't arrived. He went to find the policewoman he'd sent to bring him down.

'What happened to Michael's dad? I thought I asked you to bring him down,' he said.

'Oh, sorry, Sarge,' she replied. 'When I brought him to the cordon, the sergeant in charge there sent him home again.'

Phil was aghast. That action had deprived Michael the comforting presence of his father, and denied his father a last chance to see his son. It also meant that Mr Barnett learned of his son's death when the headline flashed up on the TV news.

Finally, around forty-five minutes later, the large fire brigade crane arrived. Rocky, Phil and the others looked on as it was driven into position, and its four hydraulic stabilising feet were deployed. The jib was rotated out over the water, and chains were fixed to the grate, with a tether support for Michael. The crane began to lift, but the steel grate was so tightly secured that the jib began to oscillate up and down. Eventually, there was a crunching sound and the grille supports gave way. As the grille rose up out of the water the pressure was lifted, and as the water drained from Michael's waders his legs fell out from between the bars.

Rocky was looking in the mirror at Cottingham police

station. He was naked except for his boxer shorts, his entire body alabaster white, having got out of his wet clothes. As other officers milled around dealing with the problems of a city that seemed to be half underwater, Rocky sipped at the hot chocolate and allowed his temperature to stabilise. Slowly, he started to feel physically normal again, but his mind was still racing.

The next day, Rocky was having breakfast with his wife and one-year-old daughter. He burst into tears, went upstairs to his bedroom and sobbed for fifteen minutes. Suddenly, he stopped. He felt as if something inside him had been turned off.

Rocky was numb, and for the next three or four months he wandered around in a daze, unable to care about anything. He felt like a failure. Much of the press coverage was critical, and Rocky believed his superiors weren't publicly supporting him enough. If they'd got Michael out it would have been seen as a heroic rescue, but because he died it was a tragic failure. There was no middle ground. No one seemed to understand that once Michael was trapped in the drain it would have taken a miracle to save him.

Things came to a head during a family holiday in Ireland, when he almost crashed the family car after going into what seemed like a trance. Rocky needed help, and began to see a police psychologist. The doctor told him that some of his problems were down to gaps in his memory; his mind was trying to fill them in, which was why he couldn't stop thinking about what had happened. Slowly, they began to complete the picture.

Phil Young was also seeing the psychologist. He too spent long hours wondering whether they'd failed Michael, and thinking up more and more elaborate plans that could have saved him.

About a week after the accident, he recognised Michael's father at a local supermarket and introduced himself. Mr Barnett had been critical of the emergency services in a TV interview, but he apologised to Phil and said he'd been misquoted. He didn't blame the police or the firefighters on the scene, and believed that they had done their best for his son.

At the inquest, a health and safety expert was scathing. He told the coroner Geoffrey Saul that numerous rescue divers had been killed in similar circumstances, and that in his view none of the officers should have entered the water without heavy lifting equipment. It was estimated that the current at the entrance to the drain was between fifteen and twenty knots, and the maximum working current for divers in normal conditions is half a knot.

The coroner also heard from local residents, as well as from Phil, Rocky, Ron and the other officers who were there. Some bystanders who gave evidence criticised the emergency services – saying they seemed to be unprofessional and lacking in strategy.

Mr Saul said the case highlighted a gap in the capability of the UK's emergency services.

'It has become clear that neither the fire service, the police nor the ambulance service have an underwater rescue capability,' he said. He added that climate change could make such freak flooding a more regular occurrence.

After hearing all the evidence, the jury returned a verdict of accidental death. The coroner turned to Michael Barnett's father, offered his condolences and said his son was a 'truly fine young man'.

When the inquest was over, reporters asked Mr Barnett outside the coroner's court if he felt the emergency services had let his son down. After reminding them that some of the emergency crews had gone into the water without any proper equipment, he paused and said: 'All I can say is they were a brave bunch of lads.'

∽◠◡∽

Dave Robinson, the dive commander, retired within a month. He had stayed on beyond his retirement date for some time because he enjoyed the work and his colleagues felt he was good at it.

Rocky Clark's marriage broke down, and he retired from the police. He now works with disabled children, taking them hiking, climbing and diving. He also works as a volunteer with a dolphin rescue group.

Phil Young is still a neighbourhood police officer. He's eligible to retire in 2015.

The following year £1.2 million was spent on flood protection for Hull and the East Riding of Yorkshire. A new £15,000 heavy-duty box cage with reinforced concrete mountings was fitted over the drain at Astral Close in Hessle. So far, residents have not removed it.

5

GUNFIRE IN THE SMOKE

'I was thinking, there's a barrier there, that vehicle's got to stop. How are we going to respond? Because they have quite a lot of weapons with them!'

PC CHARMAIN BRENYAH

It might have been the blacked out windows, or the fancy alloy wheels. Perhaps it was the way it pulled out in front of them – a little bit too fast. As if the driver had been spooked at the sight of a marked police car.

'That looks like a baddie's car,' said PC Alan O'Connor to his colleague, PC Charmain Brenyah.

'Yes, there's something not right. I'll run a check.' In the passenger seat, Charmain reached for her folder and jotted down the car's registration number, as she'd been taught, so that if it suddenly made off she wouldn't need to rely on her memory.

Charmain was just coming to the end of her two-year probationary period. Though her father was originally from Ghana and her mother from a small village in rural Ireland, she'd been born and raised in West London. She'd originally gone into banking, reaching senior manager level at the Royal Bank of Scotland. But in her spare time she'd volunteered as a special constable. She discovered that she loved policing so much that she decided to abandon banking and join the Metropolitan Police as a regular officer – despite the considerable pay cut.

Alan had speeded up a little, and tucked in behind the silver car. It wasn't exactly a pursuit, since the other vehicle didn't seem to be making any effort to get away, but the driver must have been aware that each turn he made was matched by the following police car.

Alan and Charmain had been patrolling the Kensal Green and Kilburn areas of north-west London all afternoon. They were in Alan's favourite patrol car, a Vauxhall Astra he'd christened Oliver after a car featured in the TV show *Top Gear*. The original Oliver was a forty-three-year-old Opel Kadett found in Botswana and restored; the Astra was its modern successor. After a couple of unusually exciting jobs, Alan had decided it was lucky, and he used it for his patrols whenever he could.

Alan had grown up nearby, and had studied business at university. Like Charmain, he'd considered a job in the financial services industry, but emerging one day from a gruelling interview for an analyst's job with one of the big City insurance brokers, he'd watched a police car with its blue lights on chasing down the road. 'That's what I want to do,' he thought, and joined the police instead.

Ahead, the silver car had become bogged down in traffic. Alan could see it was an Audi, but there was no way of seeing how many people were inside through the smoked windows. Suddenly Charmain's radio squawked into life as the vehicle check came back:

'Registration shows target car has been reported lost/stolen.' Charmain looked at Alan. Their instincts had been right! This changed things!

It was almost as if the other driver could read their thoughts: the Audi suddenly ducked out into the centre of the carriageway and accelerated, overtaking the long line of stationary vehicles and forcing oncoming traffic to move to the side. Alan turned on his sirens and blue lights, pulled out into the oncoming lane and followed.

Alan was a grade three driver – which meant he was authorised to drive with flashing blue lights and sirens but not permitted to actively pursue. He knew there was little chance of him overtaking the Audi with his relatively low-powered Astra, and made it his goal simply to stay with them. Now the Audi had been confirmed as stolen, Alan knew that a more highly trained pursuit team would be sent.

Although both officers had personal radios, Charmain reached forward and switched on the vehicle transmitter. This was standard procedure, as it would allow more senior colleagues to manage the chase and assess the risks, and would draw other vehicles to them. As he drove, Alan kept up a running commentary of the streets they were passing so anyone listening in would know where they were.

Alan struggled to keep up as the powerful Audi made high-speed left and right turns through the residential streets. They were now in a group of streets known as the Avenues, just on the border of West Kilburn and Kensal Town. Alan knew the streets as his own father had lived there. Alan slowed for the speed bumps, then accelerated again. Ahead, the Audi took a left turn and disappeared from view.

Alan took the turn and immediately slammed on the

brakes. The silver Audi was stationary in the middle of the road, right in front of them. Alan managed to stop with just inches between them.

Charmain shouted into the radio: 'Vehicle stopped, vehicle stopped, decamp.' She had already assumed that whoever was inside was about to make a run for it, and was opening her door to continue the pursuit on foot. Alan put the car in neutral and pulled on the handbrake. Charmain was already out of the car and running towards the passenger door of the Audi.

As she reached for the handle, at the back of her mind she started to wonder why no one had got out of the car. Suddenly, on the driver's side, a man stood up. He turned towards her, and raised a handgun. Charmain found that all she could see was the weapon. It seemed to fill the scene. She shouted 'Gun! Gun!' and turned and ran back towards the patrol car, crouching down, waiting for the man to open fire, wondering if she would be hit.

Alan was only just opening his door when he saw the rear passenger get out. The gun looked black and deadly. He saw the masked man raise it towards Charmain. Saw her turn and run. Saw him crouch down into the classic firing position. Saw his knuckle whiten as he squeezed the trigger. There was a flash and a bang and then . . . nothing.

Charmain clambered back into the Astra and ducked down into the footwell, trying to put the engine block between her and the gunman. Crouching down behind a door only worked in films, they'd told her in training – in reality, the only part of a car likely to stop a bullet was the engine.

Alan stared at the gunman. He pulled the trigger again and again – maybe four or five times. But there was no shattering glass, no bullets fizzing towards them. Alan snapped into action.

'I'll reverse, I'll reverse,' he shouted. Charmain's door was still open, but Alan gunned the engine, and it whined as the car accelerated backwards down the street. On the passenger side, Charmain grabbed the radio, shouting, 'Shots fired, shots fired,' to alert the control room.

The car travelled back around fifteen yards. Alan stopped and turned back to look at the Audi. The gunman got back in, closed the door, and it pulled away.

Without hesitating, Alan put his car in gear and followed. He was trying to stay calm, to remember his training, but the adrenaline was flooding into his bloodstream, and it was all he could do to stop shaking.

'Oh my God,' said Charmain, 'what just happened? I can't believe it!' Alan tried to focus on the driving. He remembered what he'd been taught, and tried to take in as much detail as he could. He knew he had to keep his composure, and ensure that when he followed he did so safely.

He began to think back to what had happened, remembering details. The bang he'd heard wasn't as loud as expected. Perhaps the gun wasn't real, or maybe a defective round hadn't discharged properly and had caused it to jam.

'Listen,' he said, 'I think it's probably a replica gun or something. After all, nothing actually hit us, did it?' After weighing things up, Alan was fairly sure of his ground, and anyway he wanted to reassure Charmain.

She was monitoring the radio. Most of the other units were keeping quiet – so she and Alan could transmit clearly – but from what she'd heard she knew that armed response vehicles, code named Trojan units in London, were on their way. The armed officers drove high-powered BMW 5-series cars, which were identified by the yellow discs in the lower corners of the windscreen.

After a near miss with a bus, Alan and Charmain continued to follow the Audi. Ahead, the powerful silver car was swerving around other cars, crossing onto the oncoming carriageway, using the nearside lane where necessary. 'He's a skilled driver,' Alan thought to himself ruefully.

Ahead was the looming concrete form of Trellick Tower, an imposing thirty-one-storey block of flats built in the late-1960s. Its hard, brutalist style – characteristic of its architect Erno Goldfinger – was disliked by many, but the building had recently been granted listed status.

Charmain knew that there was a sharp right-hand bend just in front of the tower, and as she watched the Audi took the corner faster than she imagined possible. Their own tyres squealed a few seconds later as Alan made the same turn.

As he drove, Alan was aware that he did not want to get too close to the Audi. He was feeling slightly guilty that he had made the decision to follow without consulting Charmain, but he was sure she wouldn't have wanted to hold back.

On either side, Charmain saw people queuing at bus stops who stared at the speeding police car as it passed. They were gaining on the Audi. Then suddenly, a hole appeared in its rear window. Then another. Alan frowned. What the . . . ?

A second later the entire rear window of the car in front exploded, showering glass fragments onto the road.

'Don't get too close! They're shooting at us through their own window!' yelled Charmain incredulously, as the police car crunched over the broken glass. Before now, she hadn't really had time to think. It had all happened so fast. But now, despite what Alan had said, it was clear the gun was a real one, and that these men were serious and desperate enough to do anything to get away.

She thumbed the radio transmitter and reported that more shots had been fired – barely able to believe what she was seeing and what she was saying. Inside the vehicle in front, they could see the gunman levelling his weapon again.

Then, without warning, Alan pulled to the side, and a faster police Vectra roared past them. It was the area response car, come to take over the pursuit. Charmain breathed a sigh of relief. They were still in the chase, but at least a trained pursuit driver in a more powerful car was ahead of them now.

The three cars travelled in high speed convoy through the streets of west London. As they passed below the concrete overbridge of the Westway, next to a bus garage and just before reaching Westbourne Park Tube station, the Audi made a sudden left turn, onto a ramp leading down towards an abandoned railway yard. The police vehicles followed.

At the bottom, the tarmac became a dirt track, and the Audi threw up clouds of dust as it weaved its way across the ground. The yard was used by the bus company for storing equipment and vehicles.

Charmain thought the gang might be planning to abandon the car and try to escape across the busy railway lines, but there was a high steel fence preventing this.

At the far end was an exit, but this was blocked by a barrier. Charmain thought the robbers were driving into a dead end. Neither they, nor the team in the pursuit car ahead, were armed. That vehicle's going to stop, she realised: how are we going to respond?

Alan was having similar thoughts. He looked in the mirror.

If they had to stop and reverse suddenly, he wanted to be sure nothing behind was blocking him in.

'It's up,' said Charmain, relieved. 'That barrier's up!' At the side of the road she could see a security guard. It wasn't clear if he'd raised the barrier when he saw the three cars approaching at speed, but as they flashed past he did an almost comical triple-take.

The Audi continued at speed, with the police cars in pursuit, but the net was closing in.

The car was now approaching the Westminster Academy, which was expecting Princess Anne, the Princess Royal, on a Royal visit. A group of parents and children had assembled in the street outside to greet her, and there were a number of Royal protection officers on duty.

Suddenly, the Audi roared out from the side street onto the main road, where it collided almost immediately with a police car trying to block it. It was a write-off. Immediately the men inside climbed out and made off.

The parents and children outside the school watched in fear as one of the men ran down the street, firing at least three shots into the air. Urgent radio messages were sent to Buckingham Palace and the royal visit was cancelled.

By now, the area was swarming with police. Alan and Charmain got out of their car and joined the search. They linked up with Cat, one of the officers from the pursuit car. Turning the corner of a block of flats, they came across a man walking unhurriedly in the other direction. Alan and Cat stopped him.

'Where are you going?' she asked.

'I've just come from my mate's,' he replied, a little unconvincingly. Alan suspected he was one of the gang, trying to bluff – or 'style' – his way out. They noticed he was wearing a t-shirt, in December. Cat wasn't fooled.

'You're nicked.'

Charmain ran on. Onlookers were pointing towards the nearby Grand Union Canal. She saw another officer she recognised, and told him to cross the bridge and get to the other side of the canal.

The canal was at a higher level than the flats, and Charmain had to climb a shallow embankment. As she reached the top she looked over the edge. The man who'd tried to shoot at her, and who she'd last seen firing at them out of the back of a speeding car, was stranded in the middle of the canal. There were officers on both banks. Hundreds and hundreds of banknotes stained red with security dye were floating in the water around him.

The water was only waist deep, and officers were advancing towards him. As she watched, they arrested the man, handcuffed him and dragged him to the bank. He was furious – struggling, shouting and swearing.

Charmain turned away and went to find Alan. He was standing near a fence where some gloves had been found. A gun was also recovered near the flats, barely fifteen feet from where the first man had been arrested. For a couple of hours, Charmain and Alan were asked to guard the crime scene, but they were both keen to show investigators where they'd been shot at, in case there were any important forensic clues there. A sergeant agreed to drive them back and record the locations.

As they got out of the car in Herries Street, where the Audi had stopped and they'd first been shot at, an old man approached them.

'I know you two,' he said. Alan and Charmain looked at him. 'Yes, I saw him shoot. I can't believe you're alive!'

∽✷∾

The two men arrested on the day were later charged and convicted. Nicholas Bidar, the gunman, was jailed for seventeen years for robbery and firearms offences. The passenger in the car, Christopher Ryan, was given a six-month suspended sentence for handling stolen goods. The driver of the Audi, Thomas Pulhofer, escaped and fled to Ireland. He was later recaptured after returning to London and being spotted by an off-duty officer; he was jailed for seven years.

Charmain Brenyah and Alan O'Connor received commendations from the trial judge, and a Commissioner's High Commendation. They were also regional winners in the Police Federation National Bravery Awards.

The weapon used was a Russian-made Baikal pistol, converted to fire 9 mm live rounds. They are cheap, accurate and reliable. Charmain and Alan still do not know why, when they were at the gunman's mercy, it apparently failed to fire.

6

TRAPPED ON THE TOR

'The girl hadn't been seen for twenty-four hours.
There's always in the back of your mind the possibility
that it's too late.'

PC JOHN NICHOLLS

It was as if the girl had just vanished. Her door was unlocked, her mobile phone was on the bedside table, and her laptop computer was switched on and lying on her bed. To PC John Nicholls and his colleague, PC James Rogers, it looked as though she'd just stepped out for a moment. But she hadn't been seen for nearly twenty-four hours.

'She only rented the room a week or so ago,' said the landlord. 'Found it on Gumtree, she did. She was pleasant enough. Told me she'd come over from Northern Ireland to check out Swansea University, see.'

John frowned. Most students in Swansea lived in Brynmill or Uplands, but this house was in Sketty, a little further away from the universities. It was a typical two-bedroom mid-terrace home that had once been a council house but was now privately owned. Then again, thought John, the student areas were significantly more expensive, and this girl had probably been room-hunting on a budget.

'And how well did you know her?' he asked Sophie, the young woman who'd called the police.

'I just met her in a coffee shop in town. She was nice. I don't have that many friends, and she had no friends at all in Swansea, so we hit it off, like,' she replied. Sophie was close to tears, and obviously frantic with worry.

'Don't worry,' smiled John. 'You did the right thing calling us. When did you last see her?'

'Yesterday evening. We went out. I thought we were going to maybe meet up today but she didn't reply to any of my texts or nothing. So I came round here and . . . well . . . it was like this. I haven't touched anything.'

The police officers looked around the small, sparsely furnished back bedroom. John walked over to the bedside table. On it was a folded slip of paper. He picked it up and read it.

'Look at this,' he said, handing the note to James. The neatly handwritten note said simply that the girl did not see any point in carrying on with life, and asked that her parents be contacted. Sophie began to sob.

'Oh God, it's so horrid. I mean, she was fine. I had no idea she was so unhappy.' She pulled a tissue from her bag as the police officers continued to look round the room. James sat on the bed and examined the laptop.

'Here's a stroke of luck,' he said. 'She hasn't got a password on her computer. Means I can open it up and look inside.' While James busied himself looking through the missing girl's hard drive, John picked up her mobile phone. Like the laptop it wasn't locked, and he was able to flick through the list of contact numbers. There weren't very many, he thought.

He took out his notebook and wrote down the number he found for 'Mum and Dad'.

'Look at this,' said James excitedly. John leant over and peered at the screen. Although he used computers at work, he considered himself something of a Luddite when it came to technology.

'I've been checking her Internet browsing history,' James explained. 'She's googled "scenic suicide spots", and been on websites that give lists of nice places for people kill themselves.'

'Any of those scenic spots near here?' asked John.

'No, not that I can find. But she's also been looking at bus routes – and she's repeatedly checked the First Bus timetables for the Gower,' replied James.

The Gower peninsula juts out roughly twelve miles into the Bristol Channel from the coastline of South Wales. Around its shoreline, wide sandy beaches are interspersed with jagged limestone cliffs. Bisecting it at forty-five degrees is Cefn Bryn: a five-mile-long red sandstone ridge protruding from the surrounding limestone and referred to locally as the backbone of the Gower. In 1956 the peninsula became the first place in Britain to be designated an Area of Outstanding Natural Beauty.

John and James looked at each other. There seemed little doubt what she was planning. It had gone midnight. James called the operations room at First Bus. Services to the Gower didn't always run, as the area was so rural and lightly populated. According to her Internet browser, the girl had also been looking up local taxi numbers. John rang round them all to see if any could recall taking a slim girl with mousy brown hair to the Gower peninsula. None could.

John was worried. There had been plenty of clues in the

room, yet nothing had given them any solid leads. Most people are surrounded by networks – family, friends, friends of friends – and usually there would be some chosen confidante who could help. But here, apart from a landlord she'd spoken to once or twice on the stairs, and a friend who hardly knew her, there was nothing.

More often than not suicide threats are really a cry for help, but in this case the girl's preparations had been so thorough and well thought-out that John had no doubt she fully intended to go through with it. The chances are, he thought sadly, she's already dead. He decided to call her parents, using the number he'd found in her phone.

Unsurprisingly, the telephone call in the middle of the night from a policeman in South Wales left them badly shaken. No, they told John, they didn't know that she was unhappy. Nor were they aware of any reason she might have chosen Swansea. They, like everyone, believed she had come to the city to visit the university.

'You got any ideas?' John asked.

'No, not really,' admitted James.

'Well then,' said John, 'we're just going to have to drive down to the Gower and see what we can find. Have you worked out those bus routes?' James nodded. They picked up the girl's phone and laptop. John turned to Sophie, who was still struggling to compose herself.

'If she's there, we'll find her,' he promised. But his long years of experience told him the search was an almost hopeless task.

Although John had only been a regular police officer for four years, he'd been a special constable for a quarter of a century before that. He'd joined Tesco at the age of nineteen, and after being promoted to store manager had worked all over Britain and in Ireland. Once his children were grown up, he decided to fulfil his long-held ambition to become a full-time officer, and at forty-four years old joined South Wales Police. Despite his age, fitting in had been straightforward – not least because he'd known many of the present inspectors, chief inspectors and superintendents when they were still young constables – in metaphorical short trousers.

On top of his regular duties he was a football liaison officer, travelling to away games with Swansea City football club supporters and providing a point of contact for police in other force areas.

It was about two in the morning by the time the police officers arrived in the Gower. Swansea lay at the base of the peninsula. The northern coast largely comprised cockle-beds; studying the maps they thought it more likely the girl would have taken one of the buses following the Gower's southern shore. For the rest of the night, they drove from beach to beach and cliff to cliff calling out her name, looking for any trace. There was nothing.

'OK, let's try Three Cliffs Bay,' said John, wearily. 'The tide's out at the moment, so we can drive right onto the sand.'

There was a distinct glow on the eastern horizon. The sun was coming up. The two officers were due to go off duty in an hour, at seven o'clock, so they'd have to give up fairly soon. As they walked along the beach, the three tall and pointed cliffs that gave the bay its name – the Great Tor, the Little Tor and the West Tor – loomed behind them. As the skies brightened, they could pick out features on the craggy rock faces. At their highest point the cliffs were around eighty feet tall – about the same as a nine-storey building.

On the sands below, the two police officers became aware

of faint calls of seagulls above. John paused. There didn't seem to be many birds about. Was that noise really seagulls? He turned round and looked up.

'Quick!' he cried. 'Look up there! It's her, it's got to be!' James followed his pointing finger and, sure enough, about three-quarters of the way up the Great Tor, he could see a woman waving and shouting. They'd found her! She seemed to be sitting on a ledge jutting out of the sheer cliff face. John waved back.

'Are you all right?' he shouted. The woman carried on waving, but was struggling to hear him. The sun was coming up, and they could see her more clearly. John could see she was in distress and needed help.

At its tallest point, the Great Tor appeared to be a huge pillar of limestone jutting forward. Luckily the action of the sea over millions of years had created numerous footholds and handholds. John took off his utility belt and handed it to James.

'You wait here,' he said. 'I'll climb up and see if I can get to her.' James did not demur. Although John was some years older, he was smaller and probably more agile.

John had always hated heights, and as he climbed he felt his adrenaline kick in. He tried not to look down, focusing instead on the route up the cliff, feeling for handholds and watching out for suitable footsteps. His hobbies were scuba diving and sailing and he had never tried rock climbing, but he knew his arms would tire far more quickly than his legs, and good climbing technique was to push up with the legs rather than pull up with the arms and hands.

The cliff face wasn't totally vertical and there were some parts where it sloped in, allowing him some respite and the chance for a breather. As he was climbing he couldn't see the girl above him, but James was shouting encouragement and directions from below. All John had to do was focus on reaching the girl to see if she was OK.

His right foot found a toe hold and he pushed himself up a few more inches. Suddenly, to his right, he could see her. Knowing he was so close gave him a burst of energy, and within seconds he had scrabbled up onto the ledge. It was about four feet wide and ten feet long.

He looked over at the girl. She was sitting upright, which surprised him, but she seemed very still.

'Are you all right?' he asked.

'I don't know. It hurts,' she replied in her soft Irish brogue. 'I think I've broken my legs. And I'm cold. I'm sorry. I'm so sorry.'

'Don't worry, I'm here to help you,' said John as he crawled over to her. She was in her early twenties and very slight. He took off his fleece jacket and wrapped it round her. Just that gentle contact made her wince with pain. He wanted to hug her, to warm her up and reassure her, but he held back in case it hurt too much.

He looked down at her legs. She was wearing plain black leggings. Both her legs were clearly broken – her feet were twisted and facing the 'wrong way' and one of her legs had a sharp bend where it shouldn't. He also suspected she'd broken her pelvis and might have internal injuries too.

John confirmed her name, then radioed the information back and requested a rescue helicopter. He gave his position, but knew that wasn't too important as his Airwave radio incorporated a GPS tracker and the control room would know his location.

'I'm sorry,' said the girl again. 'Have you spoken to my ma and da? Can you let them know I'm OK?'

'Yes, of course,' replied John, and shouted down to James, who called the girl's parents and told them what had happened. Their relief that she had been found alive was tempered by the news that she was badly hurt. They began making arrangements to travel to South Wales.

'How long have you been here?' asked John. The sun was coming up but the wind blowing in from the Atlantic was still bitingly cold. The girl had been shivering almost unceasingly since he had reached her, even though he'd given her his fleece. He noticed that at some point she had wet herself, and the damp would have made things worse.

'I don't know. I caught the bus yesterday afternoon at about four. Got here an hour or two later. I don't know exactly what time it was but the tide was in. And then . . .' She paused. 'I'm sorry. Then . . . I jumped. But the cliff wasn't steep enough, and I hit the rocks and started rolling and rolling and then I landed here.'

John looked back up. Now he was on the ledge, he could see that the lower reaches of the cliff, where he'd climbed, were considerably steeper than the top twenty feet or so. And while it was incredible that she had survived the fall, she'd then had to endure the whole night alone on the ledge, unable to move and exposed to the elements.

'How did you find me?' asked the girl, though she was difficult to understand as her teeth were chattering so much.

'It's down to your friend, Sophie,' said John, and he explained how they had found her laptop, found the bus routes and decided to follow them, searching beach after beach before arriving at Three Cliffs. As he spoke, John watched the girl. He noticed that now he had arrived she seemed to be drifting off to sleep, perhaps thinking she no longer needed to stay awake. John did his best to keep her talking.

'I'm sorry,' said the girl again. She kept apologising, despite John's reassurances that she had nothing to be sorry about. 'Have you seen my handbag?' she asked.

'No we haven't found it. Is there something important you want?'

'Just my diary,' she replied. Then she apologised again and started sobbing. John tried to console her. Where was that damn rescue helicopter? Surely it should be here by now.

He called down to James and asked him what was happening. 'The helicopter's grounded because of the ash. It can only come if it's absolute life or death. They're sending the coastguard to confirm she can't be moved,' came the answer.

'It *is* bloody life or death,' thought John, angrily. In May 2011, much of Britain's airspace was closed and hundreds of flights were cancelled after millions of tonnes of ash were thrown high into the atmosphere by an erupting volcano in Iceland. For short periods only some specialist aircraft – including rescue helicopters – were permitted to fly at all. John understood this, but knowing the facts didn't make the delay any less frustrating.

He could see the girl's legs through tears in her clothing. They were a disquieting purple-blue. John was becoming less worried now about her broken bones and more concerned about hypothermia. He was already feeling the cold, and he'd been on the ledge with her for less than an hour. He hoped his fleece would provide enough insulation to maintain her core body temperature, but she'd been out here all night, and couldn't even jump around to keep warm. The only good thing about the cold, he mused, was that it was probably numbing her legs and blocking the pain.

'What made you come here to Swansea?' he asked.

'It was just I didn't want anyone in my family to find me. I wanted to be found by strangers. I'm sorry.'

John nodded, then heard a call from above and looked up. The helmeted head of a coastguard had appeared at the top of the cliff. Most of them were farmers who knew the area well. It seemed to take an age, but eventually the coastguard dropped ropes to the bottom of the cliff, then abseiled down onto the ledge.

'Right,' he said briskly. 'Let's have a look. What have we got here then?' He knelt down and examined the girl as she apologised to him for causing such a fuss. Within seconds he realised the severity of her injuries, and called through to his control centre.

'Casualty suffering multiple fractures, possible internal haemorrhaging and hypothermia,' he said. 'Cannot be moved by us. Will require assistance of helicopter.'

John breathed a sigh of relief and pressed himself back into the ledge as they waited for the helicopter to arrive. Since the coastguard had arrived, he had not needed to give all his attention to the girl. This was a mixed blessing, because he'd had time to look over the edge. With a start he had realised how high up they were, and remembered how much he hated heights.

Within ten minutes they became aware of the sound of throbbing rotor blades, and could make out the sun glinting off the yellow RAF Sea King helicopter, call sign Rescue 169, as it crossed the Bristol Channel from its base thirty odd miles away at Chivenor in north Devon.

Although the police had no direct communication link to the pilot, the coastguard did, and he relayed instructions to John.

'Get over her to protect her from the prop-wash,' he said. John lay over the girl in a press up position, making sure that he covered her but didn't put any weight on her. As the helicopter came closer, John looked up, squinting to protect his eyes as small bits of grit, stones and foliage were thrown up all around. All John could focus on was the tips of the rotor blades, which seemed to him to be worryingly close to the edge of the cliff. 'If they hit,' he thought, 'we've all had it.'

As he watched, an orange-suited figure stepped out of the helicopter's sliding door and was lowered down to them. As soon as he was safely on the ledge, the helicopter crewman unfastened his winch cable and the helicopter banked away and stood off, hovering over the water.

The helicopter paramedic moved towards the girl, assessing her condition quickly. He had brought with him a bulky medical pack, and he took out a small hand-pump, then unravelled and inflated what looked to John like a bright blue airbed.

'This may hurt a little bit, but I'm afraid we have to do it,' said the medic to the young woman. She nodded, and apologised again for what she'd done. The man turned to John and the coastguard.

'I need you gentlemen to help me log-roll her onto the mattress,' he said, and explained what they needed to do. John was glad to have something to focus on, and as gently as they could they moved the girl onto the mattress. She cried out in pain, but as soon as she was in position the RAF paramedic reversed the action of the pump and started cranking its handle again.

The mattress was filled with tiny polystyrene balls, and as the air was sucked out the young woman sank into the mattress and it moulded itself around her, with the differential in air pressure causing it to set rigid.

The helicopter paramedic completed the preparations needed for the airlift, then called in the helicopter. As it approached, the girl looked at John.

'Please will you come with me?' she asked pleadingly. John had to refuse. Not only did he hate helicopters but he also knew that winching him on board would cause unnecessary delay. He also felt guilty about leaving James on his own on the beach.

'Look,' he said, 'you'll be fine. These guys know what they're doing and they'll get you straight to hospital. Go on, get going now!' She smiled and he waved as she was lifted up towards the helicopter with the medic attached alongside.

Once they were on board, the big yellow helicopter turned north-east and headed back across the mainland towards the Moriston hospital on the outskirts of Swansea. The hospital was the designated coastal rescue centre, and had a helipad and trauma team waiting.

Back on the ledge, John thought about how he was going to get down. It looked a lot further to the bottom than it had seemed when he was climbing up, and he gingerly walked back to the edge where he'd arrived and tried to remember the handholds he'd used.

'What do you think you're doing?' asked the coastguard, looking over.

'This is the way I came up,' replied John. 'It'll do me to get back down.'

'Not a chance!' said the coastguard. 'There's no way I'm

letting you back down there on your own. Any climber will tell you going down is more dangerous than coming up because you can't see where you're going. And one casualty on this cliff face today is enough, thanks!'

John had to admit he was probably right. The coastguard handed him a harness and he strapped it on; then the man stood behind him and linked them both together before kicking off. It was awkward abseiling down the slope linked together, and John grabbed at the rocks to steady himself.

'Stop it, stop it!' he said, nervously.

'Just relax and stop holding on to the rocks, otherwise we might get twisted up!' said the coastguard, sharply. John hated not being in control and having to put his trust in someone else, but he did his best to do as he was told.

To John it seemed to take forever to get down the cliff but eventually they reached the bottom. It was around 8.30 and the tide was coming in. John thanked the coastguard, and he and James walked back to where they'd parked their car around four hours earlier.

John had just finished a run of nightshifts, and after completing his paperwork he went home.

A few days later, the parents of the girl came to the police station to see him. They thanked him for saving her life, and, like their daughter, apologised repeatedly for all the trouble she'd caused. John shuffled uncomfortably in his chair. He found such meetings awkward, considering himself more of a man of action than a counsellor. Nevertheless, he realised that it was important for them and did his best to make them feel welcome.

They explained that they'd arrived in Swansea on the day of the rescue, gone straight to the hospital and stayed there ever since. They told John about some of the circumstances around their daughter's actions, and admitted they partly blamed themselves.

John reassured them, explaining that he too was a parent: 'Once they're eighteen they're their own people, and you don't always know what's going on in their lives,' he said.

'Besides, I was only doing my duty.'

⁂

Two weeks later, the girl was allowed to leave hospital and the family went back home to Northern Ireland.

John was sent a letter of congratulation by his superintendent. Later he learned that although James had filmed almost the entire rescue on his phone, he had edited it down to just the last few moments, when John was reluctantly being brought down on the abseil rope and had circulated it via email, much to everyone's amusement.

John still can't bear heights.

7

GUNFINGER!

'I'd never felt anything like it. It was like somebody sticking about a hundred hot pokers in you time and time again.'
PC KATIE JOHNSON, DOG HANDLER

The week between Christmas and the New Year had been quieter than anyone could remember. PC Katie Johnson had just qualified as a handler, and she was desperately keen to get into action with Chaos, her German Shepherd police dog.

Katie had wanted to work with police dogs since the age of sixteen, and after six years as a regular officer in Lancashire, working mainly in Ormskirk and Skelmersdale, she'd finally had her application to join the force's dog section approved. After a twelve-week training course, during which she and her dog learned to work together tracking, searching and dealing with criminals, she was pronounced qualified and ready to take to the streets.

Unusually, Chaos was not a puppy but an experienced police dog. She was his second handler: his first had left the unit, and as Chaos was still fairly young it made sense to find him another. The course had been hard and physical, and more than once Katie had been grateful that Chaos seemed to know what he was doing, even if she was learning.

This was her third day, but so far there hadn't been a single job for her to go to. Absolutely nothing. It was around 8.20 a.m. and she was sitting in Preston police station, chatting to Ian Tinsley. Ian had been in the dog unit for more than twenty years and it was standard practice for a newly qualified dog handler to be paired up with a more experienced colleague for their first few weeks on the streets.

Ian had joined the police in 1979 after a rugby union cup game, in which his team beat a police side by a clear 100 points. In the bar afterwards, a recruiting sergeant had written his contact details on a beer mat, and eight weeks later Ian had started. Ian worked with explosive search dogs as well as standard police dogs, and in the mid-1990s, Ian's dog Ben, a black Labrador, had sniffed out a large bomb hidden in a lorry that had arrived in Lancashire from Northern Ireland.

Suddenly, a head poked round the door.

'There's a job come in at Bamber Bridge.' It was one of the traffic officers based at Preston. 'You might be interested – it's an alarm at the Hospital Inn pub.'

'I bet it's the cleaner come in and set it off!' said Ian, but he and Katie grabbed their things and headed out to their police dog van. In the back were enclosures for the two dogs: Chaos, and Ian's dog Blitz, a Malinois.

Malinois, also known as Belgian Shepherd dogs, are becoming increasingly popular with police forces in the UK. Similar in shape to the familiar German Shepherds, but with black faces and tan-coloured coats, Malinois tend to have a slightly longer operational life and are not prone to the degenerative hip dysplasia that can afflict German Shepherds.

Having worked with both breeds during his career, Ian preferred the Malinois' temperament and ability to focus.

Ian drove, and Katie got on the radio.

'Hotel Zulu three two, we're attending Bamber Bridge with dogs.' It was sensible to let officers already there know that the dog team were on their way, so they could hang back.

Bamber Bridge was about three miles south-east of Preston. Traffic was fairly light – probably because it was New Year's Eve – and driving with flashing blue lights it didn't take Ian and Katie long to get there. Shortly before they arrived, there was another update on the radio – an officer had seen movement inside the pub, suggesting that whoever had set off the alarm was still inside. Ian glanced at Katie.

'If the burglars are still there, this could be a great chance for you and Chaos to have your first arrest!' he said. Katie nodded and smiled. Ian radioed ahead to remind officers on the scene not to go in but to wait for the dog.

The Hospital Inn was a large two-storey Victorian building painted off-white. It stood on the corner of a road junction next to a level-crossing and had probably been built for the stationmaster of a long-closed railway halt. To the side was the entrance to the car park, and Ian pulled in and drove to the far corner, facing the rear of the pub. They could see officers on each corner watching the building; they were there to stop anyone trying to leave. As requested, none had directly approached the door.

Ian and Katie got out, and went round to the back of the van. They opened Chaos's compartment and Katie put him on his lead. Ian left Blitz inside. Getting both dogs out at the same time was not advisable: they might start fighting or, more likely, confuse each other. Ian knew that rather than focusing on its handler each dog would be far more interested in what the other one was doing.

They looked over at the building.

'You go round to the front and I'll go round to the back,' Ian told Katie. She knew he wanted her and her new dog to get the glory of any arrest, but they had to cover all exits. They were facing the back of the pub. The front door was on the right side of the building as they were looking at it, under a small porch. Katie strode towards it, with Chaos pulling at the lead.

On the corner nearest them, Ian could see an enclosed area with bins and a back door – probably leading into the kitchen – and further along the rear of the pub a set of patio doors leading into a small beer garden to his left. He turned to the nearest officer.

'You wait here. Watch the patio doors, and if they come bursting out then we've got them!'

As Katie made her way around the side of the pub, she was nervous but excited. On her radio she heard one of the watching officers say he could see someone running around inside the pub – presumably the intruders had realised the building was now surrounded.

As she passed one of the front doors she heard the handle rattling, and turned to face it. The door swung open sharply, and she found herself facing a huge man with a shotgun raised to his shoulder. She reacted instinctively.

'Don't move! Drop the weapon!' she shouted. Chaos barked, and pulled at the leash. Katie stood still, scared but trying to keep control. The twin barrels of the sawn-off shotgun looked huge – like two black coffee mugs next to each other – and filled her vision. Behind, all she could see of the man was his eyes shining with fury beneath a black ribbed balaclava.

'Get on the floor – now!' shouted the man, but before Katie could obey he opened fire. There was a deafening bang and she felt an excruciating pain explode in her left thigh. Katie screamed in agony. It felt like being stabbed simultaneously by a hundred hot pokers. A split second later her entire leg went numb. The force of the blast spun her round, and she felt herself falling as her leg started to buckle. 'I mustn't collapse here,' she thought. 'I don't know what he's going to do next.'

Somehow she managed to keep her footing, and without looking up she let go of the lead and ordered Chaos to hold the man. She felt certain it was the last time she would see the dog alive, but she had reverted to training: if you see a man with a gun, send the dog.

Chaos yelped, making a screeching sound that Katie had never heard before. But instead of running straight for the door, as she expected, he began circling almost maniacally, clearly confused and disorientated, before running round to Katie's right side and biting her on the arm. It wasn't a bad bite – more of a mouthing – but it certainly wasn't what he was supposed to do and hardly what she needed.

What Katie hadn't realised was that the instant the man had fired the gun he slammed the door shut and went back inside the pub. When she set Chaos loose – a second or two later – there was no target. The dog knew he had to do something but didn't know what. Katie's voice was weakened too, meaning the tone of her command wasn't right. In his panic and confusion, Chaos went for the only target he could see with a text-book arm hold. Yet because he realised something was amiss he'd moderated the force of the bite.

What Katie also didn't know was that while dog handlers had been stabbed before, none had ever been shot. Her experience would have significant repercussions for how police dogs are trained.

Katie managed to grab Chaos's lead. She managed to half-stagger and half-run away from the door. She kept forcing herself not to look at her injury, because she knew that she might pass out if she saw her own blood, or a hole in her leg.

As she limped across the tarmac, she became aware of Ian screaming at her to take cover, and pointing to a shallow ditch at the back of the car park.

Ian had heard the loud bang and immediately realised it was a shotgun blast.

'Quick, hard cover, hard cover!' he shouted to the young beat officer with him. There was a small wall to the side of the beer garden and they jumped behind it. One of the other constables was crouching behind a small sapling. It was almost comical. Ian shouted at him to get behind the wall too.

Ian's mind was racing. He was sure Katie had been shot, in which case he needed to get Blitz from the van. There was no sign of a gunman. He was about to climb out from behind the wall when he saw Katie come round the corner, dragging her left leg. Ian stood up.

'Keep coming this way. Keep coming, Katie,' he shouted. He looked back at the pub. Any second he expected to see the gunman come round the corner to finish her off.

Then he realised that if Katie came directly to him, she would be dangerously close to the pub's rear windows and exposed to fire again. He could see a shallow ditch at the back of the car park, and told her to make for it. She changed direction and dropped into the ditch with her dog. She looked over at Ian.

'I've been shot in the leg,' she whimpered. Ian could see a dark red patch on Katie's torn black police cargo trousers. Then movement caught his eye, and he turned to see the gunman emerge from the side of the pub.

The man's face was still hidden by the balaclava, and he was wearing jeans and a black bomber jacket. The sawn-off shotgun was in his hands, levelled and ready to fire. Ian had only heard one shot, which meant there was still at least one live cartridge in the gun.

The man walked slowly and deliberately across the car park. He was between the beer garden and the marked police dog van, so there was no way for Ian to reach Blitz. It looked as though he was heading towards where Katie was hiding. She was lying with her back to the car park and her head down. Although she knew someone was behind her, she didn't look up.

Ian knew time was running out but he seemed to have no options. If the man reached the other side of the car park he would find Katie and might well kill her. He felt guilty. He'd sent her round to the front door. His keenness to let her make her first arrest, instead of taking the lead himself, had put her in the sights of this ruthless gunman. Ian couldn't reach his own dog, but perhaps he could create enough confusion to buy some time – at least enough to make the gunman think twice. He knew he had to get the man's attention, to stop him finding Katie. And that if he didn't do something now he'd never forgive himself.

Ian stood up, held his hands out together in front of him and pointed his right index finger at the man.

'Stop!' he shouted. 'Armed police! Stand still! Put down the weapon!' The gunman turned round to face him. He hesitated, then lowered his gun. He looked at Ian. The moment seemed to last for ever. Then he started to raise the weapon.

'Armed police!' shouted Ian again. 'Drop your weapon or we'll open fire.' The man hesitated again, and lowered the gun again. He looked around. He and Ian were around twenty yards apart. Ian hoped that the charged atmosphere and the sight of the police officers, as well as the verbal challenges, would make him flustered and confused.

In the ditch, Katie was listening to the confrontation. She realised Ian was trying to stop the gunman finding her. The ditch was full of stagnant water and it stank, but she knew her only hope was to stay down. She still hadn't looked at her leg. It was totally numb and she couldn't feel any pain, but she thought that would probably change once her adrenaline levels started to fall.

Ian's stand-off with the masked man continued. He wondered how good the man's eyesight was: whether he could see that Ian's 'gun' was actually his index finger. Ian was still crouched in the classic 'Hollywood' firing position and he considered whether he would have time to drop back behind the wall if the gunman did call his bluff and open fire. He kept shouting, hoping to create doubt and uncertainty in the man's mind.

Without warning, the gunman turned and ran back towards the building. Another man was waiting by the corner, and they both made off. Ian breathed an enormous sigh of relief and reached for his radio.

'Control, Hotel Zulu three two. We have an officer down with gunshot injuries, and at least one offender with a shotgun. Urgent – please send armed units and an ambulance.'

Ian and the other officer ran over to Katie and helped her up. She struggled to her feet, and gently they guided her back to the wall where they'd been hiding.

'Let's go and find him. Come on,' she said. Ian looked at her.

'No, you've been hurt. I'll go.'

Katie looked at the leg. To her, it appeared uninjured.

'It's nothing serious. Probably just an air gun or something,' she protested.

Ian knew Katie simply wasn't seeing what the rest of them could see. Her left leg was bleeding fairly heavily, and it was obvious she couldn't put any weight it.

'No, Katie, you stay here. Please don't argue. Just wait for the ambulance. Make sure Chaos is OK.' Katie realised he was right, and sat down with her back to the wall. One of the other officers stayed with her. They looked down at her leg. Katy became aware of the torn fabric, the blood, the tiny holes. The numbness was started to fade, and she was aware of a deep, dull ache. It felt like a dead leg. A really bad dead leg.

Ian knew that armed officers would be on their way. His job now was to track the gunman.

A message came over his radio. 'Offenders seen running into back garden next to railway tracks.'

Tracking the gunman and his accomplice would be a job for Blitz. Ian ran across to the van and opened the back door to get him out. The dog jumped out, and without Ian saying a word set off across the car park. Ian trotted behind. Around the side of the pub they found a bag on the floor. Ian didn't touch it, but inside he could see money and a handgun. Blitz crossed the road, and headed down the side of a bungalow opposite. Ian guessed the dog was instinctively following the smell of the cordite from the discharged gun.

As they approached the house, another message came through stating that the two fugitives had been spotted on the railway line. Ian called Blitz back and they walked round to the level crossing. At the gates they met two officers.

'Leave this part to me,' said Ian, 'as I've got the dog.' He could see the two men about 300 yards down the tracks, and took cover behind a cabin at the side. His job was simply to keep the fugitives in sight, without getting shot himself.

Ian slowly made his way along the tracks, keeping at least 300 or 400 yards between himself and the two men. He could see them clambering up an embankment to the left of the line. Ian took out his mobile phone and dialled his colleague Paul Dacre. He had a specialist dog trained to work with armed officers, and Ian knew he would want to be involved.

The firearms dog worked in a slightly different way to Ian's standard police dog. He was fitted with a Perspex ballistic shield that would help to protect him from shotgun pellets, and he was more used to working with armed officers.

When the firearms team arrived, they first searched the pub to make sure there was no one still hiding inside. Upstairs, in a bathroom, they found the pub's manager, her boyfriend, who was also the chef, and two cleaners. They'd been tied up and left face down. They also found the keys to a getaway car that was still parked in the car park; during the raid the robbers had lost them.

Less than ten minutes later, about half a mile away, a large man approached a female police officer as she was searching an industrial estate on foot. He held out his hands.

'I've just shot one of your policewomen. You can arrest

me.' The officer snapped on her handcuffs and the man was taken into custody. He gave his name as Wayne McDonald, from Manchester.

There was no apparent trace of the other man. For the dogs, the trail seemed to have gone cold, and the police helicopter with a heat-seeking camera couldn't find any sign. But police kept searching, and around eight hours later David Tyrell was found, shivering and suffering from mild hypothermia, on the railway lines. He'd been hiding under a tarpaulin in a timber yard.

Katie had been put in an ambulance and taken to hospital. When her trousers were removed, she could see twelve holes, each the size of a pen top, in her thigh. There wasn't much blood because the hot lead pellets had partly cauterised each wound as they went in. It looked, she mused, like a dot-to-dot puzzle on her leg.

The doctors admitted there was not a lot they could do. Two pellets were removed from near the surface, but an X-ray showed that the rest had penetrated deep into the tissue. Removing them would require a major operation to cut into the muscle, and Katie was warned that such a procedure would leave considerable scarring.

In the end, a surgeon told her it was probably best to leave them where they were, though for the next fortnight she was almost unable to walk.

A few days later, Katie received a phone call. It was the supervisor at the police kennels. He told her that Chaos had been suffering from sickness and diarrhoea; now he had collapsed in his enclosure. But there was nothing physically wrong with him. Although he hadn't been injured in the attack on Katie, he appeared to be in distress, and she was warned it might be kinder to put him to sleep.

Katie asked if she could try looking after Chaos at her house. Her husband was also a dog handler – with Merseyside Police – and would be able to walk him until her leg improved. They agreed.

Within twelve hours, Chaos was transformed. He came back to life before her eyes and made a full recovery. Animal behaviour experts later suggested that the dog had suffered a stress reaction after being separated from her – possibly because he thought she had been killed.

Six weeks after the shooting, Katie returned to light duties. She told herself she was not going to let it affect her; like many officers she considered herself hard as nails and able to cope. But she kept getting flashbacks of the black mask: she dreamt about it most nights, and when she awoke it was the first thing she saw.

She was given counselling, but told that techniques to erase her traumatic mental images would have to wait until after the trial: unfortunately for Katie, the memories she wanted to lose were the most important part of the evidence.

Once court proceedings were finished, she was sent on a course of psychotherapy known as EMDR, or Eye Movement Desensitisation and Reprocessing. In it she was asked to remember the man's mask while she was distracted by vibrating pads or the therapist's hand movements.

Katie was sceptical, but told herself that sometimes it took more strength to accept help than to refuse, and she decided to stick with it. She was booked in for eight sessions, but found to her amazement that her fixation on the mask began to fade quickly and she only needed six.

★

Shortly after the incident, Katie had been visited by senior officers from the police dog section. They had wanted to talk about Chaos, because no one could understand his behaviour. Forensic tests had shown that twelve pellets had hit her, seventeen had hit the dog lead and seventy or so had gone into the fence behind her. Not a single one had hit Chaos. Katie was relieved her dog was uninjured, but thought that if he had been hit it might have better explained his reaction.

In an effort to find answers, the dog unit created a scenario to replicate the incident. Every dog took part, and almost every dog reacted as Chaos had.

Until then, the culmination of standard police dog training was the Test of Courage, in which a man with a gun comes out shouting and threatening the dog handler. The dog was expected to remain still, then seize the offender when commanded.

In the light of Katie's experience, it was decided that this should change, and now police dogs and handlers are taught to take hard cover whenever a gun is seen. So far, no other police dog handler has been shot, and no other police dog has had to deal with such extraordinary circumstances.

⁂

In court, Wayne McDonald claimed he was trying to shoot the police dog, not the officer. He was cleared of attempted murder but found guilty of wounding, and jailed for life. He must serve a minimum of ten years. David Tyrell, from Tyldesley, was sent to prison for at least six years for his part in the robbery. Two other men, one a former chef at the Hospital

Inn, were also imprisoned for helping to plan the raid.

Chaos reached the end of his operational career and was retired. A foster home was found, and like many ex-police dogs he began a new life as a much-loved family pet.

Ian and Katie received a Chief Constable's Commendation, were nominated for the Police Federation National Bravery Awards, and received Lancashire Police's William Garnett Cup for the most outstanding act of valour.

Katie was assigned a new dog, Hero, and eventually returned to full operational duties with the dog unit. In her spare time, she is an ambassador for Hounds for Heroes, a charity that provides trained assistance dogs to injured or disabled members of the armed forces or the emergency services.

Ian retired six months after the shooting, and did not need to aim his finger in anger again.

8

THE FLAILING SCOTSMAN

*'Suddenly there was something not comfortable about it.
Just a feeling. I don't know if it was the layout of the
flats or what but something didn't feel right.'*

PC BRIAN MANCHESTER

The postman's wife couldn't sleep. The wailing and chanting from the flat across the landing seemed never ending. It had started well before her husband left for work at around four o'clock in the morning and now, an hour later, it showed no sign of abating.

She rolled over and tried pulling the pillow round her head to muffle the sound. Even the thick stone walls of the tenement block couldn't stop it getting through. This was the fourth night in a row. At first, she and her husband thought there were two people in the flat opposite, then they'd realised that it was just one man having a conversation with himself. When she saw him on the stairs he'd nod and say hello just like anyone else. They'd even chatted, maybe once or twice. But these last few nights had been unbearable.

What was he shouting now? She could make out the odd word or sentence here and there – Satan, crucifixion, Allah,

Saddam, samurai swords – but most of it was either wordless chanting or gibberish. Enough was enough, she decided. Maybe the police could help. She picked up the phone.

'Hello,' she said when the operator answered. 'Police, please. I'd like to report a noise disturbance ...'

'You'll like this one, guys – it sounds like a bit of a laugh!' The voice of the controller squawked from the speaker in the police patrol car. PCs Craig McCall and Andy Kendall looked at each other.

'Yeah, whatever,' said Craig quietly to his colleague. Then louder, so the microphone of the hands-free unit could pick up his voice, 'No problem. This is Alpha Mike three four; we're heading there now.'

The address they'd been given was a street of typical Edinburgh four-storey tenement blocks. Edinburgh had expanded rapidly during the latter part of the eighteenth and the first half of the nineteenth centuries. The development of Edinburgh New Town from the mid-1750s had rejuvenated the city and consolidated its position as Scotland's capital and financial centre. For many years, the planners had ensured any new buildings closely followed the designs of those in the New Town area, creating a pleasing uniformity – with row after row of almost identical four-storey tenement buildings in attractive pale sandstone. The widespread use of similar materials, and a Greek-influenced 'neoclassical' architectural style, led to Edinburgh becoming known as 'the Athens of the North'.

Craig parked the police car in front of the building, and he and Andy got out. Born in Edinburgh, Craig had been a Lothian and Borders police officer for almost all his working life. He was an instructor on police safety and crowd control tactics as well as being an expert in martial arts. Andy was originally from Fife, across the Firth of Forth, but had come to Edinburgh to go to university to study engineering. He'd loved the city, but decided he wanted to be a police officer instead of an engineer. Now, in August 2004, he was still a probationer, having only been in the police for six months.

Inside the communal hallway there wasn't much space. The walls were whitewashed and there were tiles on the floor. As they climbed the stairs, they could already hear wailing and chanting. The woman who'd dialled 999 was waiting on the fourth-floor landing. The noisy flat was directly opposite hers. Andy and Craig turned down their radios and put their ears to the door to listen.

Inside the flat was the unmistakable sound of a man urinating. Without warning, they heard a voice shout:

'The blood of Satan is now leaving me!' Craig and Andy both stepped back and looked at each other.

'It's been like that for the past four nights,' said the woman. 'He's up in the wee small hours, raving and shouting. Talkin' boot choppin' people up wi' samurai swords. Crucifixion. Ah cannae get any sleep.'

Another man came out onto the hallway. He told the officers his girlfriend wouldn't stay over with him any more because of the noise.

Downstairs two other officers had just arrived. PCs Brian Manchester and John Stirling had also heard the call, and as it was such a quiet night they decided to have a look and see if anyone needed any help.

The landing on the top floor was narrow, and with the new arrivals things were becoming cramped. Brian and John squeezed in beside the stairwell railings next to Craig and Andy. As they did so, two more police officers arrived – Rachel Straub and Ash Pitblado. There wasn't enough room for both women on the landing, so they waited at the top of the stairs.

The thick stone walls caused problems for the police radios, so Craig called in to control using his mobile phone to explain the situation.

'It sounds as if the man has mental health issues, but there are now six officers here,' he said. Drawing on his experience as a tactical adviser, he added: 'In my view we have enough resources here. I suggest we knock on the door and see what the initial outcome is.'

The inspector on duty in the control room agreed, and the officers lined up. Craig was at the door; next to him was Brian and then John Sterling. Andy, the probationer, was next and then the two female officers, Ash and Rachel. The postman's wife was told to return to her flat and lock the door.

Craig and Brian drew their batons and John unclipped his canister of CS gas. Brian looked round. Suddenly he felt uncomfortable. He wasn't sure if it was the cramped space on the landing or just gut instinct, but the atmosphere had changed.

Craig leaned forward, put his thumb over the door's peephole, and knocked sharply on the door. The chanting stopped.

'What is it?' The voice came from inside the flat.

'It's your neighbour from across the way,' lied Craig. 'Are you OK? Open the door. We're worried about you.'

'Fuck off! Do you want to die?' Craig pulled his finger away from the peephole and knocked again.

'No, it's the police,' he said, more firmly. 'Open the door now.' There was a pause.

'No, you're the masons!' came the reply; then they heard the sound of numerous locks being undone and bolts being thrown back. The officers tensed. The door was opened just a crack, and the tip of a samurai sword flashed out. It passed by Craig, who was pressed into the corner, and was thrust towards Brian.

Brian looked up and saw the man's face, contorted with anger, through the gap. Instinctively he jumped to the right to avoid the blade, and it scraped the lower edge of his body armour. Because the space was so cramped he stumbled into John, and they both fell over. Brian's CS canister snapped off his belt and he dropped his baton.

The man flung open the door and held his sword high above his head. He was a tall, heavyset figure and he filled the frame. He was wearing jogging bottoms but his torso was naked.

'Die! Die!' he shouted, and lunged towards Craig, who was now isolated from the others. Craig stepped back, and put his hand up to protect himself. He was pushed up against the door of the other flat. There was no room to move. All Craig could do was hold his baton in front of his face. The man began raining down blows again and again, occasionally hitting the wooden doorframe above his head and sending chips of wood flying into the hallway.

Realising there was nowhere to retreat, Craig moved forward towards the man. His martial arts training told him that getting nearer to the man and cutting down his angles would, paradoxically perhaps, be safer in the confined space. As Craig moved forward, the man continued striking out: slash, slash, slash with the razor sharp sword.

John had got back to his feet and sprayed his CS gas directly into the swordsman's face. It appeared to have little or no impact. CS spray is designed to be an effective non-lethal weapon, but people with mental health issues, who've taken certain drugs, who've been drinking heavily or who are enraged and angry can be resistant. It wasn't a surprise to Brian that the gas had little impact. He picked up his own canister from the floor where it had fallen when it was snapped from his belt.

Next to Brian, Andy could barely believe what he was seeing. 'My God,' he thought, 'is this for real? What do we do?' He wondered whether they should all withdraw, but decided all he could do was draw his baton, follow Craig's lead and do his best to help.

By now, Craig had managed to start forcing the swordsman back into his flat, even though he was continuing to slash and hack. Brian, John and Andy followed as they moved down the hallway and emerged into a small living room.

Behind Andy, the big wooden front door swung back under its own weight and clicked shut – locking Ash and Rachel out on the landing.

The angry man stood in the middle of the room hacking and slashing with frenzied energy with officers all around him. The focus of his anger was still Craig, who was desperately parrying blow after blow with his ASP baton. Andy and John were also trying to make baton strikes.

Craig was highly experienced in martial arts and personal safety, but nothing he'd trained for matched the sheer mad savagery of the swordsman's attack. All he could do was keep on deflecting the blows with his baton. He wondered why none of them seemed to be having any impact, and started to suspect that the sword might be some kind of a toy.

Then Andy became aware of bright red splashes of blood on his shirt. He looked around. There was blood on the man's torso, on the walls and floor of the flat and on his colleagues. Suddenly, it seemed, there was blood everywhere.

Craig looked down at his hand. The sword was no toy. His hand was gaping open, and the swordsman must have cut into an artery because blood was spraying out.

Brian was beginning to wonder if the angry man would ever tire. He was still raging and slashing with his knife, and the four officers seemed unable to overpower him. John had struck him with a baton so hard it had snapped, and yet this had had almost no effect. Though it hadn't worked on the landing, Brian decided to try CS again. He reached for his CS canister and sprayed it directly into the man's face.

For a second, the man was distracted. It was all the time Craig needed. He brought his baton down onto the man's forehead in a ferocious blow. Standing to the side, Andy watched as the skin split open and what looked like a waterfall of blood gushed out.

John took the chance to grab the man's right hand, and he dropped the sword. Brian jumped on his back, Craig reached around his neck, and as he twisted the man round Andy stepped forward and snapped on a handcuff. Because the man's naked torso was so slippery with blood, he lost his grip and couldn't snap on the second handcuff.

By sheer weight of numbers, the officers forced the man to the ground. Even so, with almost superhuman strength he pushed them off and tried to get back to his feet. Despite being overweight and unfit, and up against trained police officers, the person with the most energy still seemed to be the angry man in the middle of the room.

Craig was starting to weaken slightly because of the loss of blood, so he stepped back and found a tea towel to staunch the bleeding. Brian, Andy and John managed to pull the man to the ground again and Andy snapped on the second handcuff. The man was continuing to struggle, and Brian lay on top of him just to keep him down.

Andy ran quickly to the front door and unlocked it. Craig walked past him and made off down the stairs, covered in blood and cradling his badly wounded hand. The postman's wife had come back out of her flat and was standing there with the two female police officers. She cried out in shock when she saw him.

A huge figure appeared in the door, blocking the light. Andy looked up, and for a split second he thought it was an ally of the swordsman who was about to attack. But the giant figure moved past him, and when he stepped into the light Andy could see he was wearing police uniform.

'Get off him,' the newcomer said to Brian, who was lying on top of the swordsman, holding him down.

'We're fucking lying on him until we get him under control,' replied Brian. He'd seen what the swordsman could do and had no intention of relinquishing his grip. The big man bent down and looked Brian in the eye.

'Brian,' he said slowly, 'calm down for a second. Relax. We need to sit him up because it looks like he's stopped breathing.' It was a reality check. Brian knew from his training that positional asphyxiation – when a suspect suffocates while being held face down – was a very real risk. Beneath him, the man had stopped struggling and gone very still. He was overweight, and his eyes had rolled back into his head.

Quickly, Brian climbed off. They checked the man's airway was clear and sat him up. 'It's bizarre,' he thought. 'One minute I'm fighting for my life against this guy, the next minute I'm using my first-aid knowledge to bring him round.'

Once the man sat up, it seemed as if all his anger was gone. He sat in the middle of the room with his head bowed, mumbling to himself.

Outside in the street Craig was sitting on the tenement stairs. Brian wandered out and sat down next to him. The adrenaline was wearing off now, and both men found their eyes and noses starting to stream from the residual effects of the CS spray.

'Have a look at this,' said Craig, and opened up the towel. Brian glanced inside at Craig's hand. There was an enormous gash running from his index finger almost to the base of his palm, and another smaller cut that had almost severed his little finger. Brian could see right inside: the peeled skin, bright pink tissue and paler areas of fat. For some reason, possibly shock, he and Craig began laughing hysterically.

'Does it hurt?' asked someone.

'Can you move your fingers?' asked another. Craig shook his head through the laughter – the answer was no to both questions.

John had come outside now, and saw them on the step. He took out his radio and asked what had happened to the ambulances that had been requested.

'What do you need to hurry up the ambulance for?' asked the control.

'Because Craig's hand is fucking hanging off!' replied John in exasperation.

Not long afterwards, three ambulances arrived. The man from the flat was put in the first and Craig in the second. John and Brian went in the third. They were covered in so much blood that it was considered wise to give them all a check-up.

In hospital Craig underwent a five-and-a-half-hour operation to repair his damaged hand. In total, it required fifty-two stitches, and he was off work for eight weeks while it healed. Considerable damage had been done to the tendons, and for weeks Craig needed to do exercises with a small rubber ball to rebuild strength and mobility. It was six months before he was able to make a fist again. Craig had also suffered stab wounds to his legs, but no serious injury, and several bruises across his back. The cause of these was a mystery, until it was realised that he had probably been struck by the batons of his colleagues in what was a fast-moving and very aggressive environment.

Brian and John were checked over and treated for minor cuts before returning to Corstorphine police station in west Edinburgh, where they were based. Brian's PR24 side-handled baton was sent away for tests to establish why it had broken in use.

The last one of the four out of the tenement block that morning was Andy, the probationer. As he emerged into the fresh morning air, he blinked in disbelief at the street full of white and Battenberg-checked vehicles, and the many police officers and paramedics. He'd never seen such a response.

Standing in the midst of all the vehicles and activity, just six months into his police career, Andy was suddenly overwhelmed. For the first time he fully understood that the police force was also a police family.

The man from the flat was charged with the attempted murders of the four officers. Owing to his mental state the evidence was uncontested, and he was sent to a secure hospital.

In the light of PC Brian Manchester's experience, the plastic restraining clips for CS canisters were redesigned. Later, after a survey of their performance in numerous incidents including this one, PR24 side-handled batons were withdrawn from use.

Two years later, Craig McCall, Brian Manchester, John Stirling and Andy Kendall were awarded Meritorious Conduct Awards. They received them from the Lord Provost in a ceremony at Fettes College in Edinburgh.

In April 2013, Lothian and Borders Police was united with six other Scottish forces to become Police Scotland.

9

ON A NEARSIDE WING AND A PRAYER

'I had never been to Crown Court before. The defence barrister stood up and said, "Good afternoon, James Bond." It put me right at ease, even though he was trying to put me off.'

PC ROGER SMITH

The Romans named it Deva Victrix, and from AD70 it was home to the largest garrison in Britannia. Later, Welsh tribes called it Caerleon, literally Fortress City of the Legions. Now known as Chester, for nearly two millennia the walled city on the River Dee has been a locus for trade, law and business in the North West.

None of this was in the mind of PC Iestyn Lewis-Jones as he and colleague Roger Smith made their way through the city on foot patrol in October 2007. Iestyn was looking forward to the rugby world cup final that day. Unfortunately his own national team, Wales, was not involved, but like the majority of his countrymen he was planning to cheer on South Africa against England.

It was mid morning, and Iestyn and Roger were heading for the Cross – a red sandstone landmark in the heart of the city that dated, in part, from the fourteenth century. Chester's half-timbered Jacobean buildings and unique galleried shops attracted visitors from all over the world, and the city was bustling. However, a local health policy of generously prescribing the heroin substitute methadone had also made it a magnet for drug users – and led to a corresponding surge in drug-dealing and pickpocketing. Iestyn and Roger had been recruited into a small proactive unit with one simple mission: to clean up the town. They knew the Cross was a focal point for those arriving in Chester – particularly from Liverpool – looking to buy drugs. Following the users would, they knew, often lead them to the dealers.

Iestyn nudged Roger. 'Is that Gethyn?' he asked. Roger looked over. Sure enough, there was one of their known small-time street dealers. Gethyn was a user himself, and simply sold enough drugs to fund his own habit. They knew if they searched him they'd probably find twenty or thirty wraps of heroin or cocaine, worth between £10 and £20 each. He was small fry – but he might unwittingly lead them to a bigger fish. They decided to wait and watch.

Iestyn and Roger tried to look inconspicuous, chatting to each other while keeping a discreet watch on Gethyn. They were both in plain clothes – Iestyn in scruffy jeans and trainers, Roger in baggy tracksuit bottoms, and both wearing hooded tops. The hoodies helped to disguise their radio earpieces, though the trend among young people to wear headphones at all times meant these tended not to attract attention anyway. The talk-back function was activated by a finger button disguised as a ring, while their handcuffs and batons were on a lightweight harness that was hidden in the folds of their loose-fitting tops.

It also helped that neither looked liked typical police

officers. Iestyn was tall and lean, with the characteristic dark eyes and hair of the Brythonic Welsh, while Roger, who was originally from the Wirral, had the boyish good looks and athletic build of a sportsman. Iestyn's father was a coroner, and had encouraged his son to consider a career in the police, whereas Roger had played cricket semi-professionally and had been in the same Lancashire youth team as Andrew Flintoff, who went on to become captain of England. He'd then worked briefly for the Sports Council before joining the police. Their personalities were different too. Roger: confident and outgoing; Iestyn: more reserved and analytical. They hadn't really known each other before being partnered together on the unit, but their differences made for a balanced and effective working partnership.

Being in plain clothes allowed Iestyn and Roger to move and observe criminals without being detected, but the rules governing how they could operate were strict. They couldn't entrap suspects by trying to buy drugs themselves; only if they observed a possible drug deal taking place were they allowed to step in and make an arrest. They could use stop and search, but this tactic, though useful, was sometimes controversial. To avoid legal arguments or accusations of unfairness, they used a rigid method identified by the acronym GOWISELY. The letters stood for:

G   Grounds for the search. An officer can only stop someone if he/she has grounds for suspicion.

O   Object of the search. This must be explained to the suspect before the search begins.

W   Warrant card. If in plain clothes, the officer must identify him/herself as police.

I   Identity. The police officer must give his/her name.

S   Station. The officer also has to tell the suspect the police station he/she is operating from.

E   Entitlement to a copy of the search record. All searches must be recorded.

L   Legality. The suspect should be told what legal powers the officer is using.

Y   You are now detained. This is the last step before the search, and tells the suspect that they cannot leave and must cooperate.

Apparently unaware he was being watched, Gethyn suddenly started walking away from the Cross, accompanied by two other youths. Iestyn and Roger kept a discreet distance behind. Iestyn radioed the force CCTV monitoring room and asked the operators to keep an eye on their suspect in case he slipped out of view. The officers had stopped him before, and were worried that if they got too close Gethyn would recognise them. The trio went down into a subway below the Fountains roundabout, on the northern corner of Chester's inner ring road, and were hidden from view. By the time the officers emerged on the other side, Gethyn's associates were there but he had disappeared. Iestyn cursed. They walked over to the two youths.

'All right, lads. How's it going?' he asked. Closer, he recognised the two young men, and realised they knew him too. They were what Roger and he called 'nominals' – neither was from Chester, but both came into the town to obtain drugs for their own use. There was no point in taking action against them – they were even less important than Gethyn – and Iestyn and Roger knew from experience that they were far more likely to get information in the future if they were friendly. They had a short chat, but both youths claimed not to know where Gethyn had gone.

Iestyn and Roger were frustrated. Even though Gethyn was small fry, losing him stung their professional pride. 'What about Mason Street?' said Roger. Iestyn looked up. He remembered that address being mentioned at an earlier intelligence briefing. It was nearby. Perhaps that was where Gethyn had gone.

'Good idea,' he agreed. 'Let's go and have a look.'

They made their way north along Liverpool Road, which was an important route into Chester, with two lanes of traffic in each direction and a central barrier. They passed a tattoo parlour and a small estate agent's before turning right into Mason Street, a narrow cul-de-sac. There was no sign of Gethyn. Either side were tall brick buildings and plain, unmarked doors. Iestyn and Roger walked down the centre of the road, wondering what to do. On the left side was an alleyway and they ducked into it.

'I've got an inkling it's that door,' said Roger, gesturing across the street. 'We did a search there a few months ago. Shall we wait and see if Gethyn comes out?' They knew if Gethyn had simply gone to get more drugs from a bigger dealer, he wouldn't want to be too long.

'You know the intel is that he keeps drugs in his mouth?' asked Iestyn.

'Yeah,' replied Roger. 'I was thinking about that. If he comes out shall I grab his throat so he can't swallow?'

'Well, I don't know,' hesitated Iestyn. 'The swallowing reflex is pretty strong. I'm not sure it's a great idea – might we end up strangling him?'

Suddenly, across the street another door opened and a youth appeared, looking from side to side. Roger immediately recognised him from a previous operation, and knew he was linked to a prominent Liverpool drug dealer.

'Shit!' he said. 'I know that lad. I can't remember who he is, but I definitely know him. I bet he's involved. Come on.'

The two officers removed their earpieces and pulled down their hoods, then crossed the street. As they approached the youth, Roger asked simply, 'Is Gethyn there?'

The young man looked round. 'Who the fuck's Gethyn?' he said, unconvincingly. 'I don't know what you're talking about.'

As Roger reached for his warrant card a car turned into the road. It was a dark green Honda saloon. It pulled up in front of the door where they were standing. In the front were two men they didn't recognise, but sitting in the centre of the rear seat was a man Iestyn and Roger were all too familiar with – Liam Harvey.

Liam Harvey was the youngest of three brothers. The eldest, Granville, was in prison for using a samurai sword to attack a man in Saltney, just over the border in Wales. The middle brother, Shamus, had been arrested by Iestyn and Roger about two weeks earlier.

Iestyn and Roger had been on patrol in Chester city centre when they'd seen Shamus Harvey selling drugs to a man they knew to be a heroin and crack cocaine addict. When he saw the officers he ran off, but they chased him down and arrested him.

'He's plugged,' said Roger, referring to the standard practice among drug dealers of keeping wraps of drugs pushed up the back passage – often inside the plastic containers designed to protect the toys supplied with Kinder chocolate eggs. Shamus had even been known to hide a mobile phone in his rectum. When arrested, he had, according to police gossip, dialled for a pizza from his cell and had it delivered to the police station – much to the bemusement of the duty officers.

'He'll try to swallow them if he isn't watched constantly,' warned Iestyn as they handed over Shamus to the custody officers. Shamus refused to submit to a search, and unfortunately it soon became clear that he'd managed to swallow the drugs.

Normally, this would leave the police with little choice but to release him, but because Shamus hadn't cooperated they were able to charge him with obstructing a drug search – and keep him in custody for a few more days. He was taken to Runcorn police station, where there was a specialist cell for suspected drug dealers. In it, the most conspicuous item of furniture was a toilet with a clear glass bowl – allowing the police to see if any drugs passed through the hapless suspect. Iestyn and Roger were later told that Harvey had tried to dispose of the evidence by eating his own faeces, but the officers at Runcorn had spotted what he was doing and managed to recover two of the drugs wraps. It was enough to earn Shamus Harvey a sentence of several months in prison – meaning he was off the streets when Iestyn and Roger encountered Liam Harvey a fortnight or so later.

Iestyn was sure Liam had recognised them both, the second he saw them, as the officers who'd arrested his brother a fortnight earlier. Both officers did a double-take, and after several months working together had an almost telepathic understanding of what to do.

Iestyn had two main worries: he didn't want Liam Harvey to escape, but at the same time he didn't want the car to cause any injuries to passers-by. Almost instinctively, and while shouting, 'Police, police, police!', he darted round to the driver's side and reached in through the open window to grab the keys and turn off the engine. It was a technique that had worked before when Iestyn wanted to stop a suspected drunk driver making off.

On the other side, Roger tried the passenger door. It was locked. Bending his arm, he struck the window with his elbow, expecting to smash it. Astonishingly, the glass did not crack but appeared to absorb the force of the blow, flexing inwards and then back into place. Roger tried again, bearing down with all his weight. This time, the window shattered, and he could suddenly hear voices in the car shouting, 'Get us away, get us away, they're the police, get us out of here.' Roger looked into the back and saw Liam. He reached for the back door, but again it had been locked. Using his elbow, he struck the rear passenger door window and it smashed first time. Then Roger heard the engine start revving.

On the other side of the car, Iestyn was still trying to grab the keys, but the driver was lashing out and attempting to elbow him away from the car. Then, without warning, he reached down and quickly wound up the window. Iestyn tried to snatch his right arm back but wasn't quite quick enough, and he suddenly realised his forearm was held fast between the top of the glass pane and the upper edge of the frame.

'My arm's trapped!' he shouted to Roger, who looked over and saw the panic on his colleague's face. He ran and stood in front of the car, hoping to stop the driver attempting a three-point turn.

The driver revved the engine and slammed the gearlever into reverse. Iestyn barely had time to think before the car lurched backwards, dragging him with it. It felt as if his shoulder was about to be dislocated.

Standing in front of the car, Roger realised what was happening and, without thinking, jumped onto the bonnet. The hard metal felt warm underneath, but to stop himself sliding off as the car began to move he reached for the A-pillars on either side. Luckily, he was able to get a firm hold, because on one side the window was slightly lowered, where Iestyn's arm was trapped, and on the other he'd already smashed out the glass.

Roger shouted through the windscreen, 'It's the police, stop the engine, it's the police,' but the driver was oblivious. Iestyn turned round and yelled at him, 'Roger, get the fuck off the bonnet!'

But it was too late: the car had started to accelerate back along Mason Street. As it gathered speed, Roger held on grimly, but Iestyn found himself struggling to keep up. He barely noticed any pain from his trapped arm, being more focused on keeping up with the speeding car, and realising that if it got much faster he wouldn't be able to run fast enough and would be dragged over. It was terrifying. Suddenly, as the adrenaline surged through him, all his senses became heightened and time seemed to slow down.

'I could die here,' he thought. 'These are drug dealers. They don't care, they don't give a shit, and we're heading into a dual carriageway here.'

As the car reversed into the flow of traffic on Liverpool Road, the driver swung the wheel and slammed on the brakes. The force of the manoeuvre was too much for the window's grip on his arm and Iestyn was thrown clear, falling to the ground and rolling across the carriageway.

Roger, still clinging to the bonnet, was thrown to the side but managed to hold on. He looked on horrified as Iestyn came to rest directly in the path of an oncoming motorcycle. Somehow, with lightning reactions and considerable skill, the rider managed to swerve round the stricken officer and avoid him. Roger watched, incredulous, as the bike's wheels missed Iestyn's head by what seemed like a hair's width.

Iestyn turned and looked back at the car – Roger was still holding on. He started to shout at him to get off, but it was too late: the driver had already found first gear and was accelerating away at speed towards the big roundabout.

Iestyn reached for his radio. 'Whisky Alpha three zero,' he called in. Then, barely able to believe what he was saying, he continued: 'Officer on the bonnet. Vehicle making off with an officer on the bonnet!'

It wasn't far back down to the Fountains roundabout, and the car was almost there. Iestyn ripped off his jacket and other loose items, and began sprinting down towards the junction.

Still clinging to the bonnet, Roger remembered there were traffic lights on the roundabout. It was a Saturday lunchtime and there were plenty of vehicles around. When the car stopped, he thought he'd be able to climb off. But the car didn't stop, swerving around stationery vehicles and then going through a red light. Roger could see vehicles on either side forced to stop suddenly, and heard the blare of angry horns.

Roger was kicking around with his legs but unable to get a solid foothold on the slippery front wings of the car. His handholds were good, but shards of the broken passenger side window were digging into the fingers of his right hand.

As the car turned onto St Oswald's Way, part of the inner

ring-road, the driver accelerated hard, reaching around 50 mph. Because of roadworks, only a single lane was open. Roger could see people at the side of the road pointing and staring. Even he could barely believe what was happening. 'This is Chester,' he thought. 'Not *Lethal Weapon 2*!'

Suddenly, the driver slammed on the brakes. Roger felt his momentum pushing forward, and gripped tighter. The driver accelerated again, then hit the brakes again. The car was bunny-hopping along as he tried to throw Roger off the bonnet. Suddenly, as the car lurched to a stop, Roger noticed Liam Harvey jump out of the rear door. His instinct was to climb down or roll off, so he could give chase, but he couldn't because he might be caught under the wheels. Within a second or two the driver accelerated again, and the chance was lost.

Roger looked through the windscreen at the man behind the wheel. He still didn't recognise him. The car was going faster and faster. Roger tried shouting again. 'Stop! You're going to get done for murder! Just stop now.' The man looked up. Roger felt a sickening lurch of fear in his stomach as the man looked him dead in the eye and mouthed the single word: 'No.'

The car had passed a large furniture warehouse on the left and was approaching a side turn. The driver was still accelerating and braking in an effort to dislodge the officer, but through his own fear Roger could see the man in the passenger seat was becoming more and more anxious.

They turned left off the main road, and Roger felt the car slowing down. Before it came completely to a halt, the side door was thrown open and the passenger spilled out onto the pavement. 'This is my chance,' thought Roger, and he rolled off towards the kerb. As his knees hit the hard, solid ground, he felt a huge wave of relief. What had just happened already seemed practically beyond belief. Behind him, the green Honda drove off. Roger looked at the man who'd just got out. He was standing still, in a state of shock, staring at Roger without really seeing him.

Roger ran towards him, his emotions a combination of the heady rush of adrenaline still pumping through his veins and raw anger that this gang had almost killed him. He grabbed the man, held his arm in a standard restraint and marched him back down towards the main road. As he rounded the corner onto St Oswald's Way, he saw Iestyn coming the other way. Iestyn beamed with relief that Roger was OK; watching the car disappear from view into Victoria Lane he had been convinced that Roger was going to die.

'Are you OK?' Roger asked.

'Yeah. You?'

'I'm OK,' said Roger. 'But I'm not actually sure what we're going to nick this one for. We haven't seen any drugs, we don't know who he is and he wasn't actually the driver. What are the offences?' Iestyn didn't care; he was just elated that Roger wasn't badly hurt.

A panda car pulled up alongside them. Iestyn and Roger squeezed into the back, either side of the prisoner, as they wanted to be sure he had no chance of disposing of any drugs or other evidence – but for the entire drive back he seemed to be in a daze.

Once in custody, the detained man – who'd given his name as Kevin Corbett – was strip searched, and sure enough a packet of drugs the size of a tennis ball was found pushed part way into his anus. In all there were around thirty wraps of heroin and crack cocaine. Corbett was formally arrested.

Roger and Iestyn were both still shaking a little from the after-effects of the adrenaline. Then news came through that Liam Harvey had been captured in an alleyway not far from the scene by a policeman who'd spotted him running away. Harvey was taken to hospital after swallowing drugs during his arrest. He was kept under observation, and the drugs were eventually recovered after they had passed through him.

A short time later, the driver, John Williams, was brought in. He had been found at an address in Blacon, after parking the damaged car outside with no attempt to hide it and then apparently sitting inside waiting to be arrested.

A couple of higher ranking officers came down to the police station and congratulated Iestyn and Roger on the job they'd done. Iestyn's arm was bruised but he was otherwise unhurt, but Roger was suffering from agonising back pains and went to hospital. He'd suffered whiplash with the force of the movement on the car, and had damaged his lower back.

Some weeks later, the case came to court. John Williams was facing charges of drug dealing and dangerous driving, and both Iestyn and Roger were needed to give evidence. Williams claimed in court that he hadn't realised Roger and Iestyn were police officers because they were in plain clothes, and that he had panicked. When asked why he had repeatedly slammed on the brakes, as if trying to dislodge Roger, he said he'd done it because he couldn't see the road ahead. Roger knew the defence barrister's job was to discredit him – to create doubt in the jury's mind. Roger had never been to Crown Court before, and sitting outside, while he was waiting to be called into the witness box, was a nerve-racking experience. Finally the usher called him in.

Roger walked into the witness box and took the oath before describing what had happened. Then the defence lawyer stood up to cross-examine him.

'Good afternoon, James Bond!' he said. The comment was meant to put Roger off, but as smiles went round the courtroom Roger relaxed, realising it had backfired on the barrister.

John Williams was found guilty, and jailed for nine years for drug dealing and dangerous driving. Kevin Corbett and Liam Harvery were both sentenced to three years for drug dealing.

∽◈◈∼

The entire Harvey family – Liam, his brothers Shamus and Granville, and their parents Granville Senior and Josie – were later evicted from their home and served with ASBOs (Anti-Social Behaviour Orders).

Roger Smith and Iestyn Lewis-Jones received Chief Constable's Commendations and National Police Bravery Awards.

Iestyn did eventually watch the rugby world cup final with his friends back home as planned, but he can hardly remember any of it as he spent the entire match reliving what had happened, and thinking how lucky he and Roger had been.

10

IN AT THE DEEP END – TWICE

'I don't think anyone sat in an office, or in another police station, can assess the situation better than the people who are there …'

PC STEVE HARGRAVE

Deep below the surface of the North Sea, diver Steve Hargrave directed the high-pressure jet at another patch of algae. Very little light penetrated this far down, so though the water was clear it was almost pitch black. His suit torch illuminated a small area of the giant support pillar that he knew extended 120 feet up to the surface and around 600 feet down to the sea bed. If placed on the bottom here, One Canada Square – the distinctive tower at the heart of Canary Wharf in London – wouldn't even break the surface.

The work demanded patience and concentration. Mainly it was maintenance or inspection – opening or closing valves or removing marine growth from critical structures or machinery. Sometimes he had to use small radioactive X-ray devices to check joints or welds for fatigue or failure.

Steve was protected from the intense cold by a drysuit – two layers of neoprene fabric that kept a thin layer of air between them for warmth. An umbilical cord carrying his air stretched from the back of his suit to a pressurised diving bell nearby, which was suspended from a small ship known as a Diving Support Vessel (DSV) that floated next to the giant oil platform. It used sophisticated directional thrusters and computer software to stay in exactly the same position, irrespective of waves or water currents. Inside the bell was a colleague suited up and ready to enter the water should Steve get into difficulties. As an air diver, Steve was licensed to a depth of fifty metres. Any work below that level required the diver to breathe a mixture of gases – usually oxygen and helium – and specialist training.

Once the dive was completed, Steve would surface and be taken to a decompression chamber on the deck of the support vessel. The decompression process was vital: without it tiny bubbles of nitrogen would form in the blood, creating disorientation, nausea and even death – a condition known as the bends. The entire dive, including the time spent recovering, was usually around six to seven hours.

But after five years as a commercial diver, Steve had noticed that work was – as others had joked – drying up. Oil prices tended to go in seven-year cycles: there were plenty of contracts when the price was high, but when it fell the oil companies scaled back to the bare minimum. And the oil in the North Sea was running out. Steve wasn't convinced there was a long-term future in commercial diving. He had a new ambition: he wanted to become a policeman.

'He's been totally down since she finished with him. We don't know where he is, and I'm just so scared he'll do something stupid.' The boy's mother was frantic with worry. She'd waited until nightfall for him to return home, then called the police to report her son missing. Now she was sitting with the two officers at her home in Worthing, West Sussex, about ten miles along the coast from Brighton.

'Don't worry, we'll do our best to find him,' said Steve Hargrave. He could tell the woman was struggling to hold it together. 'Just tell us anything you think might help, anywhere you think he might be, any friends he might be staying with.'

'Well,' said the woman, hesitantly, 'I think you should know that they found him on the end of the pier a few months ago. He was talking about jumping off. I've tried all his other friends and they don't know anything. Please find him, please!'

Steve nodded to his partner that evening, PC Ben Henwood. They stood up and moved towards the door.

'We'll do our best for your son,' promised Steve, and as they sat down in their police van they called in a description of the youngster, and requested that police CCTV camera operators keep an eye out for him. They also drove down to the pier, which housed a nightclub, and spoke to the doormen, warning them to be on the lookout for the missing teenager. Deciding that there was not much more they could do at that time of night, Steve and Ben continued on their routine patrol.

It was around half past two in the morning when the 999 call came in. The voice sounded young and frightened. 'I believe you have officers looking for me. I'm just calling to tell you where you can find my body in about two minutes. My time has come. It'll be directly south of here. I'm walking into the sea now.'

The operator immediately put a trace on the call, and

identified that it had been made from a public telephone box at Splash Point, a short stretch of beach to the east of the pier. In the control room, the CCTV team knew they had a camera there, and immediately trained it on the telephone kiosk. Sure enough, they picked out a lone figure leaving the box and walking slowly but deliberately down the beach towards the water's edge.

As soon as they received the message, Steve and Ben switched on the blue lights and siren and drove at speed down to Splash Point. The road ended at a sea wall, and a path led down to the beach a short distance below. Standing on the edge, Steve and Ben looked out into the darkness.

'There he is!' said Ben, pointing. He was younger than Steve, considerably taller and had better eyesight. Now Steve could see him too – probably around 300 feet into the water. Steve grabbed his waterproof Peli diving torch – a legacy of his diving days that he always carried with him – and started to walk down the beach. Small fishing boats lay beached either side, and Steve's boots crunched on the pebbles as he walked down towards the breaking waves. Long wooden groynes on each side stretched into the water. The tide was in, so he didn't have too far to walk.

At the water's edge, Steve shouted at the young man and directed the powerful beam of his torch onto him, but there was no response. It was clear the teenager had no intention of coming back.

Steve was a qualified risk assessor, and now put that training into action. He considered the facts. He was forty years old, physically very fit, and had many years of experience in the water: first as a commercial diver and later for nine years with Sussex Police's own underwater search unit. Although he was no longer on the dive team, he always carried a tide table in his pocket – and he checked it. The tide was still coming in, which meant that while the swim out would be hard work the return, when he'd be tiring, would be easier. He was confident in his own swimming ability but also aware of his limitations. And, put bluntly, he couldn't stand at the edge and watch a teenage boy drown – even if that boy did want to take his own life. Steve had been a teenager too. He knew that nineteen-year-olds could overreact and take personal problems to heart. But the youngster had a mother who loved him, and his whole life ahead of him.

'I'm going in,' said Steve, and pulled off his stab vest and utility belt and undid his tie.

Despite being six foot seven, and younger, Ben was not a confident swimmer. 'I'm glad you said that,' he replied.

Steve waded into the water. The sea was choppy, with waves between six and seven feet high. He knew that entering the water – the first thirty feet – was the most dangerous part. It was here, where the waves hit much shallower water and break – that they expend most of their energy. Once he was into deeper water, the wave motion became more predictable and more manageable.

The water was bitterly cold, but Steve had been expecting that. He swam front crawl, but kept his head facing forward so he could keep the young man in view at all times. He briefly tried putting his torch in his mouth, but he kept getting mouthfuls of salty water with every wave crest, so he took it out and wrapped the strap round his wrist. The beam flashed crazily one way then the other with each stroke.

Steve had left his boots on when he went in, and he began to realise that this was a mistake. Although they'd protected his feet against the stones on the beach, in the water they were a liability. Because they kept his ankle rigid, he couldn't kick out properly, and it felt as if all he could do with his feet was a strange doggy-paddle.

On the shore, more officers were arriving. The critical incident inspector in the control room issued an order that no officer was to enter the water, on health and safety grounds. No one wanted to report back that it was too late: that one officer was already out to sea and closing in on the subject.

By now, Steve was about fifteen feet from the youngster. They were around 100 yards from the beach, and well out of their depth.

'Leave me alone!' he shouted. 'Fuck off and leave me. You shouldn't have come. I'm not coming back.'

'You're coming in, and I'm not going to spend too much time out here – I've got a wife and two kids,' Steve snapped back. The boy lashed out in an effort to punch him, but Steve was able to dodge the feeble blow – he could see hypothermia was starting to set in. Experience made him realise that he too was getting some of the early signs: the ends of his feet and hands were starting to tingle, and his muscle response was starting to become sluggish.

Time was running out, and Steve had to act quickly. He swam round behind the boy, and without warning grabbed him by the scruff of the neck and dunked his head under the water, down, up – then again, down, up. The boy was stunned. He hadn't been expecting it, and the sudden sensation of being fully immersed in cold water shocked him into submission. Steve took him in the lifesaver's hold and began kicking for the shore.

'You're coming in whether you like it or not,' gasped Steve, 'so you might as well help.' The boy started kicking a little and the pair headed back, with the help of the incoming tide as Steve had anticipated. On the shore, Ben and the others were shouting encouragement, and although Steve knew roughly which direction to swim in, their voices helped to guide him back.

Suddenly, Steve realised he could touch the bottom and got to his feet. The water was chest high. The other officers waded in and helped him and the young man out. Steve was shattered, and just about managed to drag himself out of the water and up the beach. He made his way over to where paramedics were checking on the boy he'd saved. They confirmed that his core body temperature was significantly reduced, and that he was well into the early stages of hypothermia. Steve had been in the water around ten minutes, the boy probably five minutes more. In the cold waters of the English Channel in March, Steve knew that the teenager would not have lasted for much longer.

As the boy was taken off to hospital, the critical incident inspector arrived at the scene. He wanted to know why his order not to enter the water had been ignored. Steve confirmed that the decision was his, and ran through his on-the-spot risk assessment. He explained that, in his view, no one sitting in the office could assess the situation better than someone at the scene. Knowing Steve's background, and listening to the thinking behind it, the inspector nodded, and agreed that Steve had done the right thing. And, of course, he had saved a young man's life.

Steve went back to the police station. He always kept a spare uniform in his locker, so he was able to shower and change. He and his colleagues debriefed, and some of the younger officers admitted that they had been scared of going in themselves. They had also worried about telling the control room that Steve had entered the water, because they didn't want to get him into trouble.

After the debrief, Steve had a cup of hot tea and a Wispa bar, and reflected on what had happened. Within an hour and a half he was back out on foot patrol. A little later he called in at the hospital. The boy was awake, and they chatted for a while. His mother thanked Steve for saving her son's life. Some time later, Steve received a letter from her explaining that after a short spell in hospital her son had gone to university, and appeared to be getting on with his life. A life, she said gratefully, that he was now able to enjoy because of Steve's courage. What Steve did not know was that within months he would be called on to show that courage again.

Four months later, Steve was on patrol in Worthing again; he and a female colleague were on foot on the sea front. They were both tasked to Operation Marble – in which the town was flooded with uniformed officers on weekend nights in an effort to counter drunken fights and other antisocial behaviour.

It was, thought Steve, a particularly disgusting evening, especially for July. The wind was blowing hard offshore, whipping up the tops of the waves into sharp, foamy white crests. A bus pulled up beside them and the driver leaned out.

'Sorry, officers, it might be nothing, but when I was stopped at that bus stop back there I thought I could hear a woman in the sea. I could hear screaming.'

Steve ran down to the beach, while his colleague put out a radio message. Thanks to the high number of police in the town, they were joined very quickly by other officers. Steve looked at the water; he could clearly hear a woman screaming and shouting. The bulk of the pier stretched out to his right, and up on the deck two of the night-club doormen were using laser pointers to highlight the woman in the water.

'Oh no,' thought Steve. 'Here we go again.' He knew the tide was going out, and there was the added danger of waves pushing him against the heavy metal legs of the pier. Nonetheless, he had done this before and prevailed. He felt that although conditions were harder this time, he could manage it.

There were half a dozen other officers on the beach. He looked from face to face. They looked back sheepishly. 'Is it me again?' he asked. 'Is it down to the old man?' There were obviously no takers. He could hear mutterings from some of them about not being strong swimmers.

Steve sighed, and took off his stab vest, belt and tie. He also kicked off his boots, remembering how they'd hampered his swimming on the previous occasion. But the rocks were sharp, and as he tiptoed down to the water's edge, wincing and grimacing, he had to remind himself that once he was in the water he wouldn't regret the decision.

As he entered the water, Steve thought he heard someone say the coastguard had been contacted and had issued instructions that no one was to go in. But Steve didn't want him to arrive and find that the woman had drowned.

As he started to swim out, he could feel the effect of the tide – it was going out and falling very quickly. Sailors and others who know the sea understand that tides move by the rule of twelfths: the water level changes fastest at the mid-point between high and low tide.

Steve called out, 'Hold on, just hold on. I'm coming,' but the woman was shouting and screaming, and he wasn't sure she had heard or understood him. As he got to within twenty-five yards, she suddenly went silent. Quickly, Steve reached for his waterproof diver's torch. She had lost consciousness, and he watched as she slipped below the waves. He swam quickly to where he'd last seen her, reached down and pulled her back to the surface. She didn't seem to be breathing, so Steve held her nose and gave her a rescue breath in the mouth. She was a dead weight, and he knew that swimming back was going to be far harder this time. Not only was he swimming against the wind and the tide, but she was unconscious and unable to help at all.

Steve kicked off for the shore, but he seemed to be making little progress. He picked a point on the water's edge to aim for, but after several strokes it seemed no nearer, and he was starting to tire. With each kick he moved forward, but then the tide took him back. Steve realised the current was also moving him sideways, in towards the pier. They were around 100 yards from the shore, but the pier was 400 yards long so there was no way of avoiding it. Steve could see the waves breaking against the metal support struts. Not only were there plenty of rough, rusty edges and corners, but most of the legs were covered with barnacles. He was tiring rapidly, though, and began to wonder whether being washed against the hazardous pier legs might be his best option.

Steve was frightened. The tide was too strong. As hard as he tried kicking, he wasn't getting any closer to the shore. He'd always had total confidence in his own strength and ability in the water, but now doubts were setting in. He was strong but he wasn't invincible. His reserves of energy were probably greater than most, but they weren't infinite. What if he fainted? Would they both drown? Before that moment came, would he have to release the woman just to save himself?

Up on the pier, Steve's colleague Ben Henwood and one of the night-club doormen were now level with those in the water. There was a life ring on the rail, and as Steve was obviously struggling they uncoiled the rope and threw the ring towards him. Steve managed to swim towards it and grabbed it. He tried to put it over the woman's head, but she was completely unresponsive and he couldn't do it on his own. With what was left of his strength, he looped his own arm through the ring. Now he was holding onto the woman with one hand and onto the ring with the other. His arms were tired, his legs were tired, and he was gasping for breath in the cold night air.

Ben started to pull him towards the shore, walking slowly back along the pier edge, but the wind and current was taking Steve closer and closer to the pier legs.

'Stop, stop pulling!' he shouted, but a wave caught them and they were pounded against the hard steel legs. Steve tried his best to take the brunt of the collision, to protect the woman. Though his lightweight Wickaway shirt offered some protection, he could feel sharp barnacle shells digging into his skin, and salt water stinging the resulting cuts and scratches.

The rope had become snagged on the pier leg, and Ben released some to loosen the tension. Using the tide, Steve managed to push himself away from the pier, and Ben took up the strain and pulled him closer to shore. Then another big wave came in. Again Steve and the woman were pummelled against the pier legs, and again he held her clear and felt the barnacles digging into his arms and back. The life ring was keeping them afloat, but Steve wondered how long he would have the strength to hold on while taking such punishment. It seemed to take a lifetime, but slowly they were working their way towards the shore, again and again being forced against the pier legs, again and again untangling the rope and managing to push his way out.

Eventually, after repeating the process half a dozen times, they reached the shallows. A night-club doorman and a police colleague were waiting, and they helped Steve pull the woman out of the water and onto the beach.

The rescue had taken much longer than planned, and Steve was physically exhausted. The woman lay totally still. She looked dead. They rolled her onto her back; she wasn't breathing. Steve tried to take her pulse, but his own heart was beating so fast he couldn't. Suddenly, the other officer snapped, 'She's got a pulse. It's weak, but there's definitely something there.'

Without stopping to think, Steve held her nose, tilted her head back to make sure her airway was clear, took a deep breath and blew hard into the woman's mouth. He paused, then gave her a second rescue breath. Suddenly, she shuddered back to life and began coughing violently. They rolled her over into the recovery position, and waited for the paramedics to arrive.

Steve sat back. He felt light-headed and utterly exhausted. The water wasn't cold enough for hypothermia; he simply felt that he had used up every last reserve of energy and strength he had. Had it gone on any longer, he felt sure that he would have had to let go of the woman, then just cling to the pier and wait to be rescued. And if Ben hadn't had the presence of mind to throw him the life ring, he knew they would have been washed right under the pier and killed.

As the paramedics arrived, Steve was helped to the ambulance. They placed a mask over his face and he gulped down pure oxygen. He shuddered, and felt the energy and strength surging back through his body, into his arms and legs, across his back.

Afterwards, when Steve returned to the police station, there was another discussion about health and safety. Steve was told that one senior officer had asked, 'Do we have a rogue officer in Worthing who stands by the beach waiting for these things to happen?' Steve had a long, hot shower, a cup of tea and another Wispa bar. He realised that he'd gone right to the limits of his endurance and strength with this rescue, and although he'd saved the woman it had been a close call. It had scared him.

For the rest of that night, and ever since, Steve has wondered whether he'll go into the sea again if the need arises. He hopes he'll never find out.

๛

In 2010, Steve was nominated for a National Bravery Award for the two sea rescues.

Originally from Lancashire, and ever the practical northerner, his wife was less enthusiastic about his heroism. She said to him simply, 'Once was brave. Twice was stupid. Three times is a divorce . . .'

11

AND SO HOLD ON . . .

*'I could have let go of him but I'm not that kind of
person. I was determined he was going to be arrested,
particularly as he'd assaulted me.'*

PC STEPHEN CARTLIDGE

PC Stephen Cartlidge had parked in his favourite spot and
now there was nothing to do but wait. It was the early hours
of the morning and still dark. He'd reversed the patrol car
off the main road into a short driveway that led to some
long-deserted garages. From his point of view, the location
had the advantage of being in a dip, which meant that the
sort of people he was after wouldn't see him until it was too
late.

Sitting next to him in the car was PC Claire Bowker.
Stephen liked working with Claire – he thought their skills
complemented each other well, and she was good company.

Stephen had wanted to join the police for as long as
he could remember; his ambition was to follow his father
and become a police dog handler. When he'd finished his
A-levels, Staffordshire police weren't recruiting, so he'd gone
to university in Leicester to read English. One year into his

degree course, some jobs became available. Stephen applied immediately and was accepted, abandoning his studies with barely a second thought.

They were on a night shift, and as usual they'd been sent to Bentilee, a large housing estate on the edge of Stoke-on-Trent. Bentilee had a high crime rate at the time and Stephen relished the challenge of policing such a neighbourhood.

Sitting in the car, Stephen and Claire both heard it at the same time – the unmistakable sound of a vehicle being driven too fast. As it flashed over the brow of the hill on Dawlish Avenue, Stephen could tell immediately there was something not quite right about the car. Apart from the speed, he saw the worried expressions of those inside. The back-seat passenger craned round to look out of the rear window to see what the patrol car would do. The officers could imagine the discussion in the speeding car: 'Do you think they suspect anything?' 'Keep cool!' 'Are they following us?'

Stephen revved the engine and accelerated into the street. As soon as the other driver saw him pull out, he accelerated and switched off his lights.

'Right,' thought Stephen, 'he obviously doesn't want to talk to me, which makes me very keen to talk to him!' Besides alerting the police, switching the lights off was a tactic of debatable wisdom anyway. Yes, it meant the glow of the head and taillights was hidden, but it also made it far harder for the driver to see the road ahead – and every time the car braked the police behind saw red anyway.

Stephen's blue lights were on and the pursuit continued. Claire alerted the control room with the radio. Most car chases are over within seconds, or maybe a couple of minutes, but this one lasted a good four to five minutes. It felt to

Stephen as if they had driven up and down the entire length of Bentilee.

Those being followed would know that the longer the chase went on the more likely they were to be caught, as the police would be able to mobilise other vehicles. Stephen was expecting them to abandon the car at any time.

Sure enough, a moment later the car mounted the kerb and drove down a gently sloping grassy bank towards the brook, a tributary of the River Trent, that ran through the centre of Bentilee. Stephen stopped and got out. It had been raining heavily and he knew the ground was soft. He was sure the car would rapidly become bogged down, and would be unable to get back up the hill.

'Claire, stay with the car,' he shouted, and sprinted off across the grass.

He could see the car ahead of him illuminated by the streetlights. As it rolled down the incline he saw the doors open. Three men climbed out and began to run. One man peeled off to the side, but the driver and another ran forward, splashing through the swollen waters of the brook and up the hill the other side. Stephen followed. His first target was the driver, purely because he'd already committed one offence by failing to stop. And if he was driving while disqualified, or the car was stolen, he would be responsible.

Stephen was confident. He'd always been a strong sprinter and had a reasonable success rate in foot chases, and he could tell he was gaining on the men. He could see from the driver's build that he obviously worked out in the gym a fair amount, but while weights build size they don't usually increase speed.

At the top of the short bank they came out onto another residential street, with a row of semi-detached houses on the other side. The driver was falling behind the other runner, and Stephen was gaining rapidly as they crossed the road and continued along the footpath. The man in front jumped over a low wall and ran up the side of one of the houses, but Stephen was focused on the driver. He reached out and grabbed the man's arm.

The driver turned and punched Stephen full in the face, hard. Stephen rocked back on his heels. He hadn't expected such an immediately aggressive response. Most of the time suspects surrendered when he took hold of them.

The man punched him again and again. Stephen could have let him go, but the attack made him more determined to make an arrest.

He reached round and tried to draw his baton. The man realised what he was doing and tried to grab it from him. It was one of the older, fixed rigid batons. 'If he gets hold of it,' Stephen thought, 'he'll use it as a weapon on me.'

As they grappled, Stephen decided to see if he could get the man on the ground, where it was usually easier to get control. He used a leg sweep and his own weight to pull them both down. As they fell, the baton flew out of Stephen's hand.

While they writhed on the pavement, the man continued to punch Stephen in the head and body. It was hurting. The man was obviously someone who was used to fighting and used to using his fists. He seemed not to be tiring.

'Kilo Alpha three five requesting urgent assistance,' Stephen gasped into his radio, but in the struggle it had got knocked onto a different channel. His garbled messages caused confusion, and because he was panting his call sign wasn't clear.

The man ignored Stephen's efforts on the radio and continued to lash out. There were no rules and no boundaries

– this was a vicious street brawl. Stephen tried to fight back, but the man was more violent and more powerful.

'Help! Somebody please help me! Police!' Stephen had never shouted for help like this before, but he was hoping that someone in the nearby houses would hear the commotion and dial 999. He realised his radio messages hadn't got through, and if someone called the police his colleagues would know where he was. He tried pulling out his CS spray canister, but it jammed.

Stephen knew he was struggling to hold on. This was a fight he was losing. There was no sign of any help, and he could feel his initial adrenaline burst starting to ebb away. He was tiring, but his opponent still seemed to be full of energy.

In a last effort, he managed to roll the man over. As soon as he was on top, he clicked on a handcuff. Because the handcuffs were rigid, even on one wrist they gave Stephen leverage and a measure of restraint. The instant he felt the handcuff snap shut, the man stopped struggling.

'All right mate, all right,' he said. 'I give up.' A wave of relief surged over Stephen. About bloody time! For a second he relaxed his grip. In that instant, the man pulled up Stephen's hand and bit hard on the deep flesh at the heel. The pain was immediate and excruciating. Stephen shouted out and snatched his hand away. As he did so, the man drew back the hand Stephen had cuffed and smashed the handcuffs across his face.

Bang! The first blow struck Stephen across his eyebrow. He felt it split open and begin bleeding. Bang! The man struck Stephen again, on the other cheek, with a backhanded motion as he drew the cuffs across.

Stephen tried to grab the man's wrist and bring it into his

body, so he couldn't lash out, but he was close to exhaustion. They were still lying on the floor, and Stephen was trying to hold him down while avoiding more blows.

'Kill him! Kill him!' The man was shouting beyond Stephen to someone else. Stephen turned his head just in time to see a white trainer coming straight towards his face. For a split second, time seemed to freeze. He could make out the markings, the laces, even the stitching and individual scuffs of dirt.

Stephen's head snapped back with the kick, and his vision blurred. He was still holding onto the first man, but as he looked up he saw the treads on the sole of the trainer as the other figure raised his foot. The trainer crashed down in a vicious stamp, and Stephen didn't feel anything after that.

He could see a face. It was blurred but familiar.

'Stephen, are you OK?' he heard a voice say. Everything was muddled, and his head was full of a throbbing, unrelenting pain.

He seemed to be in a very small room. The lights were very bright. He closed and opened his eyes a few times. Slowly, the face unblurred.

'Claire!' He remembered her name. 'Where am I? What's happened?'

'You're all right,' she said. 'You're in the ambulance now. Just relax.' Stephen was confused. Ambulance? He reached up to his head. It was bandaged, but through it he could feel swelling on either side. His hand was hurting. He looked down and could see a nasty red arc of puncture wounds.

'It's a bite. They've left it open because of infection. They're going to give you antibiotics,' Claire explained. Another face appeared at the door of the ambulance. It was Stephen's sergeant, Nigel Spooner.

'How you doing then?' he asked. Stephen started to remember: the man, the fight, the trainer.

'I think I'm OK,' he said. 'Did the guys get away?'

'Claire told me where you'd gone,' replied Nigel. 'I followed you. There was only one guy there. You were virtually unconscious but locked onto him. You just weren't letting go. I don't know how you did it. Oh, and you might like to know we found a knife in the abandoned car.'

Now he could remember how desperate the struggle had been. If the man had had that knife, Stephen felt sure he would have used it. He didn't know how he'd held on, but he was glad he had. Perhaps his subconscious mind was able to keep sending the same message to his muscles: just hold on.

Another face appeared at the ambulance door. It was a detective.

'Can you give us a description of the other man who assaulted you?' he asked.

Stephen smiled. 'Well, I'm not sure about his face, but I can give you an excellent description of his trainers!'

⤞⤝

The man Stephen arrested, Michael William Lockley, denied assault. Stephen gave evidence against him in court and he was convicted and sentenced to eighteen months. A known heroin and cocaine addict, at last count he had forty-five convictions for 218 offences, prompting one judge to say:

'You are persistent, incorrigible, you do not change your

ways, and you prey on your neighbours and people who have properties and businesses nearby.'

The second man was arrested the following day.

Stephen Cartlidge received a Chief Constable's Commendation, and was also nominated for a Police Federation National Bravery Award.

He later fulfilled his ambition to become a police dog handler.

12

BRUTAL IN BEDWORTH

'I'd resigned myself to the fact that I was getting a kicking here. These guys were obviously serious.'

PC PETER DOHERTY

Behind the steel shutters, it sounded as if somebody was tearing the shop apart. PC Peter Doherty tiptoed up to the front and listened. The alarm light was flashing and he could hear a loud banging and crashing inside. He turned round and went back to the car where his more experienced colleagues were waiting.

'I think they're still inside – we've got them!' he said. Sergeant Martin Hewish looked up at the blue-fronted newsagent's shop.

'Yes, Pete, you're right. You go round to the left there. We'll go right, loop round and meet you at the back. I'll send the two in the car round there too.'

Peter nodded and trotted off in the direction indicated. This was only his second week after being signed off to go on patrol independently. Sergeant Hewish and the other officer, PC Paul Browning, went the other way.

Born in Coventry, Peter had spent fifteen years in the army

and had served in Ireland, Germany, Cyprus and the first Gulf War. He'd left the military after becoming disillusioned, and decided to become a police officer. Because the application process had taken so long, he'd spent time working as a used car salesman and then successfully applied to be a paramedic. He'd even completed some of the preliminary ambulance training before he received his start date for Warwickshire Police.

Peter was older than most of the new recruits arriving at the training centre at Ryton. He'd been surprised at some of the behaviour that was tolerated, such as answering mobile phone calls during sessions or arriving late. His own army discipline and fitness were a great benefit, and after completing his classroom training he was sent to Bedworth, a small town north of Coventry. So far he'd loved every minute of it.

Peter turned the corner at the end of the parade of shops and carried on another thirty or so yards before reaching the access road that led round to a small loading yard at the back of the shops. Along one side was a tall hedge, and at the far end he could make out a row of concrete garages.

Peter heard a squeal of tyres and started running towards the yard. A black Lexus came hurtling around the corner ahead of him, almost on two wheels. 'That's got to be a getaway car,' he thought, and drew his baton. If nothing else he'd just try to put it through the windscreen. As the car came closer, Peter stepped to one side and raised his baton, ready to strike. As he did so, the car turned towards him. He jumped to the side, and the car turned again. Peter slipped and dropped his baton. The car was still bearing down on him. 'Shit,' he thought, 'he's going to wipe me out.' At the last moment, Peter rolled to the side and the car's wheels flashed past his face.

Peter sat up and dusted himself off. He started to look for his baton. A police car came into sight from the direction of the yard. It was the mobile unit Sergeant Hewish had sent round to check, but they'd been unable to stop the Lexus making off.

'Are you all right?' asked the driver, winding down the window.

'Of course I'm all right!' said Peter, 'Get after them!' The officer in the car nodded and drove off.

Peter stood up and looked around for his baton. As he picked it up, he noticed movement on the roof of a nearby garage. First one man, then another, both in balaclavas, clambered into view on top of the building. 'Great,' thought Peter. 'The getaway car driver must've panicked and left these two behind.'

'Stop where you are. You're both nicked,' he shouted. Another masked man appeared on the roof. The odds were lengthening, but Peter was still confident.

Then the men turned and made off. Peter called for back-up on his radio, but wasn't sure it was working. He shouted out to his colleagues in the hope that they could hear him. What Peter didn't know was that the route they'd taken round the other side of the block led to a long row of houses, with no access to the rear yard of the shop.

Peter ran into the yard. The three men had climbed off the garage roof ahead of him – but he was gaining on them. As he reached for the nearest man, he heard the sound of a revving engine behind him. The Lexus had come back for the rest of the gang. 'Piss,' thought Peter, but hopefully the car with the other two officers wasn't far behind.

The car spun around in front and stopped. Peter decided

his best option was to target the driver and put the car out of action; the other robbers would have to make off on foot, and would be less likely to get away.

Suddenly, the three men he was chasing stopped and turned to face him. One was carrying a pick-axe handle; another had a sledge hammer. The one nearest him took a swing with the wooden pick-axe handle, and Peter lifted his arm to deflect the blow. He staggered as he felt an enormous impact on his left side, just below his raised arm. 'I've been shot,' he thought in disbelief. But he hadn't heard a bang. As his left arm came down he felt it touch something, and there was a crunching in his side. They'd speared him!

'Get in, get in!' The driver was screaming with an almost comically high-pitched voice, but two robbers were still coming towards Peter.

He staggered back. 'I'm going to get a kicking here,' he thought. 'These guys are serious, and if they get hold of this thing while it's still inside me I'm fucked. They could push it in further, or God knows what.'

He felt himself becoming fired up with anger as the adrenaline surge kicked in. He reached to his side and gripped the shaft – it was thick, with angled corners but not sharp edges, and felt like cold steel.

He started to pull, and could feel it grating against his ribs. Peter had been wearing a stab vest, but it had gone between the front and rear plates through the soft webbing below his armpit, almost as if the assailant had known exactly where to strike. The weapon came out and clattered to the floor. The robbers looked at it, and then backed off. Peter realised he couldn't breathe. He reached round to the side and felt in with his fingers. There was a slight wetness – 'That's got to be blood,' he thought; but apart from a stinging pain at the entry point it didn't hurt too much. He thought it hadn't pierced that deeply.

The two robbers had run around to the far side of the car and were getting in. Peter lurched forward, stumbled, but stayed on his feet. The doors of the car slammed shut and it drove off.

Peter stood swaying and watched it leave. The wound in his side was really starting to hurt. He couldn't breathe, and as he bent over he caught sight of the weapon on the ground. It was a steel crowbar with the straight tip sharpened to a point. 'Fuck', he thought.

People started running towards him from the neighbouring houses. Peter toppled over, falling onto the crowbar. One of the onlookers tried to pick it up. 'Fuck off,' thought Peter. 'Leave it!' He tried to speak, but didn't have the breath. He could see a large pool of blood forming on the floor. A woman was screaming.

'Oh my God, oh my God, do you need an ambulance?' Peter tried to nod. No shit! He tried to stand up again, and got halfway to his feet before stumbling over again.

'What do you want me to do?' asked a man.

'Help . . .' Peter was struggling to find the breath to speak. 'Help me . . . off . . . with this . . . armour.' The man loosened the Velcro straps. Peter could see the horrified look on his face. He put his right hand up to the wound. Now the armour was clear, he could feel through his shirt. His fingers touched jagged ribs, and a hole. 'That's nasty,' he thought. Nearby, the woman was still screaming.

'Listen,' he said to the man. 'Call me an . . . ambulance. I might be unconscious soon . . . Tell them I'm losing blood

. . . and I have a . . . punctured left lung . . .' Peter sat back, exhausted with the effort of speaking. His paramedic training told him that if one lung collapsed then differential pressure meant the other was likely to follow. In that case he would almost certainly lose consciousness. If the ambulance crew were told what was wrong without having to check, it would save time – and quite probably save his life.

Peter tried to remain in a sitting position. He was worried that if he lay down, he'd pass out. He activated his radio and got through to his colleague Paul Browning.

'Mate, you really need to get to me because I'm fucked here,' he gasped. 'I've been stabbed, and my ribs are smashed in. I've got the weapon.'

'Where are you?' asked Paul.

'I'm round the back of the shop. If you see the crowd of people then you've found me.'

The man who'd called the ambulance had been passed a blanket and was trying to wrap it around Peter's shoulders.

'Look, mate, I just need some space, please,' Peter asked. It was early August, and not a cold evening. Within a minute, Paul arrived.

'Fuck me!' he said. 'Don't pass out on me! I need you to tell me what to do!'

Peter could feel he was on the edge of consciousness. It would be so easy to let the darkness wash over him. He started to lean back.

'Can you just leave me alone?' he said to his colleague.

'No!' said Paul. 'Stay with me, stay awake.' Peter sat back up. The sharp, angry pain in his side was getting worse and worse, and he felt as if he'd been winded, that he couldn't get his breath. He fought down the urge to panic; made himself stay calm. Paul helped Peter to get comfortable by leaning him on the discarded body armour.

Peter looked up. The alarm light was still flashing on the side of the shop. 'Of all the shit that could have killed me in my life,' he thought to himself, 'now I'm going to die outside a newspaper shop. That's just ridiculous. But at least if I die, my partner will be told I died doing the right thing.' For some reason, as he struggled to stay awake, he felt this was important.

When the ambulance crew arrived, Peter recognised them – he'd worked with them before. Paul Browning explained about the punctured lung.

'I'm barely hanging on here,' said Peter from the floor. 'I'm not sure if I can stay conscious.'

'Just relax. Let me check your lung,' said the paramedic, kneeling down. She felt around Peter's side.

'You've got air entry on the left side, which means there must still be some function. Air going in and out. That's good.' She felt a little more and winced. 'It's a bit of a mess, but I think you're going to be OK.'

Carefully they moved Peter onto a stretcher, though by now the pain was excruciating, and it was made worse by the grinding and grating sensation he could feel in his broken ribs.

The George Eliot hospital in Nuneaton was just six minutes away, and by the time they arrived the crash team were ready. Peter was still conscious as he was wheeled into the A&E department. Doctors, nurses and other medical staff immediately surrounded the stretcher.

The initial assessment was that Peter's wound was nasty but superficial. But there was a problem. Almost as he watched, he could see his stomach swelling up. A nurse tried to take a blood pressure reading.

'That can't be right,' she said. 'According to this you shouldn't be conscious.' She tried again. The reading was the same. Suddenly, there was an increased air of urgency in the treatment room. A consultant was called in. He pressed Peter's swelling stomach. The agony was unbearable! It became clear Peter was bleeding internally. Two very wide needles were pushed in and fluid began draining out.

Peter was sent for a CT scan, and the full extent of the damage became clear. The crowbar had struck him in a downward arc and penetrated ten inches. The sharpened tip had punched through a rib, popped his diaphragm, bisected his spleen, damaged a kidney, burst a blood vessel in his stomach and torn his bowel. He was sedated and prepared for surgery.

Peter didn't come round for two days. The first surgical team found such a mess when they operated that they realised another, more extensive, procedure would be needed. It was easier to keep him sedated and ready for the second team.

When he awoke, he found the bed was inclined at an odd angle, to aid recovery, and he had tubes and pipes everywhere. He'd been fitted with a nasal feeding tube, and discovered that the damage to his bowel meant that he now wore a colostomy bag.

He could barely move. After a few hours, the feeding tube was becoming unbearable. Peter decided he could do without it, and began pulling it. He could feel it coming up and out of his oesophagus. His girlfriend Tracey stayed with him, and explained that he'd already had numerous lucid conversations with people, and yet he remembered nothing of them.

Peter was still in intensive care, but his condition had

stabilised. The attack had made headlines in the local media, and the hospital was receiving so many phone calls and visits from well-wishers that it took the unusual step of putting out a press release asking people to stay away to allow him to recover.

After three days, Peter left hospital and went home. To start with, he could barely eat. His stomach had shrunk so much that half a slice of toast would leave him feeling bloated. He was unable to stand or sit unaided and felt constantly out of breath. Slowly things improved, and six months after the operation doctors told him his bowel had healed – and the colostomy bag was removed.

Because he lost his spleen, Peter has to take penicillin each day and is far more vulnerable to colds and other viruses than most. A year after the attack, he also discovered that he had lost a kidney. Doctors had thought it would be OK, but tests later showed that his body had decided it was too badly damaged and had reabsorbed it, leaving just a small nodule of scar tissue.

Seven months after the attack, Peter returned to work. After an intensive period of training, and passing numerous fitness tests, he was allowed back to front-line policing.

On the night of the attack, the Lexus had fled across the border into the West Midlands Police area. They'd put up their helicopter, and tracked the vehicle and members of the gang as they returned home. All but one were arrested immediately; the fifth member of the gang gave himself up a month later, realising the net was closing in.

They'd left their haul behind at the scene: a quilt cover stuffed with stolen cigarettes – hardly a king's ransom, but almost the price of an officer's life.

Peter received a Chief Constable's Commendation and was nominated for a National Bravery Award. After returning to duty following his injury, he received a second commendation for his handling of a stabbing incident.

Mark Connolly admitted causing grievous bodily harm, burglary and aggravated car theft. He was sentenced to jail for eight years and given a four-year driving ban.

In 2009, Peter Doherty was contacted by a reporter, who asked him if he'd known Connolly was being allowed out on day release. He had not. The story had emerged when Connolly went to court to apply to have his driving ban overturned. The judge, Robert Orme, said, 'I don't know what is going on with the Prison Service. A man gets eight years in 2007, and here he is on day release in 2009.'

The other members of the gang received various shorter sentences for burglary.

13

THEY ALSO SERVE . . .

*'You can feel sorry for someone up to a certain extent, and
then in the end you just want to say you're alive, you've
survived it, now pull your socks up.'*
JULIE MARSHALL, WIFE OF PC GARY MARSHALL (RETIRED)

Only the hum of the computers and the low voices of sales
staff on their telephones disturbed the quiet efficiency of
the open-plan office. Julie Marshall was sitting at her desk,
preparing for a mid-afternoon design meeting and working
on some costings. Her job importing school uniforms and
workwear often took her abroad, but this week she was based
at the company's base in Reddish, Greater Manchester. The
phone rang. Julie noticed the call had come in on her private
line.

'Hello?' she said.

'Is that Julie?' asked a male voice. 'This is Sergeant Darren
Lomas from Greater Manchester Police. I work with your
husband, Gary. Listen, I'm sorry but he's been involved in an
armed robbery and he's hurt. He's conscious and on his way
to hospital. That's all I know at the moment.'

The colour drained from Julie's face and she slumped

forward slightly onto her desk. Workmates around her looked up. They could tell something was wrong.

'What are his injuries?' asked Julie quietly. 'Has he been shot? Where are they taking him?'

'I can't say what his injuries are, and I don't know how he got them. I'm sorry. They're taking him to Trafford General Hospital. Do you want me to send a car to pick you up?' Julie wrote 'Trafford General' absently on the pad in front of her. Her mind was reeling. She was worried about Gary, but also starting to realise that whatever had happened to him would have a knock-on effect for their eight-year-old son Max, as Gary was supposed to be collecting him from school.

'No, no thanks,' she replied. 'I'll get there more quickly if I drive. Thanks for letting me know.' Julie put the phone down. Her colleague Paula came over.

'Is it Max?' she asked. 'Has something happened at school?' Julie looked up.

'No, it's not Max. It's Gary. He's been hurt at work.' Julie shook her head to clear it and automatically slipped into 'mum' mode. She started thinking through what arrangements she'd need to make and what plans she might have to cancel. Paula offered to collect Max, so she contacted his after-school club and explained the situation, asking them to tell her son that he was going to McDonald's for tea as a treat with Aunty Paula.

She nipped to the loo, and when she returned Paula had printed an AA route planner with directions to the hospital. According to the map, it would take her about twenty minutes to get there, as it was nearly the other side of Manchester. Julie thanked Paula again, and quickly walked out of the office to her car.

★

That morning, Gary Marshall had arrived for work as usual at Partington police station at 7 a.m. His usual partner was on a training course, but he'd been asked to look after Chris Tilley, a PCSO on his first day in the job.

'I've got a scheduled arrest to make first,' said Gary to Chris. 'You're welcome to come along if you like.' The young officer nodded, and they climbed into the Ford Transit Connect van that Gary used for his rounds.

Before going to make the arrest, Gary gave the new officer a tour of the area. Partington was on the south-west edge of the Greater Manchester conurbation, and had originally been a part of Cheshire. In the late 1950s, as urban planners cleared and demolished large areas of Victorian slum houses in the city centre, a housing estate had been built to accommodate the overspill population. Half a century later, it had become widely regarded as one of the most deprived parts of Greater Manchester.

As they drove around the rows of small two-storey houses and maisonettes – many with St George's cross flags draped beneath the windows or old furniture dumped in the front gardens – Gary stopped from time to time to talk to some of the local characters. As often as not, the arrival of the marked police van would be greeted with V-signs and jeers.

'It's like anywhere really,' said Gary. 'There's a lot of nice, honest people round here but a few undesirables. Now let's go and make this arrest.'

The man they were looking for had breached a court order, and needed to be taken into custody. He had the resigned amenability of someone for whom arrest was a regular occurrence. After handcuffing him and sitting him in the back of the van, Gary drove to Stretford police station to hand him over. The custody sergeant asked if they could take the prisoner to Manchester Crown Court, because he could be dealt with immediately. Gary shrugged and agreed. There were no other urgent matters he had to deal with.

Once they'd delivered the man to the cells in the centre of the city and returned to Partington, it was lunchtime. Another PCSO, Steve Bright, had just arrived for his late shift. Gary poured himself a cup of tea and sat down with something to eat.

'Panic alarm activated at Partington Leisure Centre. Immediate response.' As soon as he heard the message on the radio, Gary put down his drink and got to his feet.

'Come on, lads,' he said. 'Probably a false alarm, but we have to go.' Gary told the control centre that he was heading to the location. As they were leaving the building, another call came through.

'Cash in transit armed robbery at Partington Leisure Centre.' Such a report probably wasn't a false alarm, and Gary jumped behind the wheel of the van. Steve sat next to him and Chris in the back.

'Don't bother shutting the gate behind us; we need to get going,' said Gary, and he switched the blue lights on, though he didn't bother with the siren as it was a residential area and the traffic was light. Besides, he didn't want to give the robbers any warning that the police were on their way.

Partington Leisure Centre was a large, blue, corrugated steel building at the end of a gated 200-yard drive. Either side of the narrow road leading up to the entrance were playing fields and tennis courts. There were schoolchildren playing on some of the pitches. On one side was a row of steel railings. As they turned in, Gary could see a white security van and, parked next to it at an angle, a black BMW. The boot was open and three hooded figures were standing at the side of the van. One appeared to be using a large angle grinder to try to get into the security vehicle, and sparks were flying. Another was attempting to lever open a panel with a heavy steel crowbar.

Gary thought for a split second: What to do? He decided to try to block the getaway car, and see how many of the gang he could arrest. He drove up to the front of the BMW and stopped – bumping his van up against the front. The men looked around, but instead of running in all directions as Gary had expected, one climbed behind the wheel of the black car while the other two came purposefully towards the police van.

Both were wearing balaclavas, and all Gary could see were their eyes. He pressed the emergency button on his radio to call for immediate back-up, and shouted to Steve and Chris to stay where they were. Gary opened the door and got out. As he did so, the man approaching hesitated. There was a loud bang as the man on the other side slammed a crowbar into the van's windscreen, cracking it.

Gary heard the BMW's engine revving up, and felt the van lurch backwards. The black car's driver was flooring the accelerator, and the two masked men climbed quickly back inside as it began to gather speed, pushing the police vehicle backwards.

Gary found himself caught between the driver's door and a steel fence. As he tried to move back, he tripped on the kerb and was thrown onto the ground.

'Gary, watch out for the car!' Steve was screaming from the passenger seat. As he looked up, Gary watched in disbelief as the BMW's passenger side wheels bounced onto the pavement. The last thing he saw was the familiar wide grille, with its quartered-circle blue and white badge, before the front wheels struck him. Gary was rolled over and over by the impact. He had a brief glimpse of the underside of the car's sill, then the back wheel, and then it was gone.

Gary lay on the ground face up, staring at the sky. His first thought was, 'I'm not dead.' He could feel a tremendous burning sensation, as if he was lying on hundreds of shards of glass. Below his navel everything was numb. He couldn't move at all.

Although he was aware of the sound of voices on his radio and of sirens approaching, he felt oddly detached. He could hear things but he couldn't take them in. Steve and Chris were there, and some people had come out of the leisure centre to help. A woman in a bright blue top held Gary's hand. He heard her voice as she tried to comfort him.

'Stay with me! Stay with me! Don't give up!' said the voice. Gary was unable to respond. His eyes were fixed on the sky and the clouds. All he was thinking about was Julie and Max. Nothing else mattered at that point. Look at the clouds, think of Julie and Max, he told himself.

After what seemed like a long time to Gary but was probably just moments, he started to focus. Another woman was talking to him. She put her face in front of his. Gary struggled to make sense of what she was saying.

'. . . and you're police officer Gary Marshall. I want you to concentrate on my voice. Can you hear me, Gary? I'm a paramedic and I'm going to assess you.' Her words started to make sense, and he began tuning in to the surroundings. He could see feet, legs, further back a small crowd of people and some schoolchildren crying.

'The ambulance is on its way. It'll just be a couple of minutes. Don't worry, we'll get you to hospital. You'll be OK.' The woman paramedic kept talking to him; the woman in blue was still holding his hand.

'Where does it hurt?' asked the paramedic.

'It feels like I'm lying on glass,' said Gary, snapping out of his catatonic state. 'I can't move my legs.'

The ambulance crew arrived, and Gary felt himself being lifted gently and carefully onto a stretcher. Within minutes, he was being wheeled into the accident and emergency unit at Trafford General. He was aware of doctors, nurses and orderlies running around, putting in drips and cutting away his blood-soaked and torn clothing.

Another figure came into his field of view – his sergeant, Darren Lomas.

'It's OK,' said Darren. 'I've spoken to Julie and she's on her way.' Gary wanted to say something, to respond, but he couldn't seem to get the words out. There was nothing he could do. 'Just get on with it then,' he thought, as the hospital staff went about their tasks. 'Just do whatever you've got to do.'

In the car, Julie was trying hard to be positive. She was clinging to the knowledge that, whatever else, Gary was conscious. Which surely must mean it wasn't life threatening. When she'd first heard the news in her office she'd had to focus on making arrangements for Max, but now, in the car, her mind was racing. If it was an armed robbery, had Gary been shot? Or stabbed? Would he be paralysed or left with brain injuries?

'Come on, Julie,' she told herself, 'think positive. At least he's alive!'

Julie felt as if she and Gary had been together forever. They'd met at work in 1985. She was the office girl and Gary worked in the warehouse. They used to joke that their eyes met across crowded boxes. They'd started going out together a couple of years later, and married in 1990.

Julie had stayed with the company and progressed steadily through executive roles and into management. Gary had joined an engineering firm, then become the transport manager for a food delivery company and then trained as a bus driver. But he'd always been interested in police work, and in 1997 decided to become a special constable. At the age of thirty-seven, he decided to apply to become a regular officer. He and Julie didn't hold out much hope, because of his age, but to their delight he was offered a job, and he started in May 2003.

As she walked into the A&E reception Julie had no idea what to do. There seemed to be people milling about everywhere, so she joined the line at the reception desk and waited her turn. Several minutes later, the queue hadn't moved, and Julie began to feel ridiculous and frustrated. Surely there was someone who could tell her what was going on.

Glancing round, she saw a police officer behind a glass door. He must know something about it, she thought, and walked over. She tapped on the door, explained who she was and was ushered through.

A detective took her to one side and told her what had happened. He also warned her that because of the dramatic way in which Gary had suffered his injuries, the story was likely to be in the newspapers and on TV. Julie listened, but all she wanted to do was see her husband.

'One last thing,' said the detective. 'So they know it's you when you call the hospital for information, use this codeword: Strawberry.'

Gary was in the far corner of a small side ward with four beds, with a curtain round his bed. His sergeant and an inspector were there, along with various medical staff. Julie walked over to the bed and approached the gap in the curtain, half-dreading what she was about to see.

Gary was lying on the bed. Nearly all his clothes had been cut away. There seemed to be blood everywhere. There were braces on both his legs, and he had a deep cut on his shin. As she watched, a doctor was cleaning it out. She could see his fingers pressing into the wound as he rinsed it. She could see the pink flesh and the creamy white bone. 'Why am I looking at this?' she asked herself. But she couldn't seem to take her eyes off it.

Seeing that all his injuries were below the waist was a relief. None of Gary's vital organs had been damaged, and there was no internal bleeding. Gary's waist and torso had been protected by his belt and body armour, which had formed a protective cocoon. It was bad, of course, but some of the visions Julie had had in the car driving over were far worse.

'We need to take him down to X-ray,' said a nurse, and Julie walked alongside as they wheeled Gary's trolley out. After they'd X-rayed him, and Gary was being wheeled out, he seemed to notice Julie for the first time.

'I've not done this to get out of the decorating,' he said. Julie smiled. Gary had taken two days off later in the week because they wanted to redecorate their bedroom. Once Gary was back in the ward, he was soon asleep again – but now Julie had to tell his parents.

She went outside and called them from the car. They were both in their seventies, and she didn't want to alarm them unduly. She explained what had happened, but underlined that Gary was expected to be OK. Julie asked her mother-in-law to collect Max from her friend's house, but not to say anything to him.

Julie arrived home at around 8 p.m. Her son was in the kitchen. She sat down next to him.

'You'll never guess what's happened,' she said. 'Daddy has only tried to be a hero and stop some robbers, and they've run over him. But don't worry, we can go and see him tomorrow.' She then asked Max to help her pack a bag for Gary, and they put in a wash-bag, some clothing and a packet of biscuits. There were no tears, but that night Max asked if he could sleep in Julie's bed rather than his own.

The following morning, Julie sent Max off to school as normal. She'd written a note to the teacher explaining what had happened, just in case. Later, the teacher sent a note back saying that Max had left the classroom upset, and every now and then there were indications that the accident was placing an added strain on him.

Gary was in hospital for just over two weeks. He'd suffered two broken ankles, and his right kneecap, his right wrist, a left rib and his right toe were also fractured. He'd suffered numerous cuts and lacerations, both from being dragged along the hard tarmac and also from the sharp metal edges on the underside of the car. His anterior cruciate ligament was torn. At times, it seemed to Julie that the hospital was finding a new injury every day. It wasn't until the third day, for example, that the hospital called her to say they'd discovered that Gary's wrist was broken.

Gary's legs were put in braces and his wrist into a cast. When he arrived home, he had to stay on the ground floor because he couldn't make it up the stairs. Julie had arranged with Social Services for wheelchair ramps to be installed, and because there was no downstairs toilet at their home in Stockport a commode was supplied.

For the next few weeks, while he waited for his bones to knit, Gary's life was spent almost entirely on the sofa. He was almost completely immobile. He couldn't walk; he couldn't even get out of his wheelchair unaided; he had to eat with one hand.

The family got into a routine. Julie and Max made a pile of cushions on the sofa bed and tucked Gary in at night, then they went upstairs to bed. In the morning they came down and gave him breakfast, then settled him down on the sofa for the day. For the first two weeks, Julie's boss allowed her to work from home; then she went back to the office.

Nurses came each day to change Gary's dressings, and every lunchtime Julie came home to empty the commode. To cap it all, Gary was diagnosed with MRSA, and had to take even more drugs.

He couldn't seem to concentrate on anything; he'd watch TV for a few moments then switch it off. He'd read, then pick at food. In the hospital they'd warned him that his broken joints would probably cause discomfort for the rest of his life, and they were right so far. The pain meant he couldn't sleep for more than an hour or two at a time, that he could never get comfortable, that he became frustrated and short tempered.

Even as the weeks passed and Gary's casts and braces came off, it was still difficult. Because he'd been immobile for so long, he'd suffered severe muscle wastage. Gary looked at his thin, emaciated legs. They'd given him thick bands and a rubber ball to do strengthening exercises. It was hard. The first time he stood up, he felt like a toddler learning to walk again. He used a crutch to help him move around, but the doctors warned him not to become too reliant on it – because he'd find it harder to relinquish when the time came.

The physio was gruelling and monotonous, but Gary had to do it: he still needed an operation to repair his torn knee ligament, and that couldn't be carried out until he'd built up his muscle mass.

Gary was still having sleepless nights and bad dreams. In one recurring nightmare, he pictured the car running over him, as it had done, but then it stopped, reversed and finished him off.

Julie had noticed the change. Gary had always been a real 'people person', outgoing and with formidable social skills. Now he was introverted and sullen. He seemed to have had too long to think about things. He became bitter about what had happened and why it had happened to him.

Because Gary had always worked long days and shifts, Julie had become quite independent and wasn't used to having him around the house. She was working full time and trying to run the house, as well as taking the lion's share of the child care, and she found it hard to recognise the Gary she loved in the ratty man who was feeling sorry for himself.

'You're getting on my nerves,' she said to him on at least one occasion. 'You're alive, you've survived, now pull your socks up!' And of course as soon as she said it she felt guilty, knowing that Gary was trying hard to do just that.

In the spring of 2011, eighteen months after he had been

injured, Gary tried returning to work. Both he and Julie felt that Greater Manchester Police (GMP) had done everything they possibly could to help him, and it had been agreed that Gary might be able to carry out light duties that did not involve contact with the public.

Gary knew he couldn't go out on the front line again. His injuries meant he couldn't complete the self-defence training that was required, and in a dangerous situation he could be a risk to himself and a liability to his colleagues. He was given a job in the intelligence unit, but Gary hadn't joined the police to sit in an office – and he struggled.

A couple of weeks after he started, he was chatting in a corridor with one of his colleagues. Suddenly, the officer got an urgent call. He apologised to Gary and left immediately. Gary just stood there. What's he going to? Is he going to be safe? Are any of them going to be safe? The questions kept repeating, over and over again, in a mental loop that Gary couldn't break out of.

He had another meeting with the occupational health team and GMP. They told him they could offer medical retirement.

The company Julie worked for had recently been taken over, and the new head office was in Wiltshire. She'd been asked whether she could transfer south permanently, and she talked it through with Gary. He'd never planned to leave the police, but this was a chance for them to put everything behind them and start again. Max was nearly ten, and if Gary was medically retired he'd be able to play a greater role in his son's life. They agreed to move, and set a date for July 2011.

The decision to move came as Gary was preparing for the trial of one of those accused of taking part in the robbery.

Christopher Jones had been arrested shortly after the raid in Partington, after a police chase, but at the time wasn't linked to the robbery. He'd been given bail and had fled to Holland. In late 2010, he'd tried to slip back into England by ferry, but he was spotted, and after a desperate attempt to escape from police by abseiling down the side of the ship he'd been arrested.

By now, forensic work had revealed his involvement, and he was charged with robbery and GBH. Gary had to attend court to give evidence.

What Gary hadn't known at the time of the robbery was that the whole incident was being filmed by a man inside the leisure centre on his mobile phone. The footage was later uploaded to the Internet, and Gary and Julie had watched it together. To Julie it felt like watching an action film, but knowing it was happening to someone she loved. She could feel Gary's pain.

At the trial, the judge said that as the jury had already seen what happened on the footage, they didn't need Gary to relive it in court. The questions he was asked were fairly brief, and at the end of the trial Jones was found guilty and jailed for nineteen years. No one else has been charged or convicted in connection with Gary's injuries, but he believes the other two raiders may have been among those killed in a car crash following a cash machine robbery in Holland a month later in November 2009.

∞∞∞

In July 2012, Gary, Julie and Max left Stockport and moved to Wiltshire. Living in more rural surroundings enabled Gary to take up golf; he also did voluntary work for the British Heart Foundation for a while; and with Julie's encouragement he became a governor at Max's school.

Julie believes the change of scene has helped, and that Gary is slowly turning back into the easygoing man she married.

Although he'll probably be in pain for the rest of his life, Gary is determined to keep as active as possible.

And when he's out walking their pet dog, Rolo, or having a quiet moment with Julie and Max, he reflects that at least he isn't just a name on a plaque on the wall of a police headquarters building.

14

OFF THE RAILS AND ON THE TRACKS

'We heard the transport police shouting, "the train's coming and can't stop", as it came round the bend. It's so sharp we couldn't see the train coming.'

PC MATHEW WINTERBOTTOM

With its boxy, grey girders and eleven unevenly spaced stone piers, some added as an afterthought sixty-four years after it was first opened, Dinting Viaduct in the north-west corner of the High Peak in Derbyshire is not an attractive example of Victorian railway engineering.

It was built as part of the Woodhead Line, the first railway to link Manchester and Sheffield, and for more than a century and a half it has carried passengers and freight over Dinting Vale and Glossop Brook.

At the viaduct's northern end, on the high ground, is Dinting Station. Here the line forks: one branch continues north to Hadfield while the other curves sharply south-east to Glossop, where the line terminates. The route beyond to Sheffield was closed in the early 1980s.

In 1855, not realising their train had stopped slightly short of the platform, three passengers, Jane Eliza Hadfield, Thomas

Priestnall and John Healey, stepped out and fell to their deaths. A stone plaque nearby marks the tragedy. Since then, many more have killed themselves or threatened suicide at the bridge, and 999 calls to the local police are relatively common.

'Bravo Hotel one six, we are responding.' PC Mathew Winterbottom and his colleague Leigh Gyte had just started a nightshift and were driving through Glossop when a 'concern for safety' call came in of a potentially suicidal woman. They were already heading to a different job, but the possibility that someone was in danger took priority.

'Shall we go and have a quick look at Dinting?' said Mathew. They both knew that the viaduct was a good place to start when looking for someone unhappy or distressed enough to want to take their own life. And they knew that more often than not such cases were more of a cry for help than a genuine desire to end it all, and police officers were often able to talk people out of jumping.

Mathew had lived in Glossop for twenty-six of his twenty-eight years; he knew the town and the people very well. He'd considered a career in the police while still at school, but at the age of nineteen had been offered a job as a football, or rather 'soccer', coach in the Midwestern United States. He'd moved to the small town of Grand Blanc, on the Michigan peninsula between Lakes Huron and Michigan, and spent two years training the Genesee Stars.

When he returned home he decided to fulfil his ambition to be a policeman, but his first application was unsuccessful. For nine months he worked as a PCSO, gaining experience of typical police situations, before applying again and being accepted.

Leigh was older than Mathew, and had seen considerably

more of the world. Born in Stockport, he'd joined the army aged seventeen and had had postings in Norway and Saudi Arabia. He'd left after the first Gulf War with the ambition of becoming a police officer. It took a couple of goes, and while waiting he worked as a lorry driver, quarryman and at a water bottling plant, before starting with Surrey Police in 1999. After three years he transferred to Nottinghamshire, and then to Derbyshire in 2006.

It didn't take Mathew and Leigh long to reach the viaduct, and they parked their marked Vauxhall Astra near the base of one of the huge stone pillars that carried the railway 120 feet above the dale. Mathew checked his watch: half past ten. It was already cold and dark. They started walking along the public footpath leading up towards the edge of the valley, lighting the way with their small pocket torches.

They had no chance of seeing anyone on the viaduct from so far below, but they knew there was the chance they might hear something or find abandoned belongings. They found nothing. When they reached the entrance to the station, at the top of the footpath, they saw a British Transport Police (BTP) car was already there. They'd probably had the same idea about checking out Dinting Viaduct first, thought Mathew.

Mathew and Leigh walked past the deserted booking office and onto the platform. Like many old stations that have been rationalised, Dinting now merely echoed former glories. Solid red-brick buildings that once housed porters, guards and a stationmaster were boarded up. High-ceilinged waiting rooms were locked shut or had been sold to private owners. The only sanctuary from the bitter Pennine winds was a spartan shelter that Mathew had mistaken, at first glance, for a bus stop. There seemed to be very little romance in a journey that started at Dinting Station, he mused.

Mathew walked out to the pointed end of the platform, where the two diverging rail lines came together, and looked out along the viaduct. The beam of his small torch failed to illuminate more than ten feet or so. In the darkness beyond, all he could see were the shining ribbons of the railheads narrowing into the distance, and, well beyond the far end of the viaduct, the unblinking glow of a yellow railway signal. As he watched, it turned green.

Where he stood, the air was still and quiet. He listened, but the only sound was the occasional clicking pop of the high-tension overhead power lines.

'She's not here, lads – we've been here twenty minutes.' The BTP officer had seen Leigh and Mathew walk onto the platform and had wandered over.

'Oh, right, OK,' said Leigh, and went back to swap notes with the other two officers.

Mathew walked down the angled ramp at the very tip of the platform and stepped down to track level. He looked out again across the viaduct. It was so dark they probably wouldn't be able to see her even if she was there. He had a sudden thought. What was it his tutor used to say? 'Assume nothing, believe nobody, check everything.' The aphorism had served him well, and he wasn't about to disregard it now.

He reached into his pocket. He'd been given the woman's mobile number, and he dialled it . Barely a second or two after he had finished, the synthesised notes of a mobile ringtone sounded in the distance – directly in front of him. Mathew looked again. Now he could see a small, flashing, white square and realised it was the display of a phone indicating the incoming call.

'Leigh, I think she's down here, or at least her phone is. See if you can get them to stop the trains.' Without waiting, Mathew started walking briskly towards the light.

The stone ballast crunched under foot, and he had to be careful not to trip on discarded sleeper bolts, rail fixings and lengths of pipe as he made his way out onto the 450-yard-long viaduct. The woman appeared to be about a third of the way along.

'Police! Police! Can you hear me?' Mathew called, but there was no response. He could hear shouting behind him, and assumed it was Leigh catching up.

The woman was lying face up across the rails, her pose reminding Mathew of the helpless victim in a silent film. It was clear that if a train came it would sever her head and feet.

Her phone was in her hand but the screen was visible – explaining how Matthew had been able to spot it and identify her position.

As Leigh came up, Mathew became aware of loud voices again. It was the two BTP officers shouting and waving their torches.

'There's a train coming! There's a train coming and it can't stop!' As Mathew and Leigh looked back, they could see the glow of the train's headlights as it came round the curve from Glossop. Despite the frantic torch gestures and warnings of the BTP officers on the platform, it was clear the driver would have no chance of stopping the 120-tonne train before it reached them.

Mathew and Leigh could feel the viaduct starting to

vibrate, and heard the high-pitched fluctuating whine of the steel rails as the train wheels approached.

'Quick, grab her. We've got to get her off the tracks.' The two police officers knew they had mere seconds. As they reached down to help her up, they realised the woman was almost catatonically drunk: she was a dead weight. Leigh grabbed her armpits and Mathew her legs. When she felt the officers trying to lift her up she started shouting abuse, and ordered them to leave her alone. Fortunately, thought Mathew, she was too drunk to put up much in the way of physical resistance.

The rumbling had turned into a roar and the train was almost upon them. Its headlights were illuminating the tracks and the officers tried hard to avoid being dazzled. The beam seemed far brighter than a car headlight.

Despite the woman's weight and uncooperative behaviour, with a last heave Mathew and Leigh managed to drag her off the tracks and down into the narrow gap between the edge of the rail and the parapet of the viaduct. There were just seconds to spare.

As the carriages rumbled past, Mathew and Leigh crouched down. The noise was deafening. They hunched over, shielding the woman from the sound and from any stones or grit blown up by the passing train. They also held her down, in case she tried to get back onto the tracks and into danger.

The driver had applied the emergency stop procedure as soon as he saw the commotion on the platform, and Mathew could hear the wheels squealing and smell the pungent aroma of overheated brake fluid as the heavy train slowed.

The sharp projections and angled corners of the running gear and under-floor equipment passed by within inches of their heads. Leigh was wearing a hi-viz jacket, and when Mathew looked up he could see curious and worried passengers staring down at them from the windows. Eventually, the train drew to a halt, and there was a long hiss as the brakes shut off.

Mathew and Leigh looked up at each other in relief. Somehow they were still alive, and so was the woman. Once the train had stopped, the BTP officers walked along to them, and helped Mathew and Leigh carry her back to the station.

One of the BTP officers went back along the line to speak to the train driver and to reassure him that all was well. Hitting someone on the tracks – even if they are intending to kill themselves – is a traumatic experience, and the driver might not have been certain Mathew and Leigh had got the woman out of the way in time.

As the train continued on its way, the transport policeman walked back to them.

'OK, we'll have to take it from here. It's our responsibility as she's on railway property. We'll get her to hospital.' Mathew was happy to agree, so the BTP officers helped the woman into their car and drove off.

Suddenly, Dinting Station was quiet again.

'That was a bit close,' said Mathew. Leigh nodded. It had been a bit *too* close.

There was nothing more to be done at the railway station, so Mathew and Leigh started to walk back down the hill to where they'd left the car.

And just before midnight they finally called it a day.

∽◈∾

The woman was diagnosed with mental health problems and treated. She still lives in the Buxton area.

Leigh and Mathew received Chief Constable's Commendations that summer. Early the following year, they were invited to the National Police Bravery Awards as the Derbyshire nominees.

The award ceremony was to take place in London; it was only the third time in his life that Mathew had been to the capital. He and Leigh decided to travel by train from Dinting Station. Unfortunately, their train was delayed by over an hour, as there was a vulnerable adult threatening to jump off the viaduct . . .

15

THE PERSUADERS

*'We don't lie to anybody, because if you tell one lie
you have to tell fifteen more to get yourself out of it. And
we don't make promises.'*

DCI DAVE MCCAUGHREAN

The morning of Saturday, 8 January 2011 was cold but bright in Liverpool. At around 7 a.m. Anthony Paine left his home in the south of the city to go to work. As he walked, a Ford Focus pulled up alongside him. The driver beckoned him over, and Mr Paine saw that he was holding a black handgun.

Panic-stricken, he turned and ran away along the pavement. He could hear the car behind him, following. There was nowhere to hide – only a six-foot wall nearby. He turned and looked back at the car. The driver was raising the gun again, as if to fire. Without thinking, the terrified pedestrian clambered frantically over the wall and managed to escape.

Around fifteen minutes later, a short distance away, two builders working on a house looked up to see a Ford Focus stop and a man get out. He brandished a handgun at them, but before they could react he got back in the car and drove off.

Sean Turner, a paramedic, was driving along Woolton Road in Liverpool when he saw a car in his rear view mirror approaching at speed and flashing its lights. The driver appeared to be shouting abuse. The car, a Ford Focus, sped past, then stopped just in front of him. He saw with horror that the driver had a gun. He levelled it, and his hand seemed to tense as if about to pull the trigger.

The paramedic accelerated away, and decided to drive straight to the nearest police station at Garston. However, in his panic he drove into a 30 mph speed limit sign. The gunman, who had been following behind, sounded his horn scornfully and drove away.

By this time, Merseyside police control was receiving numerous 999 calls about a gunman on the rampage. Some described shots fired at a petrol station; others said he had shot at a house. There were conflicting and contradictory reports about where he'd been seen. But they all agreed on two details: that he was carrying a live 9 mm handgun, and that he was aggressive, abusive and dangerous.

Detective Chief Inspector Dave McCaughrean was at home. Although he was off duty, he was the on-call police negotiator, and parked outside his house was the plain blue van used by the team. His phone rang.

'Dave, it's the force incident manager at control. We've got a containment issue and a siege on. Can you get down to south Liverpool as soon as possible?'

Dave was on his feet and ready to leave before the call ended. He had all the equipment he would need in the van. It was around sixteen miles from his home to the location, so he switched on his blue lights and sirens and headed off.

Although it was a police vehicle with sirens and lights, the van was otherwise unmarked. At first glance it was unremarkable, and could park near someone's house without immediately flagging up the presence of the police, though the concealed lights and roof aerials wouldn't bear close scrutiny.

His route took him down into the centre of Liverpool and through to the southern edge of the city. As he drove, he received another call.

'We've had several discharges during the morning. There's a male with a 9 mm pistol with live rounds. Shots fired at a garage and male threatened with a firearm. Armed officers now containing the male at an address in Aigburth.' The information was sketchy, but at least it gave Dave something to go on.

Though Liverpool born and raised, Dave had joined the Metropolitan Police in London, because in the late 1980s Merseyside's recruitment criteria were far more stringent. After six years in the capital he transferred to Merseyside, and returned to Liverpool before a stint with the National Crime Squad. By now, he was a detective, and he spent five years travelling around the world working on serious and organised crime. Returning home, he was made a detective inspector shortly before the murder of eleven-year-old Rhys Jones shone an unwelcome light on the gun and gang culture that was becoming endemic in parts of the city.

For the last year and a half he had been a trained hostage negotiator, working on a voluntary basis to ensure that cover was available every hour of every day of the year.

Driving at high speed through Liverpool's bustling Saturday afternoon traffic, Dave's overriding thought was,

'How am I going to stay calm and arrive at the scene in the right frame of mind?'

For hostage negotiators, the basic tenet is 'Save life and buy time'. Everything Dave did was aimed at securing those two goals. Although he was a police officer, as a hostage negotiator at a scene he was detached from the main operation. His role was not to gather evidence or be operationally involved with the police investigation. He was kept out of the loop by the incident commander so he could focus on establishing a rapport with the suspect, building up trust and steering the incident to a peaceful conclusion.

He ran through the usual mental checklist, asking himself key questions. Top of the list: was he mentally up for it? Almost from day one, trainees are told to be honest with themselves about their own mindset, and about whether they are just too tired, too stressed or too preoccupied with other things on any given day.

Did he know enough about the situation? With the sketchy details he had so far, the answer to that was a resounding no, so he began considering whom he needed to speak to.

As he drove through Liverpool city centre, Dave half-expected a call to come through saying the job was cancelled, as many end with suspects surrendering before the negotiators arrive. His route took him right past Merseyside police headquarters then onto the streets of the south of the city, alongside the banks of the River Mersey, before he arrived in the suburb of Aigburth and came up against the police's outer cordon.

It was a huge job. The street was full of Merseyside's distinctive yellow police vans, and there seemed to be uniformed officers everywhere.

The street had been sealed off with police tape and a small crowd had gathered. The officers on the cordon checked Dave's ID, then waved him through. He parked his blue van and went to find the Silver Commander.

On any critical incident, police procedure is to have three different levels of command. At the top is the Gold Commander, usually a high ranking officer such as an assistant or deputy chief constable. Their role is to set the overall target and consider policy. Immediately below is the Silver Commander. Typically a superintendent, their job is to ensure the policy formulated by Gold is implemented on the ground. Below that is the Bronze Commander. He or she is in command on the ground, and is tasked to make sure that orders given by Silver are completed. It's a command model used by the police and, increasingly, copied by other organisations – with varying degrees of success.

Dave walked towards the front line. To one side, he caught sight of the firearms team pulling on their ballistics jackets and helmets. Although Dave's usual negotiating outfit was jeans, a t-shirt and a Berghaus jacket, he did have body armour and a SWAT-style helmet in the van.

Up ahead, he saw a familiar face.

'John! Are you the Silver Commander here?' Dave had known Chief Superintendent John Martin for many years. They respected each other, and that could be helpful if the situation became more challenging.

'Come on, Dave! Can you sort this out? I've got rugby to play in an hour!' John and Dave played rugby together for a police team.

'What have we got?' asked Dave. John explained what they knew so far. The man was named Alan Grant. At a party the night before, he'd got into an argument, pulled out a gun and fired a shot. No one had been hit. Then he'd left the party, stolen a car and spent the next few hours driving aimlessly around south Liverpool, firing the gun intermittently, stealing petrol from a garage and terrorising random passers-by.

Now, he was believed to be hiding in the loft of his grandmother's house a short distance down the street.

'What do you know about cocaine?' asked the chief superintendent. 'We think he's taken some and been drinking all night.'

Dave was part way through a Master's degree in psychology at the time, and purely by chance had just completed an essay on the effects of cocaine use. Medical data suggested the effects of cocaine lasted in the body for roughly the same amount of time as alcohol.

'My advice is that if we can keep him up there he'll start to calm down quite quickly once the drugs wear off.' Dave felt that the longer Grant stayed up in the loft, the more rational he'd become – provided he didn't have more drugs or booze.

The chief superintendent knew the situation was delicate. He had to balance the needs of the wider community with the time and resources needed for this operation.

There was also a question of motive: 'death-by-cop' – where suicidal individuals left armed police with no choice but to shoot them – was a growing issue. And at the back of their minds they were also thinking of Raoul Moat – the man who had killed himself after shooting his ex-girlfriend, her new boyfriend and a policeman in north-east England a few weeks earlier. The case had caused national headlines, as Moat had evaded capture for several days.

'Are the family around?' asked Dave. They might be able to help with possible motives. And they might have other background information that could be useful in any negotiations.

The man's parents and grandmother were sitting in a police van nearby. Dave climbed in and explained why he had been called. He asked whether the gunman had any mental health issues, whether he'd done anything like this before, or if they knew why he'd done it today. They weren't helpful. The man's mother told Dave that she wasn't surprised at what had happened, and blamed the police. Dave decided he was wasting his time.

'Are you a cop?' one of them asked, looking at his jeans and t-shirt.

'I'm working with the police,' said Dave. It was his standard answer. When negotiating, a uniform could be a barrier. Distancing himself from other officers, without actually lying, often helped.

He thanked the family and left. As he walked away, the man's grandmother shouted, 'Good luck – because he's mad!'

Normally on a job this size, especially with firearms teams, Dave would have a second negotiator. He or she would be the link with the Silver Commander, and could also provide words of encouragement or fresh ideas if the lead negotiator was running out of options. Dave was on his own; and he wanted back-up. He called a colleague – Detective Inspector Justin Danu – who agreed to come down and provide support.

The firearms team was about ready to go in, and Dave returned to his van. His body armour carried no police insignia, and simply had 'Negotiator' written across it. Regulations demanded that he wore it, together with his helmet, when deploying with armed officers. As he pulled it over his head, he thought about how he'd start the negotiations.

'What's my opening line?' he wondered. 'What's my hook?' There was no one to rehearse with – and no time – but he wanted to find something to make the man engage with him. Favourites were family, or simply a few questions about why the person has got themselves into the situation they're in. Football was another, though Dave tended to avoid it, because in a city like Liverpool, with two prominent teams and partisan attitudes, mentioning the wrong name could do more harm than good.

Dave thought back to his training, eighteen months earlier. The gruelling three-week course at the Metropolitan Police Training School at Hendon, north London, was widely regarded as one of the best in the world, and Dave's group had included an FBI agent from the United States.

By day they'd studied topics including emotional intelligence, techniques and mindset, then in the evening they'd spent hours in practice and role play, with psychology students playing the parts of other characters in the scenario. They'd worked sixteen hours each day, and at the end were simply awarded pass or fail.

Best practice changes over time, and the course had evolved since it was created in the 1970s. Techniques that had been originally developed after sieges at Entebbe airport, and at the bank in Sweden that originated the concept of Stockholm Syndrome, had been modified as experience and understanding grew, but the underlying principle, of protecting life and buying time, had remained constant.

As Dave returned to the front line, the firearms officers

were waiting. Each was carrying a firearm and a ballistic shield, and they formed up and shuffled forward, the shields angled to provide protection from in front and above. Dave was somewhere in the middle. Nearby, probably in the house opposite, Dave knew a sniper would have a gun trained on the front of the house. As they entered, Dave was pushed quickly into a bathroom by the front door.

'ARMED POLICE! ARMED POLICE!' It seemed as though all the officers were shouting at the tops of their voices as they took up positions in the hallway.

Then silence fell again. There was no answer to the entry or the shouting. At this point it became Dave's responsibility. He cleared his throat.

'My name is Dave, and I'm here to help,' he said, 'Hi, Alan, it's Dave here. I'm here to help you.' There was no response. Dave tried again, the same basic message.

'Alan, my name is Dave and I'm here to help you.' Dave waited, and repeated the message. Again and again. The minutes ticked by. Dave wondered if the intelligence was wrong. It wouldn't be the first time he'd negotiated with an empty house. The family had said the man was somewhere in the house, but Dave wasn't sure he trusted them.

'I can hear noises in the attic.' One of the firearms officers was gesturing towards the stairs on the left side of the hallway.

'Alan,' said Dave again, raising his voice. 'I'm Dave. I'm here to help. Are you up there?' At that point, a voice emerged from the loft hatch at the top of the stairs.

'What do you want? Piss off!' The voice had a thick Scouse accent and was heavy with aggression, but it was a response. Dave felt a rush of excitement – they were on! He immediately shouted back the same message:

'I'm Dave, I'm here to help.' He crept forward and stood behind the two firearms officers at the bottom of the stairs.

Dave's goal was to build a rapport with the man. Often, he knew, armed men tended to think of themselves as all powerful, and he was happy to let them. One technique was known as emotional mirroring: Dave would match his energy level to that of the suspect, then slowly reduce it, and more often than not they'd come down with him.

Dave decided it was time for a reality check.

'Alan, it's Dave. You're surrounded by armed police. But I want to help you get out of this. I want you to come down safely.'

Dave strained to hear a response, or any noise that would give him an indication of the man's state of mind. There was a banging in the loft; it sounded as if he was agitated and pacing around. Dave tried again.

'OK, Alan, this is the situation you're in: we're in the house, I want you to come down safely, I'm working with the police. I'm here to help you. What's happened today? Why are we in this position?'

'Dave . . .' started the man, and Dave felt a quiet twinge of satisfaction. The man's using his name was the first step in creating a meaningful rapport.

'Dave, just clear off. If yous don't all go I've got an AK47 and a hand grenade.'

At the bottom of the stairs, Dave could see the firearms officers tense up. If a grenade dropped out of the loft hatch things could get very nasty. But Dave wasn't sure. Getting hold of a handgun was one thing; getting hold of a grenade and an AK47 assault rifle was something else.

'You don't want to use that AK47 and that hand grenade,'

shouted Dave. 'You don't want to kill yourself. You've got a lot to live for.'

For the next ten or fifteen minutes, there was no response from the loft. Dave kept talking. Another tactic was simply to become an ear-worm: a constant presence, not threatening or adding to the tension but persistent, unwavering and simply trying to hook the man back to reality. And with the same message repeated over and over: 'My name is Dave, and I'm here to help.'

'What about your mum and dad?' asked Dave. 'Do you want this to be their last view of you? Do you want to be doing this at your nan's house? Remember, I'm here to help.' Dave had inched forward, beyond the protective shields, and one of the firearms officers pulled him back.

'Fuck off – or can you get the charges dropped?' came the voice from the top of the stairs. Dave paused. A core principle was that negotiators never lie, because once you told one lie you had to tell another fifteen to get yourself out of it. And he couldn't make promises either – any authority had to come from the Silver Commander.

'You've got plenty to live for. OK, you may go to prison, but even if you do you'll get out again. Think of all the things you've got.' Dave kept trying to hook Alan back to normality, but he still seemed irrational, and continued to threaten to drop the grenade or open fire through the closed loft door.

Dave looked up at the hatch. He felt it was a real barrier to the negotiations, and not just physically. If he could get the hatch opened, they could start talking face to face. Of course, if he could see Alan then Alan could see him, and that could potentially put him directly in the line of fire.

'Look, Alan, why don't you open the hatch? We can see each other then. I'm here to help and I won't hurt you.'

'Fuck off. I'm not doing it. Yous can all fuck off.'

Dave kept on trying to be reasonable, trying to make the man see sense, trying to be that ear-worm, hoping that soon the effect of the drugs would wear off. At one stage the man asked him to shut up, so he did – for ten seconds. Then he started talking again, with the same core message.

'I'm not going away, because you're in this situation and I'm here to help you.'

Three-quarters of an hour later, the man agreed to rotate the loft hatch a quarter turn – creating triangular gaps in each corner. A few moments later, Dave's colleague Justin Danu arrived. And he had one thing Dave didn't have: a packet of cigarettes.

Dave had been looking for something to offer the man, because if he accepted it, then Dave could ask for something in return, and they could start a bartering business that would end, Dave hoped, with the man surrendering peacefully.

'I want a cigarette,' came the voice from the loft. It was music to Dave's ears. Now they had common ground. He wanted something from Dave, and in turn Dave could get something from him. The negotiator opened negotiations.

'If I give you a cigarette, what are you going to give me?' asked Dave.

'What do you mean?' said the man.

'Well, are you going to come down to get it?' While the man thought this over, Justin confirmed quietly that Silver Command was aware and had okayed the cigarette offer.

'I wanna smoke it here,' came the reply. Dave explained

the problem:

'I'm going to give you a cigarette. You're going to smoke it. But if you smoke it in the loft, how do I know you aren't going to start a fire?'

'Trust me, trust me,' said the man. This was what Dave had been waiting for. He had something the man wanted, and that thing required a bond of trust. And Dave could hold out for as long as is necessary.

'Well, how can I trust you when you've been shooting at people?' said Dave, reasonably. 'If I give you a cigarette, when you've finished it can I trust you to come down?'

Suddenly the man became angry, using the Liverpool slang for police officers.

'Why should I trust you? You're all bizzies. You're just gonna shoot me when I come down.'

Dave thought about it from the man's point of view. He was obviously looking through the corner of the hatch and seeing lots of armed police, and the negotiator talking to him from the middle wearing a helmet. Dave considered taking off his helmet but decided against it: partly because the man had said he had a grenade, and also because the armed officers would have a hissy fit if he tried.

'How are we going to get this cigarette up to you?' Dave tried to get the man to focus on what he wanted. The man thought about it, and after more discussions he found a black plastic bag that he tore and stretched out, almost like a fishing line.

He lowered it down. Dave folded the cigarette in tin foil and tied the plastic around it. The man pulled it back into the loft space. There was a pause.

'Where's the lighter? Where's the match?' Dave had been

waiting for this. It was yet another step in the negotiating process.

'Alan,' he said, 'why should we trust you with that? You asked us for a cigarette and we've given you that.'

As if on cue, the firearms officers moved rapidly halfway up the staircase. Alan was immediately panicked, and started shouting and screaming:

'Get them back! Get them back, Dave!'

Dave loudly said, 'Come down,' and the firearms officers withdrew. He looked up at the hatch. 'Look – there are a couple of things you asked for. You asked for a cigarette, and I got you that. You asked me to get the firearms officers to come down and I did that.'

'Yeah, OK.'

'You can trust me. I'm not going to lie to you. You're going to get arrested at the end of this, but you're going to be treated fairly. And I'll walk out with you every step of the way.' Dave thought it was time for another reality check, as the man was calming down.

'OK. But I'm not coming down until I've smoked my cigarette.' So, after more discussion, a single match was wrapped in foil and the man reeled it up on his plastic bag fishing line. By now, the hatch was fully opened, and Dave could just make out the shape of the man inside the loft space.

The smell of burning tobacco drifted down the stairs. The man went silent. Dave started to feel a little twitchy, and he could sense the unease in the firearms officers around him. They all knew they'd reached a key moment. What was he going to do? Was he going to keep his word and come down? Dave decided to reinforce the message.

'You said I can trust you. You said you're a man of honour.

You said you're going to come down. Make sure you come down after that cigarette.'

The man had nearly finished smoking. 'I'm not fucking coming down. I've got an AK47. Yous can all fuck off.' The reply didn't surprise Dave, but he wasn't about to give up.

'I thought I could trust you. This is what I've done for you . . .' Dave listed what he'd arranged, then rewound the loop and started again – telling the man he was there to help, asking him about his family, just keeping on talking.

Dave had been there for just over two hours. Throughout, he'd been aware that the man had at least one weapon and might open fire at any time. He was starting to get tired.

'What's going to happen when I come out?' The man's words gave Dave fresh hope and energy. The fact that he was imagining a surrender was a big step forward.

Again, in slow and laborious steps, they discussed and negotiated a process for the man to surrender without being shot. Dave knew he needed to explain the coming-out plan to the Silver Commander, but the man was restless. Having decided to come out, he became impatient and fidgety. Suddenly he disappeared back into the loft. 'Oh no,' thought Dave. 'Don't go and do something stupid. Not when we're so close!'

Without warning, and completely ignoring the agreed plans, the man dropped through the hatch onto the landing below and disappeared from view. At the bottom of the stairs, the firearms officers tensed up.

'Suspect in the front bedroom, now drinking a glass of wine . . . stand by, stand by,' the audio feed came from the sniper across the road who could see into the house. 'Suspect has now picked up a gun.'

Aghast, Dave shouted up the stairs, 'Put the gun down, put it down!' The man was on the landing, walking back towards the top of the stairs. Through the banister, Dave could see the outline of the gun. Beside him, he heard quiet rustling as the firearms officers raised their weapons. Dave knew the man whom he'd spent more than two hours talking, cajoling and arguing with now had only a few more seconds to live.

Then there was a thud as he dropped the gun and walked slowly round the corner to the top of the stairs, unarmed. Everyone held their nerve. No shots rang out.

'Well done,' said Dave, genuinely elated. 'Well done. You've done really well.'

The man was arrested, and Dave walked with him, as he'd promised, out to the waiting police van. And as it drove off, Dave sat down and began to tremble. He never knew whether it was an after-effect of the pent-up adrenaline or an echo of the life he'd just saved.

⁂

Alan Grant was given an indeterminate sentence for public protection, serving a minimum of six years and only eligible for release when judged no longer to be a danger to society.

Dave McCaughrean received a Chief Constable's Commendation. The ceremony took place at Aintree, and lasted three hours – twenty minutes longer than the siege in Aigburth.

16

LEAP OF FAITH

'In mid-air it's too late for second thoughts. I just hoped I was going to make it. I didn't really have time to think.'

PC ROGER MORAN

The sun was shining and children were laughing. The open day at Port Edgar marina, on the south side of the Firth of Forth and in the shadow of the giant Forth road bridge, was in full swing. Sea cadets were out in dinghies learning to sail, younger children were playing in kayaks and canoes inside the protective breakwaters, and more intrepid customers were queuing for powerboat rides out to the bridge and back.

On one side of the marina was the black police boat, a 6.5 metre RIB, with twin Yamaha engines. RIB stands for Rigid Inflatable Boat – the vessel had a rigid central hull with inflatable rubber sponsons around the edge. It was designed for speed, and in calm water could reach up to forty knots. The boat was operated by the Lothian and Borders Police marine unit, and was based at the marina.

'The marine unit is for surface searches, and we also counter any criminal activity on the water.' Senior Helm

Brian Suddon was explaining their role to some visitors. The unit had been created in the mid-1990s, and Brian had been the first officer recruited. Born in Kelso, in the Scottish borders, he'd served in the Royal Navy for six years before joining the police, and was also a volunteer on the South Queensferry lifeboat, making him an ideal candidate.

Roger Moran, his colleague on the boat, had no such seafaring background. Originally from Fort William in the western Highlands, he'd eschewed a career in the local paper mill and moved to Edinburgh for a taste of big city life. When he joined the police in 1982, officers still carried whistles on chains and worked out of police boxes. Looking back, thought Roger, it seemed almost Dickensian.

After qualifying as a panda car driver – his first car was a Vauxhall Chevette – Roger spent ten years as a traffic officer before moving to the new unit created to police the new Scottish Parliament in 1999. From there he went into specialist operations, and eventually joined the marine unit. Roger was chatting to Clarissa Berry, the third member of the team on duty that morning.

The police boat was a popular attraction at the Port Edgar marina open day. Brian and the other members of the crew enjoyed posing for photographs and answering questions. They'd just finished a successful operation policing the G8 summit, which in the summer of 2005 had taken place at Gleneagles in Scotland.

'You know, that wind's getting up a bit,' said Brian. Roger nodded, and looked out past the breakwater. The water was starting to look choppy, and some of the smaller dinghies were leaning over worryingly.

Brian and Roger knew that conditions on the Firth of

Forth could change without warning. At its narrowest point, there was just twelve miles between the River Clyde, on the west of Scotland, and the River Forth, which flowed to the east. These were the lowlands of the Scottish central belt, and when Atlantic Westerly winds hit Scotland they were funnelled into this narrow gap between the Trossachs and the southern uplands. The wind could whip up with alarming speed, and the changing conditions could easily trap an unwary sailor or yachtsman.

One of the marina staff came over.

'Guys, we've got one of the little dinghies gone over just outside the breakwater. Do you think you could help?' Brian nodded. The boat's powerful twin engines were already ticking over. Clarissa had nipped off the boat, but she wasn't needed for this. Roger cast off and they eased towards the marina entrance.

As they passed the breakwater, both men could feel the conditions change. It was just after lunch, and already the winds were blowing up to a force six. The little dinghy was floating on its side just outside the marina in the choppy water. They put a line on it and towed it back in to Port Edgar. As they were approaching one of the floating piers, a panicked voice came over the marine radio.

'Mayday, mayday. I'm in difficulty. Near Rosyth. The *Ilex* – it's a white yacht. The skipper has sustained an injury and is unconscious, and I've no idea how to sail.' The call had come in on Channel 16 – the international distress frequency. Brian and Roger looked at each other.

'That's us,' said Roger, and Brian nodded. They both knew it was time to go to work. Rosyth was on the north side of the Firth of Forth, but no more than three miles away. Brian handed the dinghy rope over to a member of the marina staff, then gunned the engines again and the police boat headed back out to sea.

'Sierra Oscar one zero.' While Brian took the helm, Roger operated the radio. 'We're responding to mayday.' Roger switched on the flashing blue stroboscopic light to indicate that this was a genuine emergency.

'Sierra Oscar one zero, understood,' replied the coastguard controller, recognising the call sign of the police marine unit. 'We're launching RNLI lifeboat but your attendance much appreciated.'

The nearest lifeboat was at South Queensferry, next to the giant red Forth rail bridge, and was further away and slower. It would also take a few minutes to launch, as it was crewed by volunteers who'd be travelling from their homes or workplaces.

Out on the open water, the conditions were worsening almost by the minute. The winds were now a steady force six – a strong wind – and the waves were peaking at around eight to ten feet with foam crests.

To maximise speed while maintaining control, Brian used a technique known as power on and off. He used maximum power to climb the side of large waves, but just as he crested he throttled down, to ensure the bow dropped down the other side. If he'd kept the throttles on full power there was a strong chance the lightweight RIB, with its inflatable sponsons, would fly into the air, be caught by a strong gust of wind and flipped over.

In the open cockpit Brian was on the right side, steering, while Roger was in the left seat. Both men were wearing their police drysuits, one-piece watertight overalls with integral rubber boots and elasticated cuffs and collar to keep the water out.

Both were also wearing helmets, which combined with the engine noise, wind and splashing to make communication difficult. As they headed out onto the Firth of Forth they looked around. They could see at least seven white yachts, and in the rapidly worsening conditions all seemed to be rolling heavily.

The nearest yacht was probably around a mile and a half away. As they reached it, one of the crew gave a thumbs up sign when he noticed their flashing blue light. Not this one, thought Roger and Brian. Brian turned towards the second yacht. As he did so, Roger caught his arm. Beyond it, a lone white yacht was corkscrewing – looping uncontrollably in a figure of eight – heaving more and more seriously from side to side.

Brian knew immediately that this must be the *Ilex*. He steered the police boat towards the stricken yacht. As they approached, he could see the large horizontal boom swinging crazily from side to side as the boat tossed first one way, then the other. The main sail was still taut, and each time the wind caught it the boat leant over dangerously. With each wave and each gust the mast seemed to be leaning further and further over. 'It won't be long before she capsizes,' thought Brian. As it tilted towards them, they could see the deck. A man was lying, apparently unconscious, near the aft section of the boat, while the man who'd put out the mayday call was sitting nearby, holding on grimly and looking, to Brian and Roger, terrified.

Roger tried to shout over to him but the man couldn't hear above the wind, the flapping of the sails and the crashing water. He looked over at the heaving yacht. 'I'm going to have to get on that,' he thought.

'You're going to have to get on that yacht!' shouted Brian, pointing with his head.

'Yes, I know!' replied Roger. He looked over at the *Ilex*. She was about twice the length and a little higher than their RIB. It was also clear that she was leaning over further and further as the wind got up; when she tilted away from him, he could clearly see the keel coming half out of the grey and foamy water.

'I'm going to try to get in closer, and time it for you to jump over,' said Brian. Roger nodded. The inflatable sponsons down either side of the police boat formed a point at the front; they were not unlike the components of a bouncy castle. If he could keep his footing, then maybe he could use the bounce to give him a slight boost when making the jump.

'There's just one problem,' shouted Roger back to Brian. 'I've only been on a yacht once before. What do I do when I get on board?'

Brian thought about it. He couldn't leave the police boat himself, as he had to pilot it. He could give Roger detailed instructions about how to bring the jib down and let the halyards out, but he realised such sailing jargon would probably mean nothing to his colleague.

'All you need to do is just get that sail down,' he said. 'Just release any rope you can!'

Brian looked at the yacht. Ideally, he'd get as close as he could, but there were ropes and sails dragging on the water next to it. If these wrapped round or fouled the propellers of the police boat then they'd both be out of action. He decided he'd have to approach at an angle, then immediately reverse back.

Feathering the throttle, Brian brought the police boat closer and closer to the reeling yacht. Roger prepared to jump. 'OK,' he thought, 'OK . . .'

Suddenly, Brian slammed the police boat into reverse and drew back. The timing wasn't right. The big yacht lurched over, and the large horizontal boom slapped into the water where they'd been floating just a second or two before.

Up on the deck of the *Ilex*, they could see the wounded man. He seemed to be in considerable pain, but it looked to Roger as if he was conscious now.

Brian turned the RIB round and came back for another pass. Ideally, he wanted to time it so they approached just as the yacht was in the trough of a wave, to give Roger the best chance of jumping on board.

Roger was still standing near the front, next to the sponson. He knew it was vital that he didn't finish up in the sea, or hanging off the side of the yacht, because the police boat might crush him. In the centre of the *Ilex* there was a low cabin with a chrome handrail running along its full length. Next to it was a narrow ten inch strip of deck. Roger decided his best chance was to aim for the deck with his feet and to try to grab the handrail with his hands. He braced himself ready to jump again as Brian steered their boat back in towards the yacht.

'Go Roger, go now!' yelled Brian, but Roger didn't need telling. The moment was right. The bow of the police boat was rising just as the deck of the *Ilex* about six feet in front of him was falling. Roger held his breath, ran forward and jumped. He bounced into the air and across the gap. 'It's too late to change your mind now, Roger,' he thought for an instant, then focused on the handrail and the deck ahead. His legs hit the narrow, slippery wooden deck with a bang, grazing his shins. He scrabbled for the chrome handrail and managed to get a firm grip with both hands. He knelt down and steadied himself, then breathed a huge sigh of relief. He was on!

Behind him, Brian had immediately put the powerful motors of the RIB into reverse, to ensure that if Roger did slip and fall then he wouldn't be trapped between the two boats.

Roger had landed on the *Ilex* amidships, and ensuring he maintained a handhold at all times, he moved aft. His instinct was to attend to the injured man, but he knew the priority was to get the sail down and bring the yacht under some kind of control.

As the boat heaved back and forth, Roger reached the deck at the rear of the yacht. The injured skipper had regained consciousness.

'Can you tell me how to get the sails down?' asked Roger. If the skipper was at all surprised that his seagoing rescuer was ignorant of such procedures he didn't show it.

The ropes holding the sails – the halyards – passed through simple friction grips, and under the yachtsman's instruction they were freed. The *Ilex* calmed as soon as the tension was released. The sail was still flapping in the wind, but it was generating no force and was no longer a threat. The yacht was now only rising and falling with the movement of the waves, and wasn't being dragged by the winds. The only hazard was the boom, which was still swinging lazily from side to side, but under instruction Roger was able to secure it with ropes.

Once the boat was under control, Roger turned to the injured man. He was holding his arm across his body.

'Are you OK? Is it your shoulder?' he asked.

'No. I was holding the tiller and suddenly the wind grabbed it and snapped it over. It's broken my arm.' Roger was no medic, but he knew that a lateral arm break – where the bone is simply sheared apart by extreme force – could be incredibly painful.

The man explained that he owned the *Ilex* and was a competent yachtsman, but his friend had never been sailing before. He'd slipped into unconsciousness very quickly after breaking his arm, and his friend had had no idea what to do other than put out a mayday call. Roger looked over at the other man. He'd calmed down by now and was very quiet.

Roger had probably been on the *Ilex* about four minutes when the lifeboat from South Queensferry arrived. They'd made good time, largely because they'd spotted the blue flashing light on the police boat so there'd been no confusion over which yacht to aim for.

Now the yacht was under control, it was relatively easy for the lifeboat to come alongside and for one of the crew to step on board. He assessed the wounded man, and decided not to try to move him onto the lifeboat. Instead, they would tow the *Ilex* back to Port Edgar marina.

The lifeboatman fixed a line to the front of the yacht, and with a police escort from Brian they made their way back. Roger stayed on board the *Ilex*, and carried on talking to the injured man to help take his mind off the pain.

As they approached the marina, Brian accelerated ahead to prepare a berth near the ambulance, and the wounded man was carried off and taken to hospital.

Brian and Roger went to the marina café for a hot drink. Clarissa joined them.

'What happened to you two?' she asked. 'I can't leave you alone for a second!'

༄

The injured yachtsman made a full recovery, and continued to keep his yacht, *Ilex*, at Port Edgar marina and sail regularly.

Brian Suddon and Roger Moran received a Chief Constable's Commendation, and were also given Royal Humane Society awards for saving life.

Roger retired from the police in 2012, and now works as a tour guide on the Royal Yacht *Britannia*, permanently moored in Leith. Among his former colleagues he is still known as the Gazelle.

17

FLAT COKE AND HULA HOOPS

'I could feel the fear and panic building and knew I had to keep it down. It was getting harder and harder to keep conscious, and I was thinking, "I might not make this one."'

DC LUKE SIMMS

Thames Valley Police were hunting for a serial sex attacker. Already he had abducted and sexually assaulted two girls aged sixteen and fifteen, and tried to kidnap a third aged fourteen. The attacks had all happened in Bracknell, a usually quiet town in Berkshire. Online debate and speculative rumours were sweeping the area, leaving residents looking suspiciously at their neighbours and keeping their teenage daughters indoors. With each attack, the level of violence seemed to be escalating. There was a very real chance that in the next attack, or the next but one, he would kill. The police created a major investigation team to find the attacker, and called it Operation Nemesis.

Lying ten miles south-west of Windsor, Bracknell had been designated as a new town in the aftermath of the Second World War. The centre was a homage to then-fashionable urban planning concepts of ring roads, flyovers, pedestrian precincts and underpasses. It had been successful in attracting new and high-tech businesses and was popular with commuters, being on the main railway line between London and Reading.

Detective Constable Luke Simms was one of those drafted into the investigation. Normally he worked on burglary – a priority at that time – and had been targeting so-called 'vamoose' thieves, who break into homes to find the owner's car keys and then steal their car off the drive. Despite numerous crime prevention initiatives, householders still seemed determined to keep their car keys next to the front door, and thieves had even been known to put a long stick or fishing rod through the letterbox to snatch them.

Luke's team had had some success against such criminals using ANPR (Automatic Number Plate Recognition) software to track and identify vehicles and drivers. But when Operation Nemesis was launched, Luke was one of many detectives transferred away from their regular duties.

On the morning of 19 May 2010, Luke had been assigned to drive with a colleague, DC Lisa Child, to the Birch Hill shopping centre, a parade of shops in a residential estate south of the town centre.

The Operation Nemesis team was gathering as much CCTV as possible in the hope that somewhere within the hundreds and thousands of hours of footage there would be a clue as to the identity of the mystery attacker. Luke and Lisa had been asked to collect recordings from businesses at the shopping centre.

Luke had originally trained as an electronics engineer, working for an Internet company in Devon, but had lost his job when the dotcom bubble burst. He'd toyed with the idea of joining the police, but his local force was not recruiting.

Then he saw a newspaper advertisement for jobs with Thames Valley. He applied, and after a lengthy recruitment process he was taken on. After five years in uniform, he moved into CID and became a detective.

Luke and Lisa drove into the car park in the centre of the shopping parade and pulled into an empty space. It was late morning. It was a warm, bright day, and they decided to leave their stab vests and other equipment in the car. Both were in plain clothes, and as detectives on a fairly routine assignment they were not expecting any trouble.

They looked around. The car park was bordered by a parade of blocky, red brick buildings. Facing them were a pub, the Silver Birch, and an Aldi supermarket, while to the right they could see a newsagent, a dry-cleaner, a betting shop and the entrance to a community centre.

They decided to start at the pub and work their way round. They were cold-calling, without appointments, partly to avoid giving anyone any notice and partly because it would have been too time-consuming to try to arrange timed visits to every business.

In each one, they asked for around eight or nine hours of CCTV. Many shops use a tape loop to save money, recording over previous footage, so to ensure they get the material they need officers have to act quickly. They usually prefer to take the tapes away to prevent them being accidentally erased. For any tapes that are removed, paperwork has to be completed confirming its provenance, and a receipt given to the owner.

About three-quarters of an hour later they reached the Coral bookmakers. There were banks of televisions showing either horse or dog-racing, and a few punters watching the screens and checking the odds. Luke noticed CCTV security cameras dotted around, so he knew they would need to collect footage.

They walked up to the counter at the back of the shop. As they approached, the cashier looked up. She was a slim woman in her twenties with dark hair, and she knew at a glance that the smartly dressed man and woman who'd just walked in hadn't come to place any bets.

Luke showed his ID badge, and explained what they wanted.

'That should be OK,' said the girl, 'but all the signals are fed back to head office and it's all recorded there. I'll have to ring my manager.'

'OK,' Luke replied. The counter was an enclosed unit that protruded into the room, and Luke and Lisa stood in the small area beside it while the girl made her phone call. There seemed to be no other staff in the shop. She spoke briefly, then listened, nodded and hung up.

'He's not there, but should be back in five or ten minutes. I've left a message asking him to ring urgently.' Luke nodded, and turned back towards Lisa. They both had their files; Luke toyed with the idea of getting the paperwork started while they waited for the manager's call.

'Are you joking?' said the girl, suddenly and loudly. Luke started. Something in the tone of her voice wasn't right. He turned round. Standing at the counter was a man in a hooded top with a bright purple scar running down the right side of his face. Luke's first thought was that he looked like the kind of man you'd cross the street to avoid. His head was shaved, and he appeared to be resting a newspaper on the desk. Luke looked directly at him, but he appeared to be oblivious, instead pushing a note across the counter to the woman.

The writing was large enough for Luke to read. It said, *'Give me all the money and their won't be a seen.'* The spelling may have been poor but the meaning was clear. The man didn't speak, but nodded and pushed the note nearer to the cashier.

'Yes, that's fine, I'll get that,' she said, again loudly enough for the police officers to hear.

Luke looked again at the man standing at the counter. He'd never seen him before, but he knew him. A day or two earlier, at one of the regular morning briefings, they'd been shown a photograph of a scar-faced man – with a warning that he'd just been released from prison after serving a seven-year sentence for a series of knifepoint robberies. His name was Kes Nattriss. Luke was certain it was the same man, and although he couldn't see a weapon, it looked as though Kes was up to his old tricks.

Given the man's distinctive appearance, Luke briefly wondered why he hadn't bothered with a mask when it was fairly obvious there were CCTV cameras in the betting shop. He also wondered why Nattriss hadn't noticed the two officers, with their clipboard files prominently marked 'POLICE'.

Lisa was concentrating on paperwork and was oblivious to the drama unfolding at the counter. Everyone else in the shop was absorbed in the TV screens or their newspapers. Though they'd left their police radios in the car with their other equipment, Luke had a mobile phone with him – but he could hardly dial 999 in front of a potentially violent robber with so many people around. He wondered if he could get behind him and make an arrest at the counter, but if Nattriss was armed, confronting him in the shop would not be a good idea. Luke decided to leave, so they could raise the alarm, and he could grab his handcuffs and protective equipment to make an arrest.

He took Lisa's elbow and whispered:

'Lisa, let's go. Robbery in progress.' She stiffened, and walked with him to the front door. Neither of them looked at Nattriss, who was still standing at the counter and apparently waiting patiently for the cash.

'You get onto control and get back-up, so we can contain the situation. I'll run and get my gear on,' said Luke when they were outside, and Lisa nodded, taking out her mobile phone.

As Luke started across the car park, he looked back over his shoulder and saw Nattriss emerge from the shop, still carrying a newspaper and clutching a bag. 'This is too quick,' thought Luke, realising there wasn't time for him to get to the car, get kitted up and return.

Nattriss turned to the right, towards a pedestrian-only passageway, and Luke realised that if he didn't act immediately the robber would probably get away. He could see Lisa and other members of the public looking on, and wondering what was happening. There was an expectation that as a police officer he would act.

Luke walked up behind Nattriss, and said firmly:

'Police officer! Stand still! You're under arrest.'

Nattriss stopped, turned and looked at Luke. Luke shivered a little. The robber simply looked evil.

Luke walked forward, closing the distance between them. He felt sure there was either going to be a physical con-frontation or Nattriss would try to run. Luke had a sense there was going to be trouble. He knew Nattriss had a history of using knives, and half expected him to pull one out now, but as far as he could see Nattriss only had the newspaper and the bag.

Before joining the police, Luke had learned karate; he was a brown belt. He'd developed the habit of going into fights side on, a martial arts tactic to reduce the size of the target and protect the vital organs. Luke moved forward and grabbed Nattriss's arm – the one carrying the bag. As he did so, Nattriss wheeled in with his other hand and struck Luke hard in the left side.

Lisa screamed. As Luke grabbed him, Nattriss started shaking his other hand. Out of Luke's view, the pages of the newspaper unravelled and fluttered away to reveal the large, shining blade of a ten-inch kitchen knife. Kes leaned in towards Luke and plunged the knife in, pulling it up and sliding it out.

All Luke knew was that the blow had made him much more aggressive than usual. He had no idea he'd been stabbed, but he recognised his response: it was the same seething anger he'd felt at karate contests when he was hurt. Kes Nattriss moved in, possibly to stab again. Luke still hadn't seen the knife, and before Nattriss could use it, he delivered a right-hand punch to the chin, knocking Nattriss to the floor, stunned.

Nattriss climbed onto all fours, tried to stand up, then slipped back onto his haunches. He slid back away from Luke, then got to his feet and made off.

The entire confrontation had taken less than eight seconds.

Luke had been expecting Nattriss to come at him again. He looked over at Lisa.

'Come on, we've got to get him,' he said.

'You've been stabbed!' she replied, 'Look!' And she pointed

at the side of Luke's shirt, where a rich red stain was just starting to spread.

'It's nothing. I'll put a plaster on it when I get home,' said Luke confidently, looking down at the blood. He decided to go back into the bookmakers, to check everyone inside was OK. Lisa followed close behind.

Just then, Luke started to feel slightly faint. He tried looking for a rag to put on the wound, then became aware of Lisa telling him to lie down.

'I'm not feeling good at all,' he said, increasingly worried that he was about to pass out.

'Lie down,' she said. 'Just relax.' Luke lay down as instructed. 'I'm out of this one,' he thought. 'I can't physically catch him.' Realising this, his training cut in and he went into detective mode. Through the haze, it seemed very important to tell Lisa that the man who'd attacked him was Kes Nattriss, and that they'd be able to get his DNA off Luke's hand – because he'd punched him in the face.

Luke wanted to fall asleep, but told himself to keep calm and stay awake. He heard Lisa on the radio – 'Officer down, please send an ambulance' – and he began to find breathing very difficult. He also kept blacking out.

Before joining the police, Lisa had been a paramedic, and she could see Luke was fighting for breath. His vital signs were still strong, but she'd seen the stabbing and suspected he had a punctured lung.

'Lie on your side; it should make it easier for you to breathe,' she said. Luke did as he was told and rolled over. He immediately noticed the improvement, and gave her a weak thumbs up.

More police were arriving, along with an ambulance

crew. Luke was being lifted onto a stretcher when he saw his sergeant.

'I punched him in the face. There's DNA,' he said again, and then he was wheeled off into the ambulance. Lisa wanted to go with him, but she was told to stay to brief the other police officers now flooding the area.

In the ambulance, Luke was asked for details of his next of kin. He also gave them contact details for his girlfriend, Belinda. He was determined not to lose consciousness.

Paramedics have a grading system to quickly assess patients, from one, the mildest, to four, the most critical. Luke was classed between three and four. 'Keep breathing,' he told himself, 'keep calm.' It was getting harder and harder to stay awake. He felt fear and panic building, but knew he had to keep them down. Until now, he'd been confident he was going to be OK, but now he started to wonder. 'I might not make this one,' he thought, with a sickening jolt of regret. 'This might be the end.'

Luke was admitted to Frimley Park Hospital. It was used for treating military wounded, and the doctors and other medical staff were experienced in dealing with trauma patients.

'Luke Simms, male, thirty-five years old, has been stabbed.' Luke heard a nurse reading dispassionately from a clipboard. He felt his clothes being cut off, and fingers being pushed inside the wound. The pain was immediate and overwhelming, and Luke let out a cry.

'Yes! I felt that!' he said. The doctors told him they were going to anaesthetise him, and Luke felt a huge sense of relief that he could finally go to sleep.

He came round after sleeping for nearly twenty-four hours, to discover that he seemed to have tubes everywhere.

His mother, his father and his girlfriend were in the room with him. He could tell by their expressions that they thought he was in a bad way.

'You're in intensive care,' said his mother. 'You've lost your spleen, and the knife blade cut through your diaphragm and punctured your lung. They had to do an emergency operation to stop the internal bleeding. The blade went in ten inches.'

It didn't sound good. He chatted for around five minutes, but soon felt tired and went to sleep again. The pattern continued: sleep for an hour or two, then a five or ten minute period of wakefulness, then more sleep. Luke wasn't sure if it was the drugs keeping him drowsy, or simply his body's way of healing.

Soon he was itching to get out of hospital, and exactly a week later he was discharged and sent home. He had two scars: one on his side where he'd been stabbed, and another on his front where they'd operated to remove his spleen, which had been cut in two by the blade. Luke's girlfriend gave him tampons to absorb any fluid leaking out of the drainage tubes that were in the wound.

Luke was having trouble with digestion, and the doctor asked what he was eating.

'Only healthy stuff,' he replied. 'Greens, that sort of thing.'

'No,' said the doctor. 'We need to bind you up. I prescribe flat Coke and Hula Hoops. And plenty of ice lollies, to keep you hydrated.'

The following day, the chief constable, Sara Thornton, visited him. Luke was anxious that he'd made mistakes; after all, he'd been stabbed and had failed to arrest a suspect – but she reassured him he'd done nothing wrong. His case was even mentioned in a speech by the Home Secretary.

Luke was told that Kes Nattriss had been arrested not long after the stabbing. As he'd run off he'd dropped the knife, then boarded a train at Martins Heron, the nearest railway station. He'd travelled about five miles to Wokingham, but was spotted there and kept under surveillance as he took a taxi. Armed officers were alerted, and intercepted the car a short time later. Nattriss was arrested without a struggle.

Over the summer, Luke's condition improved. He trained hard to get his fitness back, and the occupational health unit sent him to see a trauma psychologist. By autumn, he was ready to return to work. But overshadowing all this was the forthcoming trial. The Crown Prosecution Service (CPS) had decided to charge Kes Nattriss with attempted murder, even though it's notoriously difficult to prove in court.

Both Luke and Lisa were required to give evidence, but they'd no idea how Nattriss's lawyers would try to defend him – and catch them out.

The trial date was set for 29 November, Luke's birthday. A car was sent to collect him, and Belinda went along too, even though he was worried that she was more nervous than he was. The first day was taken up with legal argument, as Nattriss's legal team tried to argue that the jury shouldn't be told of his previous violent crimes. The prosecutor argued that the previous convictions were important, because they explained why Luke had recognised him and gave Nattriss a motive for wanting to escape by any means possible. The judge agreed, and the prosecutor won the day.

The following day, it was Luke's turn in the witness box. It didn't go well. Nattriss's lawyer claimed the whole thing was an accident – that his client had collided with Luke, and the knife had inadvertently penetrated him.

It sounded far fetched, but the CPS lawyer said the defence counsel was simply trying to inject a note of doubt: to stop the jury being sure. As predicted, the defence lawyer pounced on contradictions between Luke's and Lisa's evidence, and by the end of the day Luke was feeling glum.

'He's going to get off,' he whispered to Belinda. They returned home with heavy hearts.

On day three, however, things looked up. The jury heard evidence from a woman walking her dog who'd seen Nattriss stabbing Luke and then disposing of the weapon. She vividly described the stabbing motion; it was exactly as Luke had said. Some other evidence corroborated Luke's version of events as well. Luke started to believe they might have a chance.

The following day, Nattriss had been due to answer questions, but he refused. Instead, the judge summarised the case and sent the jury to a room to consider their verdict.

After two days with no result, the judge called the jury into court. When he asked them if they'd reached a verdict, the foreman replied that they hadn't. They were down to eleven because one juror had been snowed in, and unable to get to court. The judge asked them to continue their deliberations.

Kes Nattriss stared at them from the dock, with the contemptuous air of a man who knows he's about to be cleared.

Luke was deflated. It only needed a couple of doubters, he brooded. The defence barrister must have done enough to stop them being sure. Going for a charge of attempted murder, instead of a lesser charge of assault, was starting to look like a miscalculation.

'Look,' said the prosecutor, 'if we lose we can always appeal.'
'No,' thought Luke. 'I can't put Belinda and the witnesses through this again.'

Suddenly, after just ten minutes, there was a tannoy announcement:

'All parties in Nattriss to court please.'

'Was this it?' thought Luke, as he, Belinda and Lisa filed into court with the others. Once everyone was settled, the jury were brought back in.

'Have you reached a verdict on which you are all agreed?' asked the clerk.

'We have,' replied the foreman.

'Do you find the defendant Kes Nattriss guilty or not guilty of attempted murder?'

'Guilty.' For a second the word hung in the courtroom, then it was drowned out as a cry of 'yes!' echoed around the court. Luke, Belinda and Lisa hugged each other. Belinda whooped with joy, and Luke felt a breaking wave of elation and relief.

Looking across the court at the dock, Luke wondered whether Nattriss himself – with that sneering, arrogant stare – had finally helped the jury to make up its mind.

⁓

Kes Nattriss was sentenced to twenty-five years in prison for attempted murder. He pleaded guilty to robbery and having a weapon.

Three months after Luke was attacked, Terry Bryant, from Tottenham in London, was arrested and charged with the Bracknell sex assaults. He admitted a total of fourteen offences and was jailed indefinitely for public protection. He was caught as a result of CCTV footage obtained by Operation Nemesis detectives.

Luke Simms was awarded a Chief Constable's High Commendation, and nominated for the National Police Bravery Awards.

Lisa Child received a Chief Constable's Commendation.

18

NOT FIRING BLANKS

'I think you spend a lot of your time thinking, "When a job like that does happen, how am I going to react? If there's someone with a gun would I go towards them or would I run away?"'

INSPECTOR MARK GAMMAGE

Andrew Humbleton walked up to the familiar white door. He'd been here so many times before to see her. But this time would be different, he thought to himself. There'd be no payment, no 'see you next Wednesday'. This time, she'd be coming back home with him. He didn't believe her when she said she wanted to end things, that she didn't want him visiting. She'd be much better off building a new future with him. And if she didn't want that ... well, that was her choice. But if he couldn't have her, then no one would. Andrew felt the weight of the shotgun below his coat, opened the door and started up the stairs.

'Where is she? Where's Teresa?' he said as he walked in, making sure they could all see the gun. Teresa came out.

'You're coming with me!' said Andrew, and before anyone else could react he walked her out of the door at gunpoint.

One of the other women in the massage parlour picked up the phone and dialled 999 . . .

In the control room at Crewe police station, Sergeant Mark Gammage and Inspector Alan Allman were chatting.

'A man's got a girl. He's got a gun and he's just left a massage parlour,' was all the call said, giving the location and little further detail.

Mark knew it would be a job for Cheshire's armed response vehicles, but they were likely to be at least twenty minutes away. The massage parlour was on one of the main routes into the town centre. It was a Friday evening; businesses were closing, staff were going home and the street would be busy with pedestrians. They couldn't just leave a man wandering around with a gun.

They had another reason for going: they didn't want any unarmed beat officers trying to tackle the gunman and getting shot; if they were at the scene they'd be able to control that.

'Come on, let's go!' said Alan, and he and Mark went down to one of the large police Transit vans. The address they'd been given was on Nantwich Road, leading south-west out of Crewe and just a few hundred yards from the town's famous railway station.

Although born in Winchester, Mark had grown up in North London before moving to Carlisle. At college he'd studied business, but had no real career plan until his then girlfriend said that because he was fairly big and liked rugby he'd make a good cop.

They split up, but he thought about her words and joined the Metropolitan Police in London. Five years later, they reunited and decided to marry. She wanted to live in Crewe, her home town, so Mark agreed to move to Cheshire.

Transferring to a smaller force, Mark was very anxious not to act the 'big time Charlie' and alienate his new colleagues. After a couple of years, he was promoted to sergeant, and now, in March 2002, he had just passed his inspector's exams.

It was already dark and the roads were busy. Driving on blue lights, it took Mark and Alan about five minutes to reach their destination. Although the massage parlour was located in a building on the main road, the entrance was round the back, off Brooklyn Street – undoubtedly, thought Mark, to ensure the privacy of the clientele. There was a large college a short distance further up the road, and he could see students with their files and books among the many pedestrians. He was surprised how normal everything looked. There wasn't the expected crowd of onlookers and rubber-neckers. It all seemed a little surreal.

'Is it a false call? Think it's being blown out of all proportion?' Mark said.

Alan shrugged. More radio messages had come in, suggesting the man was a client of the brothel, and had kidnapped the woman after becoming infatuated with her.

On one corner of Brooklyn Street was a two-storey redbrick working men's club, on the other a glass-fronted fashion shop with mannequins in the window. A few yards up, Mark saw a small crowd of people, and they waved when they saw the marked police van. He pulled over and stopped. Alan was in the passenger seat, and he got out to talk to them. As he did so, Mark wound down his window.

'He's just round the corner. He's got a gun!' Everyone seemed to be speaking together, but saying pretty much the same thing. 'That's where he is, round the corner.' They pointed up the side street towards a T-junction that Mark knew led into Furnival Street, a residential street that ran parallel to the main road.

Mark considered the situation. Alan was dealing with the small crowd of people, and it didn't need both of them to take down details. If the man was planning to kidnap the girl then he'd probably have a car waiting. Was there time to intercept him before he could get away? He decided that if he saw them in a car then it would be better to ram them and try to contain them than let them leave.

He put the van into first gear and crept forward slowly, barely revving the engine, before turning into Furnival Street, which stretched about a hundred yards ahead of him. Parked cars lined the kerbs. On one side were traditional Victorian bay-window terraced houses, on the other newer houses, and further up a fenced-off children's play area. Mark knew it wasn't a high crime area; it was popular with students, and indeed he'd lived nearby himself when he was at college in the town. The street lights were more widely spaced than Mark would have liked, and there were large patches of darkness.

He had turned off his blue lights, and as he continued slowly up the road he suddenly saw the heads of a man and a woman. He was taller than her, but not by much. They were standing on the pavement behind one of the parked cars, clearly visible in the pool of light from one of the street lamps.

Mark braked, stopping short of the couple, who appeared to be rowing. Because they were largely hidden by a car, Mark couldn't see if it was the gunman and the woman he was attempting to kidnap, or just a quarrelling couple who happened to be in the wrong street at the wrong time.

Although he couldn't see clearly, it seemed to Mark that when the woman caught sight of the police van she came out from behind the car and started running towards it. But instead of banging on the door or trying to climb in, she simply ran alongside.

The Transit had a solid bulkhead behind the driver, so Mark had no idea where she'd gone. 'Oh shit,' he thought. 'What's going on here?'

He decided to get out of the van, but his seatbelt was stuck. It was a regular problem: the edge of his body armour had trapped the top of the fastener, and he struggled to unclip it. For some reason, the girl had run right round the van, and was at the driver's door. She rattled the handle, trying to open it, then ran off again round the front of the van.

Mark had got his seatbelt undone, and he turned to open the door. The girl was now clearly illuminated in the headlights – she must have tripped on the kerb because she was lying on the ground. As he watched, the man appeared out of the darkness and stood over her, holding a dark, ugly shotgun.

There was a flash and a thunderous bang: he had shot her at point blank range. 'Oh God, no.' Instinct took over, and Mark launched himself at the gunman.

Time seemed to slow down as he moved forward, his mind racing as he listed the facts and calculated the odds: He still played rugby regularly and knew how to deliver a bone-crunching shoulder barge. The man had a shotgun, was prepared to use it, and probably had another cartridge ready to fire. But Mark was braced for the impact and the gunman was not. That, he thought in the fraction of a second as he moved forward, gave him the edge.

Mark smashed into the man, and the pair of them flew

across the road. The gun skidded away across the tarmac, fortunately without going off. The man was stunned into immediate submission, and Mark was able to take hold of him, roll him over and handcuff him in a single fluid movement.

He leaned back, took in a big gulp of air and felt a wave of relief breaking over him. But what about the girl? Was it his fault she'd been killed – because she'd come running to him? Had the sight of the police van enraged the gunman? If he'd stayed away would she still be alive?

He turned to look round at her. The body was gone. Mark blinked, and looked again. He'd just seen a woman shot at point blank range with a shotgun. He'd seen the flash, heard the bang, even felt the pressure wave through his jaw and the ringing in his ears. It was impossible. He turned to the gunman, prostrate beneath him.

'Were you firing blanks?' he asked. It was the only possible explanation.

'No!' replied the man. The adrenaline was surging through Mark's veins, and he was utterly confused. He heard his radio.

'Shots fired! Police officer down!' Mark guessed someone else must've heard the bang, come round the corner and seen him in front of the van struggling on the ground.

'It's OK!' he shouted back towards his colleagues. 'I've got him. He's secure.' Adding to himself, sotto voce, but where's she gone?

While he was waiting for the others to arrive, Mark searched the man. In his pockets he found more shotgun cartridges and a canister of CS spray. He examined the cartridges. Mark wasn't a firearms expert but he'd used a shotgun before and could tell they weren't blanks – just the standard type used for hunting rabbits or vermin. The gun itself was a few feet away at the side of the road. Mark left it alone for the firearms officers to deal with.

As other officers arrived, Mark described the woman to them and asked if they'd seen her. None had. It was a mystery.

Mark knew he had work to do, but his mind was racing. If he'd held back, would she have been killed – or not shot at all? He knew armed officers were on the way – should he have waited? Why did he make that decision? Was he just being a glory boy?

Mark turned back to his prisoner, and lifted him to his feet. He'd given his name as Andrew Humbleton, and he was from Bentilee in Stoke-on-Trent. Mark took him back to the van and drove him to the police station to be questioned. He booked him in on suspicion of attempted murder and for possessing a prohibited weapon, the CS canister.

Mark started on the paperwork. A short time later, a call came in from the local hospital telling them that a young woman, twenty-two-year-old Teresa Williams, had been admitted with what appeared to be gunshot injuries. Detectives went to question her, and later relayed to Mark what she told them.

Teresa said she'd been lying on the ground when she saw Andrew looming over her with the gun. For some reason, she'd flinched to one side, and this had saved her. The main blast from the shotgun had passed beneath her armpit, though her tricep and breast were hit. She'd staggered to her feet, run down the road and almost immediately been picked up by friends, who drove her straight to hospital.

Andrew, she said, had been a client of hers at the massage parlour and had fallen in love with her, or so he thought; but she had decided to end the relationship.

Mark was tempted to visit her in hospital, but decided not to. He knew that both he and the girl would be key prosecution witnesses in Andrew Humbleton's forthcoming trial, and any such meeting would be alleged, by his defence lawyer, to be an attempt to collude against the accused.

There was also a problem because of her profession. An old police officer's saying warns that the things that'll get you into trouble are prisoners, property and prostitutes.

But simply learning she'd survived was an enormous load off his mind. Mark had always wondered how he would react if confronted with a gun. Would he face it – or run away? For a few terrible hours, he had the nagging feeling he'd got it horribly wrong – but now he knew he'd got it right. Because the first shot had only winged Teresa, there was every likelihood that Andrew Humbleton would have used his second to finish her off. Mark Gammage's shoulder charge ensured he didn't get the opportunity.

❧

Mark Gammage received a Chief Constable's Commendation for bravery and was also nominated for a Police Federation National Bravery Award. A short time later, he was promoted to inspector.

Andrew Humbleton had several previous convictions for violence. He was charged with attempted murder, but the case never reached court. He hanged himself in prison while awaiting trial.

19

THE STRONG ARM OF THE LAW

'If you're the police there's an expectation that you'll do something. If it was my dad, I'd want the police to do something.'

SERGEANT ALISTAIR LIVINGSTONE

It was hot on the top floor of the multi-storey car park. Sergeant Alistair Livingstone looked at the man standing the wrong side of the safety barrier, about fifty yards away. He tried talking to him again.

'Look, we just want to help you. Let's talk about this.' Alistair tried to edge closer across the grey tarmac roof. The man was facing him, his feet on a narrow ledge, his back to the drop, holding onto the top of the steel rail. He began shaking his head, and it was clear he was becoming more anxious and agitated. Alistair stopped moving and held up his hands. 'OK, OK, calm down. I won't come any closer. I'll give you all the space you need.'

Alistair had dealt with potential suicides before. For many police officers, it was a regular occurrence. In Suffolk, many of those who wanted to kill themselves went to the high concrete bridge that takes the A14 trunk road high over the wide estuary of the River Orwell. Like many officers, he'd developed an instinct for whether a potential suicide jumper was serious or not. And his impression now, nine storeys up on the roof of a car park in Ipswich town centre, was that this one was no time-waster.

The man had left a bag positioned neatly inside the barrier, and although he didn't seem at all hostile or aggressive it was clear he just wanted to be left alone. Alistair wondered whether his presence was making things worse. If he left, would the man just shrug, climb back over the railings and return to his life? Or would he go through with what seemed like a very real decision to kill himself? Alistair couldn't take the chance.

His colleague, PC Alastair Maidment, always known as Ally, was waiting out of sight at the top of the stairwell. For the time being, there was very little they could do. They didn't want to make things worse, but on the other hand they were much too far away to reach the man should he decide to jump. Parked cars might have offered some cover, and a way for Ally to get close to the man while Alistair kept him talking. But because it was mid-morning on a Saturday the private car park was closed, and the neatly painted parking spaces were empty.

Alistair's hands started to feel clammy, and not just because of the heat and the brisk jog up nine floors.

The call had come in around ten minutes before. Someone at a builders merchants next to the car park had looked up and spotted the man climbing slowly and deliberately over the barrier. They had watched transfixed with grim curiosity as the man stood there. Then they'd dialled 999 and called the police.

Alistair Livingstone and Ally Maidment were on duty at Ipswich police station when the alarm was raised. They realised the car park was just a few hundred yards away, and went there immediately. They managed to get a security guard to let them in, and made their way up to the roof using the vehicle ramps. However, owing to some misunderstanding, the security guard had then locked up and left, so other officers arriving shortly afterwards couldn't get in.

For far longer than they expected, they were on their own.

On the roof, Alistair continued to assess the situation. He'd had training in negotiating techniques, having spent some time with Suffolk Police's firearms unit, and he understood the basic principles: try to empathise with the subject and don't make any promises you can't deliver. But all his attempts to engage the man in conversation and open up a dialogue were ignored.

A CCTV camera on the top corner of the car park had picked up the man standing on the edge, and operators in the council-run monitoring centre had patched the images through live to the police control room. Suddenly, after about ten minutes, the control room called out to Alistair, 'He's gone over the edge. The man has just lowered himself down and appears about to jump!' Without stopping to think, Alistair sprinted towards the edge, with Ally following a dozen or so yards behind. The man's fingers were visible, clinging onto the top of the barrier. This was made of solid metal, but there was a gap of a few inches at the bottom. It seemed to Alistair that he'd get a better grip if he reached in there, rather than trying to bend over the top.

He stooped down and reached through the gap with his

right hand. Although the solid panels of the barrier prevented him seeing, he managed to get a good, firm grip on the man's left wrist. He then put his left arm through and felt for his own fingertips – gripping them from the other side to lock his right hand in place. That instant, the man let go. Alistair's arms were pulled forward, and his face and shoulders pressed against the cold steel. Above him, Ally Maidment had reached the barrier and leaned over, scrabbling to reach the man's other arm, his clothing, or anything that would provide a grip.

In the council and police control rooms, all eyes were on the images from the security camera. As the two officers held on, the man seemed to be struggling – wriggling and kicking. Surely it could only be a matter of time before he managed to loosen their grip – and plummet to the ground below.

There was no sound with the live pictures, and it was impossible to talk to the officers, as neither could let go of the man to reach their radios. All those gathered around the screens could do was watch in silence as the dramatic struggle played itself out second by second.

Nine storeys up, Alistair was desperately holding on. It had probably only been a minute since he'd grabbed the man, but already his arms, wrist and fingers were beginning to ache. He'd managed to brace his shoulders against the lower edge of the hard metal barrier and his knees against the kerb. In this position he felt firmly anchored, so now it was just a question of ensuring that his grip didn't fail. He didn't like heights, but the solid barrier meant that he couldn't see over the edge. That, he mused, was a small blessing!

The man was still struggling and kicking. 'You're hurting my shoulders,' he whined. 'Let go of me, let go of my wrists ...'

Above, Ally was having difficulty. Both his hands were holding the man's right forearm, but it wasn't a strong grip and the man kept twisting, trying to get free. It was hot, and Ally's palms were sweating. Suddenly, his grip failed, and the man's right arm slipped free.

In the control room there were gasps as Ally Maidment fell back, and the man dropped for a split second. He kicked out his legs, and it was clear that only Alistair's grip on his left arm was preventing him tumbling to the ground. The clock readout in the corner of the image showed that Alistair had been holding him for two minutes.

Alistair was now taking the man's entire weight. He was a keen squash player, playing four or five times a week. He'd always thought he had strong arms – but they were starting to tire.

'Look,' he gasped, 'we're trying to help you. Let us help you. Just work with me and we can pull you back over.' The man's only response was to keep struggling.

During the second or two that he wasn't holding on, Ally Maidment quickly reached down and pressed the emergency button on his colleague's radio to open up the communication channel. Now, everything they said would be transmitted back to the control room.

Ally reached back over the top of the barrier: 'Give me your hand, give it to me!' he shouted. The man had lowered his arm, in an effort to stop him reaching it, so Ally grabbed the shoulders of his t-shirt. He knew this was a tenuous hold, and that if Alistair lost his grip the flimsy fabric would almost certainly rip and the man would fall.

Alistair could feel his hands becoming slippery with perspiration. Sensing this, the man tried a new tactic: clenching and unclenching his fist in an effort to loosen Alistair's grip. Alistair could feel the muscles and tendons flexing, expanding and contracting. Every tiny movement seemed to require him to tighten his hold. The aching in his own fingers, wrist and arms was becoming unbearable. He imagined it must be the same for Ally. They'd done their best, hadn't they? They'd tried. After all, the man seemed determined to fall. It wouldn't be so bad if they let go now, would it?

NO!

'Just keep holding on, Ally,' he said to his colleague. 'No matter how hard it is, we've just got to keep going. We've got to do everything we can, because if we let go we'll always think to ourselves we could have held on a little bit longer, we could have done a little bit more . . .'

But where were their colleagues? Over the radio Alistair and Ally could hear garbled messages about access to the car park, and about alerting the fire brigade, but they were unaware that their would-be helpers were watching helplessly below, unable get into the locked car park.

In the control room, the digital display at the corner of the live video feed ticked on remorselessly. While operators were putting in frantic calls in an effort to locate the car park attendant, the rest simply watched the grainy images and waited.

The control room inspector had made contact with the on-call negotiator, who was a superintendent from Ipswich.

'We've now reached a critical phase,' said the negotiator.

'What does that mean?' asked the inspector.

'It means that there's no time left for negotiating. It's now down to those officers. And what will be will be.'

The searing, aching fatigue in his fingers, hand and arm was unrelenting. It felt as though his entire conscious mind – every neuron, every cell – was focused on the pain. He felt that his muscles might suddenly fail any second. Alistair had grown up in Ipswich, and had joined the police because of the job's variety and the chance to make a positive contribution to the town. He always relished challenging situations – but he was beginning to wonder if this was one challenge too far. He tried to think of a distraction. Was there anything else they could do? Was there something simple they weren't thinking of that might help alleviate some of the pressure?

'Ally, how are you doing?' he gasped. An affirmative grunt came in return. 'Do you think you can get handcuffs on him? Is there some way of fixing him to the railing?

'I don't know,' replied Ally. 'Maybe. But can we get them on tight enough? If we get it wrong his hand could slip through and he'll still fall.'

'Yeah, that's what I thought. And the fast-straps aren't really any good either.'

Fast-straps are narrow fabric strips with Velcro on one side used for restraining violent prisoners. They're worn round the waist like a belt. Usually they're wrapped around a suspect's legs, but Alistair considered putting one round the man's wrist. But any solution involved one of them letting go of him – and that was something they couldn't do. Not after holding on for so long!

By now, Alistair and Ally had been supporting the man's entire weight for more than four minutes.

Every now and then, Alistair tried to reason with the man: 'Look, come in, try to climb up, help us to help you.' But he refused.

Alistair began to feel that all along the man hadn't wanted to take responsibility for jumping but wanted the police officers to drop him. That annoyed him – and made him more determined than ever to hold on. He wondered how much more he could take. The pain in his fingers, wrists, arms and shoulders was so intense! All he could think about was maintaining his grip. It was getting harder, as the perspiration continued to make his palms and fingers slippery. Every now and then, especially when the man struggled, Alistair felt his grip starting to fail. And somewhere he found the strength to tighten it a little, just enough to stop the man sliding from his grasp and plunging to his death.

He and Ally also shouted encouragement to each other: 'Keep going!' 'Keep holding on – the rest of them will be here any second!' 'We've got to live with this for the rest of our lives if it doesn't work out. We've got to be happy we've done everything we possibly could.' 'Don't let go now – we've held on for so long . . .'

But Alistair was tiring. He knew the communications channel was open, and he directed a message at control.

'You've got to get here now. If you don't get here in the next few minutes, we can't hold him any longer and he's going to fall. You've just got to get someone here. We can't hold on any longer.' One of Alistair's colleagues said later that it was the most chilling ten seconds of radio he'd ever heard.

Alistair was desperate. Where was everyone? They'd tried

so hard, held on so long. It was so unfair. Very soon, Alistair knew, the muscles in his fingers and hands would go into spasm, and the man would slip from his grasp and fall 100 feet onto the hard concrete roadway below.

Suddenly, there was chaos. There were hands grabbing at the man and at Alistair. There were voices shouting, bodies barging, black boots around him. The barrier trembled as more officers pressed against it. The parking attendant had been found – finally – and had opened the doors, allowing half a dozen officers to sprint for the roof.

Alistair felt a massive surge of relief flood through his body. They were here! 'I've never been happier to see you!' he laughed at two of them he knew - Johnny Firman and Matt Jay.

But the relief soon turned to concern: Alistair was desperate to let go, but he didn't dare do that until he was 100 per cent sure the others had a good strong grip of the man. But had they? He could hear lots of voices: 'Let go, I'll pull him over!' 'Have you got him yet?' 'You grab his left arm, I've got his right shoulder!' 'I'll get his other arm.' Alistair, as the sergeant, had to get a grip – and not with his hand.

'RIGHT! WILL EVERYONE JUST SHUT UP AND STOP TALKING!' he shouted. Suddenly, there was quiet. 'Thank you! We just need to all work out what we've got. Matt?'

'Right wrist.'

'OK. Johnny?'

'Left wrist. I've definitely got his left wrist.'

In turn all the officers checked in, and once it became clear the man was properly supported, Alistair gave the order. Even though he was still struggling half-heartedly, the team were able to pull him to safety – and Alistair was finally able to release his grip.

In control there was a small cheer – and a big sigh of relief. According to the digital display in the corner of the picture, Alistair had been holding the man's wrist for four minutes and fifty seconds.

Back on the roof, Alistair crouched down exhausted. Others were milling around. One officer had tears streaming down her face; a short distance away another was retching. They'd been watching the drama from the bottom, unable to help until the car park could be opened. In some ways it had been far harder for them than it had for him, mused Alistair.

The man was still angry about being rescued, and angry with the officers. Alistair didn't care. If he was angry, that meant he was alive.

Alistair spoke to the man, and found out that he'd been shopping with his wife. He called her, and she explained that they'd come into town together that day but her husband hadn't returned to the car, and she'd started to worry. She'd reported him missing. Alistair told her they'd detained her husband for his own protection, and he was about to be taken to hospital.

Alistair saw the car park security attendant and wandered over to him. 'I'll need your details.' He pulled out his pen and pocket-book. The attendant started to reel off his phone number and address – then tailed off. Alistair couldn't write. His right hand was completely seized up. Both hands and arms were trembling and shaking. The marks he'd made on the paper were illegible – he could barely hold the pen. His arm and hand hurt, especially in the joints: he imagined the discomfort must be similar to arthritis. The previous year he'd broken a finger, and that one was particularly sore. But he was also filled with a sense of euphoric relief that, however excruciating the pain, it had not been in vain.

Once the man had been taken off the roof and driven to hospital, Alistair, Ally and the rest returned to the police station for a debrief. One of the control room staff had recorded the security camera footage and offered to play it. The team quickly agreed, and for the first time Alistair and Ally were able to see the drama unfold from the point of view of those who could only watch. It was compelling viewing, but for Alistair the most frightening part was at the end – when the rest of the team arrived. They'd piled up to the barrier and one of his colleagues – Johnny Firman – had reached right over to grab the man. Alastair remembered how flimsy the barrier was, and it dawned on him how lucky they were that it hadn't given way.

It was around a week before he could use his right hand properly again, and although he had no sleepless nights, Alistair found himself replaying the events over and over in his mind. He considered the fine line between success and failure – between things ending well or going unpredictably, catastrophically wrong. He re-examined his doubts. Had his visible presence on the roof put additional pressure on the man? If he'd walked away, would the man have jumped? Did the man plan to die by making the officers drop him, rather than jumping himself? He decided that if it was his own father or another loved one, he'd want officers to act; that there was an expectation that the police would get involved.

～≈～

Some weeks later, the man's wife wrote to Alistair, thanking him for saving her husband's life.

Sergeant Alistair Livingstone and PC Alastair Maidment were honoured by the Royal Humane Society and the National Police Bravery Awards, while they and their colleagues Jonny Firman, Matt Jay, Michelle Webber, Lauren Brady and Cliff Baldock received a Chief Constable's Certificate of Merit.

The following year Alistair hit the headlines again, being dubbed 'supercop' after making nearly 530 arrests in twelve months – more than any officer in Britain – a feat he put down to being a workaholic and having a gift for remembering a face.

20

ANYA

*'Even though Anya had never bitten anyone properly I knew
what she was like. I didn't have to say anything. She knew
what she was doing. She was in Exocet mode.'*

PC NEIL SAMPSON

Neil Sampson felt terrible. His wife Mandy passed him a
Lemsip as he sat at the kitchen table.

'Don't go in if you're not well,' she said. Neil took a sip.
He hated being off work, partly because he loved his job and
partly because he hated letting his colleagues down.

'No, it's all right,' he said, getting to his feet. 'I'll be fine.
And Anya needs the exercise.' Anya was his German Shepherd
police dog. He'd only had her six months and she was still
young.

Neil walked outside to the kennels at the back of his
house in Swindon. He put Anya and his search dog, a springer
spaniel called Alfie, in the back of his van. It was a Peugeot,
with 'Police Dogs' clearly marked on the side. He always took
both dogs with him because he never knew which one he
might need.

Neil had joined Wiltshire Police in the mid-1980s. His

family had always owned dogs, and as soon as he could he applied for the police dog section. A general-purpose police dog tended to have a working life of around seven years, and Anya was his fourth. If Neil timed it right, he hoped that he and Anya might retire together.

'Male with a knife at Briarswood Court, Liden. Armed Response requested to attend.' Neil heard the message over the radio. He knew the location; it was a block of flats on an estate in East Swindon. It wasn't far away, and he knew he could probably get there before the firearms team.

'Whisky Delta seven eight Delta, I have my dog and can attend,' he said. The control operator thanked him, and relayed the location of the forward rendezvous point.

Two female police officers, Jo Field and Louise Dean, were already there. They'd been sent to speak to a man outside the flat. Neil heard them radioing back in that the man wasn't making any sense, and requesting permission to go into the flats and have a look for themselves. Permission was refused and they were told to remain outside.

Neil pulled into the car park a moment or two later. As he got out of the car he noticed a man with the two officers. Neil walked over to have a chat.

'I hear he isn't making much sense,' said Neil. Louise nodded.

'I can't really understand much of what he's saying,' she admitted. 'He's Somali, doesn't speak much English.'

Neil looked around. They were standing next to a row of concrete prefabricated garages. In front of them were three blocks of flats. A path led from each block into the centre of the grassy communal area, where they merged into a single footpath stretching to the garages. There were a few shrubs and hedges dotted around.

Neil tried talking to the man, but Louise was right; it was hard to understand anything he was saying. The man was wearing a polo shirt and appeared to have some blood on his collar. All Neil could make out was that something had happened in the flats involving another man and a knife.

'I'm going to get the dog out and keep an eye on these flats until back-up arrives,' he said to Louise and Jo. 'See if you can get a description of the man who's supposedly got the knife.'

Neil drove the van to the corner of the garages and took Anya out. Apart from anything else, at least she could have a breath of fresh air.

'This is control. Initial assessment is that we would like a containment put on the flats.' Neil smiled; that was exactly what he'd decided to do.

'Ahead of you on that control; yes, we're putting in a containment,' he replied. It was a bitterly cold day, and he zipped up his jacket and put on his new fleece-lined beanie hat. He found a sheltered corner by the garages and watched the flats.

No one seemed to know what the suspect might be wearing. The man kept giving conflicting or contradictory accounts. First he said the man had a brown shirt, then that it was yellow, and that his trousers were brown. 'Seems like I'm looking for Joseph and his amazing Technicolor bloody dreamcoat,' thought Neil.

As he stood by the garages, two armed officers, PC Mick Mansell and PC Ciarian Magee, arrived in a BMW X5. They climbed out of the vehicle and looked around. It was around two o'clock in the afternoon.

Ciarian walked over to Louise and Jo. The Somali man was still mumbling, and the officers were struggling to understand what he was trying to say. Ciarian passed him a piece of paper and a pen and asked him to write down the flat number. He did – and it was completely different to the address they'd been given by control.

Mick Mansell was getting shields and other protective equipment out of the vehicle. Although it was optional, he decided to put on his body armour. It was bulky, and when worn for long periods could cause a stiff back, so he and his colleagues tended to wear it only when they felt they might need it.

Ciarian walked back to Mick. They looked over at the flats, and could see Neil standing at the edge of the garages with his dog, about forty yards away.

'Can we get authority to use taser?' asked Ciarian. Mick radioed through the request to the force incident manager at control. At this time, only armed officers had been trained to carry tasers, and although they were permitted to self-deploy it was considered good practice to get authority from a senior officer first.

'Negative,' came the response. 'We understand a knife's been mentioned by one witness, but we believe it's unlikely he'll come outside with it.' Mick and Ciarian sighed. Their plan was to move their containment position up to the door of the flats; then they could consider going inside and searching the building. They started discussing tactics and options.

Over by the garages, Neil was still watching the flats when he noticed a man come out of the middle block. The man looked similar to the witness, and appeared to be wearing a brown puffer jacket. He started walking away.

'Hey!' Neil called out. 'Can I have a word?' The man turned immediately, and began walking towards him.

'Can you tell me where you've been today?' asked Neil. If nothing else, he might be able to eliminate the man from consideration.

The man kept walking towards him, and as he approached Neil could see he had a slight smile on his face. Neil was confident: he had Anya beside him, and the man was considerably smaller than he was.

As he came closer, Neil noticed that the man's jogging bottoms appeared to have blood on them. He glanced over; Mick and Ciarian were still deep in discussion.

His eyes had only flicked away for a split second, but when he looked back the man had a knife in his hand. He held it out in front of him and began slashing it from side to side.

'Stand still and drop the knife!' Neil shouted as loud as he could, remembering his training: challenge, and challenge loudly! He also wanted to shout loudly enough that the others heard.

Over by their car, Mick and Ciarian looked round. They saw the man in the brown jacket and the knife.

'Press the fucking emergency button!' shouted Ciarian to Louise as he and Mick dropped their shields and helmets and sprinted towards Neil, drawing their yellow plastic tasers as they ran. Forget authority from control – this was exactly the kind of circumstance in which they were fully entitled to self-deploy!

Anya could tell something was wrong. She reared up and started barking at the approaching man as she'd been trained to do. 'That's my girl,' thought Neil. 'Good noise and good aggression!'

The man with the knife showed no sign of stopping; he was getting closer and closer. Right, decided Neil, you're getting it. Even though Anya had never bitten anyone properly before, Neil had seen her in training and expected the knifeman to get seriously hurt. He didn't have to say anything; Anya knew what she was doing. She was in Exocet mode.

Neil dropped the lead, and Anya sprinted up to the man and hit him hard. Up on her back legs, she jumped up, putting her paws on his chest. A textbook attack. Then, much to Neil's surprise and horror, she bounced off him and disappeared from view. 'Oh shit,' he thought. A second later, Neil became aware of a growling black and tan blur coming back in from the left, but in that instant the man was upon him and he went down.

As Neil was subjected to a frenzied attack, he was aware of Anya mauling the man's arms and legs, desperately trying to protect him.

Ciarian saw Neil on the ground with the man over him, and the knife blade flashing. He and Mick fired their tasers almost simultaneously and watched the darts fly out, trailing their fine power wires behind. Both hit their target.

On the ground, Neil heard the crackling sound of 50,000 volts being discharged.

Mick and Ciarian expected the man to collapse almost immediately: the electrical charge from the taser was designed to hurt and to cause a loss of control. The man should have dropped to the ground, but instead he turned to face the other two officers, raised his knife and took a step forward.

Taser officers are trained to take a step back as soon as they have fired to allow space and time to remove the spent cartridge from the front of the gun and fit a new one. As he did this, Mick caught his foot on a low concrete step and tumbled backwards to the ground. A second later, the knifeman was on him, stabbing and slashing. Mick could hear and feel the hollow dull thud of the knife blade punching at his body armour. The knife was everywhere! Mick remembered his combat training in the gym, and tried to bring his knees up to get his feet underneath the knifeman's body.

Ciarian binned the taser – that hasn't fucking worked, he said to himself – and reached for his canister of Pava incapacitant spray. Pava works on the soft tissues of the eyes – causing burning pain and watering. Wiltshire Police had recently upgraded to Pava from CS spray because it was supposed to be more powerful, and also because it worked on dogs.

He shouted at the man, and as he turned round Ciarian emptied the entire can into his face. 'Have some of that,' he thought. There was no reaction.

Mick had managed to get his feet under the man's body and kicked out, pushing him away and back into a hedge. Unfortunately, their assailant landed on Neil, who was crawling towards them, and started attacking him again, slashing and stabbing at his head.

Anya had been biting the man up and down his arms and legs right from the start. Mick got up from the ground and reloaded his taser, firing it at the knifeman again. The man turned away from Neil and lunged back at Mick. Mick preferred to fight on the ground, so he tripped the attacker and they both went down. As they grappled, Mick tried to keep his head away from the man and his jabbing knife.

As Ciarian drew his baton, he watched as Neil staggered to his feet, walked over to the knifeman and tried to kick him. He missed completely and fell to the ground.

On the ground, Mick was trying to get a firm grip on the attacker. The man was physically much smaller, and yet so strong! Mick had his taser in his right hand and pushed it into the man's chest – drive-stunning him. The drive-stun was a technique used at close quarters: the taser was pressed firmly against the target and the trigger pulled.

Ciarian was now striking the man repeatedly, but this too seemed to be having no effect. They seemed to be running out of options. Jo Field was there too, trying to use her baton. Nothing seemed to be working.

'Taser him. Just taser him,' gasped Mick from beneath the man.

Ciarian picked up his taser. What to do? Where might he be vulnerable? Gripping the taser, Ciarian leant forward and jammed the taser right into the man's testicles. 'Go on,' he thought, 'have 50,000 volts in the bollocks!' He pulled the trigger again and again – eight or nine times.

Amazingly, it worked. The man dropped the knife and went limp.

'Ouch!' he said. Mick and Ciarian looked at each other. It was almost comical. Before he could recover, they bundled him onto his front and slapped the handcuffs on.

'Can I have a drink of water, please?' asked the man. Ciarian and Mick ignored him and looked over at Neil. He looked dazed and was covered in blood. Jo helped him to his feet, and led him away towards the parking area.

Anya was still mauling the suspect, and Mick grabbed her by the collar. There was a tiny pool of blood near her feet. Ciarian blinked. He had been so focused on the attacker, and the knife, that this was the first time he'd even noticed the police dog.

The knife was lying on the ground nearby. It was a six-or seven-inch-long serrated steak knife. The blade had bent and the tip was broken off.

He and Mick searched the man lying face down, and found a similar knife tucked in his sock. Ciarian was later told that among Somalis it was customary to carry two knives. The man's eyes were bright red. The officers weren't sure if it was the effect of the Pava or the drugs he'd been taking.

'You bunch of bastards!' The voice belonged to a bystander who had just appeared. 'Leave him alone.' The man had only seen the last few seconds of the struggle, and had no idea what had happened.

Mick and Ciarian stood up. A paramedic was checking over the suspect. The area was a mess of blood, snot, bandages and kit. Mick went back to the car to pick up the helmets and shields they'd had to leave on the ground, while Ciarian picked up the discarded Pava canisters.

'I'm cold and I want to go to sleep,' said Neil, plaintively. Jo looked at him sternly.

'Don't you dare go to sleep, Neil Sampson!' she said. 'You stay with me here. You're going to be fine!' A paramedic came over and started to examine Neil's head wounds.

'Where's Anya?' asked Neil. Jo and the paramedic looked at each other and shrugged.

'Anya!' called out Neil, and within moments a familiar shape appeared. Neil breathed a sigh of relief and gave her a hug.

'Good girl! Well done, Anya!' He handed his keys to a PCSO and asked him to put Anya back in his van.

'You've been stabbed in your leg as well,' said the paramedic. 'I need to take off your trousers.' Neil looked around. It was half past two in the afternoon. There were colleagues and onlookers gathered around.

'You're having a laugh, aren't you?' he asked. No one was seeing his pants! The paramedic had a penknife but it was too small to cut the fabric. 'I've got a ruddy great knife on my belt,' thought Neil, 'but you're not having it to cut off my trousers!'

Then another paramedic arrived, and Neil was put in the back of an ambulance. He was able to give Ciarian and Mick the thumbs up before being taken off to hospital.

Back at headquarters, Mick and Ciarian were debriefed separately. Their clothes and equipment were seized and they were asked if they wanted a Police Federation representative to be present. Mick found this a little sinister, and struggled hard to shake off the idea that they were somehow under suspicion. He also became aware of blood under his chin that had been hidden by his goatee beard, and realised that he had been cut by the knifeman during the struggle.

Ciarian was unhurt, and once the incident was done his overriding concern was his long-planned house move. Despite not getting back home until one o'clock in the morning, he managed to move house the next day without incident.

Because Neil had been taken to hospital, Anya was taken to the police kennels that are usually used when handlers are on holiday.

She'd arrived covered in blood, had been given a clean up and a meal, and put in a kennel to rest. Later, when the keeper checked on her, she didn't get up. This was uncharacteristic, and he examined her more closely. He discovered a puncture wound in her chest, and immediately contacted the vet. Anya was seen straight away. Luckily, the wound, although quite deep, had not hit any vital organs. A single staple was put in to close it up and Anya was soon back on duty.

The knifeman was identified as Essa Suleiman. He'd previously worked as a Somali translator for the Metropolitan Police in London. The man who'd called the police was his cousin; they'd had a falling-out, and Essa had slashed him on the shoulder with the knife. He was a habitual user of the drug khat, a plant that's chewed in many North African cultures. At the time, it wasn't illegal in the UK but can in rare cases induce psychosis.

It was later found that his thick puffer jacket had protected him from the electric shock of the taser barbs; these were redesigned and made longer.

Suleiman spent three and a half weeks in hospital recovering from the bites inflicted by Anya, who'd continued to attack him and protect the other officers after she'd been stabbed.

In hospital, Neil Sampson's biggest worry was his wife. He pestered the nurses to let him call her.

'Look,' he said, 'I don't want some policeman turning up at my home and telling her about this – she'll go ballistic!' Eventually they relented, and he phoned home to explain the situation.

Neil had suffered two four-inch-deep stab wounds in his leg, but fortunately both had missed major blood vessels. The knife had slashed his face and gone through his lip, and doctors fixed this with super-glue. The most serious wounds were on the back of his head, where he had three glancing cuts and a deep wound from the crown of his scalp right down to the top of his spine.

Neil kept thinking about the radio message that Louise and Jo had made before he got there, asking to go into the flats to investigate. It was so fortunate that control had had the sense to tell them to stay put; undoubtedly it had saved their lives.

Neil's wife Mandy arrived so quickly at A&E that the policeman who was sent to his house missed her. She strode into the ward. Neil tried to smile, though it was difficult with his super-glued lip. She looked at him and folded her arms.

'I bloody told you not to go to work today!'

❧

Essa Suleiman admitted three assault charges for the attacks on his cousin and the two police officers, and a charge of criminal damage for stabbing Anya.

The chief constable of Wiltshire at the time, Brian Moore, had only been in post two days when the incident took place. He immediately ordered new, more up to date body armour, and insisted it be worn at all times. He also changed debrief procedures, and encouraged senior control room officers to be more willing to sanction the use of tasers and firearms.

Eyewitnesses described the fight as lasting fifteen minutes. Data from the officers' tasers showed the entire incident lasted just one minute and forty seconds.

Neil Sampson, Ciarian Magee and Mick Mansell received Chief Constable's Commendations and Police Federation National Bravery Awards. They were also nominated for the Queen's Gallantry Medal.

Anya won the Police Dog Humanitarian Action Award for 2008. She was also awarded the People's Dispensary for Sick Animals Gold Medal – widely regarded as the animals' George Cross, and the highest civilian award that can be given.

In July 2013, the Home Office announced plans to ban khat and classify it as a category C drug. This brought the UK into line with most other European countries and the United States and Canada.

21

THE STRENGTH OF TWENTY MEN

'I was shit-scared. If we don't keep hold of him, do whatever we need to do, and I mean whatever, we're dead. That's it. Because this bloke isn't giving up.'

SERGEANT CHRISTOPHER FLINT

Hardly anyone in Moston looked twice at the battered black Honda parked inconspicuously in a side street in the early hours of the morning. The paint was peeling off and the upholstery was ripped in places. But what the casual observer wouldn't have known was that mechanically the vehicle was immaculate: the engine was scrupulously maintained and the tyres and oil levels regularly checked.

Inside, the two men in dark clothing watched and waited. The people they were looking for would be alerted by the sound of a car engine, so they tended not to cruise around but park and bide their time.

About a year earlier, Sergeant Christopher Flint had been asked to put together a proactive police team to tackle the massive problems of burglary, robbery and drug use in parts of Greater Manchester. He'd recruited a team of plain-clothes officers and they targeted trouble-hit areas: building intelligence, maintaining a presence, focusing on the relatively small hard core of criminals who were usually responsible. They called it Operation Swag.

When recruiting his team, Chris had looked for officers he wouldn't have to spoon-feed; that he could trust to get the job done. They needed to have some experience of surveillance work, be good at procedural matters such as obtaining search warrants, and above all have a degree of common sense. One of those he recruited was Phil Bainbridge.

Phil had a military background – he'd spent seven years in the RAF before joining Greater Manchester Police. In the air force he'd travelled widely. His training was in mobile ground radar, but he'd also worked on cooling systems for aircraft hangars, and on humanitarian missions he'd found himself building shelters for refugees.

That evening Chris and Phil had taken their little Honda – a police car designed to look anything but – out into an estate in north Manchester where there'd been a sudden increase in burglaries. As usual, they had some intelligence on a few individuals believed to be responsible, but knowing a criminal was up to no good was one thing; proving it was something else. They'd decided to go to the estate in the hope that if anything came up they could react quickly enough to catch the offenders in the act.

Chris had been a police officer all his working life. He'd joined the cadets first, then moved straight into regular duties. After fifteen years in London with the Metropolitan Police he decided to transfer to north-west England, because his wife was from Runcorn.

Both were wearing personal radios and stab vests under their baggy tops – the fashion for hoodies was a godsend to undercover police officers who wanted to wear concealed equipment – and they also carried a baton, handcuffs and CS spray.

On operations they usually used two radio channels. One was the main police net, but they also had a second just for the team. They knew from experience that uniformed officers tend to be nosey, and would come for a look if they heard of an interesting job taking place – even though the sight of uniformed officers might scare off the suspects.

'Burglary in progress on Rudd Street. Thieves on. Male or males armed with knives.' The report on the main channel was short, but Chris and Phil sat up. Rudd Street was barely half a mile away, and 'thieves on' meant the burglars were still on the premises and could be caught in the act.

'This is what we're here for,' said Chris, and switched on the engine. They both knew that callers to the emergency services often exaggerate, either in good faith or because they hope to get a more speedy response, but they were still excited. The Honda didn't have lights or sirens, but at this time of the morning they didn't need them, and a silent approach gave them the benefit of surprise.

As they turned into Rudd Street, they saw on one side a patch of nondescript open grass and on the other a series of T-junctions leading to row after row of traditional Victorian terraced houses, originally built for Manchester's many textiles and industrial workers. At the far end, the road was a dead end. It opened out and there were some newer houses either side. These were set back from the pavement, with small front gardens and entrance porches.

Phil and Chris got out of the car. The house they'd been sent to was behind a short privet hedge. The front garden was full of broken glass, pieces of wood, pots and other debris and the white front door had been smashed in, with just a few parts of the frame left and some shards of glass and reinforcing mesh around the edges.

Phil picked his way through the door, being careful to avoid the sharp glass edges. His trainers crunched on the broken fragments underfoot. The house was a common design in this part of Manchester, and Phil knew the layout before he walked in. In the half-light he could see a staircase leading up and next to it a small alcove containing a pram, some coats and various other household items. On the left was a meter cupboard, a door to a small store and another door leading to the kitchen and then through to the living room, which extended across the rear of the house.

Phil hadn't drawn his baton as he always preferred to use bare hands. This was partly because he'd had martial arts training in aikido and ju-jitsu, the Japanese unarmed combat of the samurai, and partly because it was usually he who handcuffed the suspects, and he didn't want to worry about putting his baton down.

As they entered the hallway they heard muffled sounds from the back of the house, and then a woman screaming. Suddenly, a man with a hood pulled over his head emerged from the door on the left.

'Police, police!' shouted Phil and Chris simultaneously.

The man's eyes widened and for a split second he froze – before turning and running back through the kitchen door and round into the living room at the rear of the house. Phil and Chris gave chase, and as he entered the living room Phil saw a lot of things all at once. To his right were a woman and a teenage boy cowering in the corner, a large man standing over them, while in front of him the hooded man was scrabbling at the back door.

The hooded man at the door was closest, and Phil's training was to focus on the nearest threat. When the man turned back towards him with something in his hand, Phil reached into the large centre pocket of his top. He'd cut a hole in the lining, and he grabbed the CS canister from his equipment harness, pulled it out and sprayed the man in the face. Some people can resist CS spray, but the young man collapsed to the ground almost immediately. The spray wouldn't permanently harm him, but Phil knew from his time in the military, when he'd been exposed to it as part of the training, that it would put him out of action for a while.

The bigger man in the corner spun round to face them, shouting and swearing. He was around six foot four and taller than both Phil and Chris. Without pausing, he lunged at Chris, making a stabbing movement with his right hand. Chris twisted out of the way, to his left.

Chris couldn't see a knife, or any kind of a blade, but he suddenly felt an agonising pain in his right forearm. 'That fucking hurts,' he thought. 'I'm in trouble here.' His arm began to get warm and wet very quickly.

'I've been stabbed!' he said to Phil, then he fell backwards. The big man stepped over him, heading for the kitchen door.

Phil turned round in time to see Chris reeling backwards. His blood ran cold – he hadn't seen the blow or a weapon, but from the way he fell he was sure Chris had been badly – perhaps fatally – wounded. As the intruder moved past Chris, Phil sprang towards him, trying to get him into a headlock and pull him to the ground. He knew that if he could get him down to the floor it would be easier to control him – and harder for the big angry man to do him serious damage.

As they were tussling, Phil felt the man punching at his legs. Suddenly, he felt a sickening pain shoot up towards his groin and had to let go. The big man climbed to his feet and started for the door again. Chris was still in trouble on the ground. Even though Phil was in pain, he was determined that the knifeman shouldn't get away. He leapt at him as he rounded the corner into the kitchen and rugby tackled him. The two burst through the other door that led back into the hallway, then fell together onto the pram and the pile of coats in the alcove beneath the stairs.

As they grappled on the floor, the man tried to headbutt Phil, who noticed he kept reaching for the pockets of his grey hooded top. 'I bet he's got another knife,' he thought, and concentrated on stopping his assailant from getting his hands free. In these circumstances, Phil's martial arts skills were of limited use. If there was space, he could try to get in blows to the man's jaw or body to daze or wind him, always striking with an open hand, never a fist, to avoid breaking his knuckles and incapacitating himself; but grappling on the ground there was no way of striking a meaningful blow.

It was all about holding on, preventing the opponent getting in a punch or a dangerous hold. It was base instinct. But the man seemed to have superhuman strength, and his energy levels seemed not to be falling at all.

In the living room, Chris was shit scared. The intruder had been like a man possessed. He knew that if they couldn't subdue him he'd kill them. Chris was grateful for his thick, black Keela jacket. It meant he couldn't see the wound to his right arm, though he knew it was bleeding heavily. He could hear the sounds of the struggle in the hall, and climbed woozily to his feet. He had to go back and do what he could to help Phil.

In the alcove, Phil could feel himself tiring, his strength ebbing away. His power and energy levels had always been more than enough in fights before, but now he was flagging, and the other man, if anything, seemed to be getting stronger. Suddenly, Phil felt a glancing blow to his back. He realised Chris was standing behind him with his baton drawn, trying to get in strikes on the knifeman. He managed one or two, but then lurched backwards and collapsed again.

Phil and the man continued to writhe around in the alcove. The pain in Phil's knee was causing some difficulty – he thought he must have twisted or dislocated it at the start of the struggle. The fight seemed to be going on forever. Behind him, he heard Chris on his radio asking for help, and the knowledge that reinforcements were on their way seemed to give his aching muscles a surge of strength.

But the fresh energy dissipated all too quickly. Phil knew the neighbourhood officers would still be some minutes away, and at the rate he was tiring, he didn't have minutes left – it was becoming a question of how many more seconds he could last.

Chris couldn't feel any pain, probably because of the adrenaline in his system, but his arm was wet with the blood pouring out. 'Is this my last day of work?' he wondered. He couldn't believe what was happening. The man was tall, but not heavily built. Normally, he and Phil would have easily got the better of him. But he seemed to have the strength of twenty men. Chris was sure he must be on drugs: there was no other explanation for his superhuman strength and stamina. Wearily, Chris climbed to his feet again.

In the hall, the man was still getting stronger and stronger. There was no stopping him, and he seemed to feel no pain. He'd dealt Phil a couple of blows, and at least once had struck Phil's handcuffs with his fist. 'That must've hurt,' thought Phil, but the man had barely flinched.

This was a fight to the death, and Phil was losing. It wouldn't be long now, he thought, before his muscles would no longer have the energy left to obey him. Chris was dead or dying, and soon he would be too. 'I'm done,' thought Phil. 'I've thrown everything but the kitchen sink in here, and he's just not stopping. Soon, when my very last vestige of strength is gone, he'll be able to reach for a weapon and I just won't be able to stop him. This is it.'

As he continued to struggle, almost exhausted, Phil became aware of dark feet approaching. He assumed it was the man he'd sprayed by the back door come to help his accomplice. 'Idiot,' he thought to himself. 'Get ready for a kick in the head.'

But the kick didn't come. The feet were those of the first officer to arrive in response to the emergency message. Unfortunately, as he ran into the house he didn't notice the shards of glass in the doorway and ran into one – suffering a deep cut to his scalp.

Then, with a surge of strength, the assailant forced himself up, despite Phil's eighteen stone weight bearing down on him, and burst towards the stairs. Phil grabbed his legs and the man fell forward, banging his head against the wall and temporarily dazing himself.

Chris, standing behind, realised this was the chance they'd

been waiting for. He dragged the man back down the stairs, and Phil rolled him over and managed to get handcuffs snapped round his wrists. Standard technique is to put the suspect's hands behind his back, but on this occasion Phil was just glad to get some kind of restraint on him. He gave the caution, then lay across the man, physically spent, gasping for air.

'You're dead. You're already dead. You're finished,' the man was snarling insults and threats. 'There's a bullet in your head already.'

'Yeah, whatever,' thought Phil. He couldn't draw breath to reply. And threats from arrested men – while unpleasant – were nothing new.

More uniformed officers were arriving to take over.

'I need to get outside, get some fresh air,' said Chris, and went to sit down in the front garden. A paramedic gave him oxygen, and they cut off his jacket to inspect his wound. The knife had caused a vicious, U-shaped cut and the skin around it had completely peeled back. Chris had lost a lot of blood.

Inside the house, Phil stood up. The other officers were preparing to get the intruder to his feet and take him out to the police van, but the man was still struggling, kicking and shouting.

'You're not going to hold him like that!' said Phil to one of the uniformed officers. He was a fresh-faced probationer, only a couple of weeks in the job. He tightened his grip on the man's arm and nodded. Phil wasn't convinced.

'Are you sure you've got him? I just need to go outside and check on Chris.

'I've got him, yeah,' replied the young officer. Phil turned and walked towards the door. He'd barely managed three steps when he heard a sharp slap and a crunching sound followed by a groan. He turned round. The man had managed to free his hands, and had struck the officer on the face with the handcuffs. The probationer was on the floor with a broken jaw.

Phil ran back, and helped the others restrain the man. He seemed to have become enraged again, and was struggling, lashing out and even trying to bite the officers who were holding him. Eventually, four officers took a limb each, and the man was carried out of the house towards the front gate.

'I'm going to kill you. You're dead. You're going to get shot. Your family are dead!' The man continued to shout threats at Phil and the others.

The street was full of flashing blue lights. There were police cars and vans, firearms vehicles and two ambulances. In the middle was the small black Honda.

As they approached the van, still carrying a wriggling, shouting, spitting suspect, a firearms officer levelled his taser.

'Stop struggling! You're going to get tasered!' he warned. Phil looked up. He knew tasers gave a high voltage charge – would it not have an effect on those carrying the man?

'Don't taser him now while we're all holding him,' he said. 'It'll be one for the papers, this!'

Luckily, the van that had been sent was one of the larger Ford Transits with a large door, making it easier to load an unwilling prisoner. Once the Perspex cage door had snapped shut, Phil relaxed a little, and wandered back down to the grass.

'Are you all right?' asked one of his colleagues.

'Yeah, why?' replied Phil.

'Look at your trainer.' Phil looked down. His trainers had

been white when he put them on, but now the front of one of them was a deep red.

'It must be Chris's blood,' he said. 'It was him got stabbed, not me. Don't worry.' Nevertheless, Phil rolled up the leg of his tracksuit bottoms. Blood was pumping down his leg from wounds on his knee. A paramedic wiped it clean, to discover that there were three deep puncture wounds – one in Phil's knee and two below.

Phil and Chris were taken in one ambulance to a hospital in north Manchester; the officer with the injured head and the probationer with the broken jaw in another.

The woman and her son were shaken but unhurt. They told police that the men had burst into their home, held a knife to their throats and threatened to cut off their hands. The alarm had been raised by the father, who'd escaped by jumping from a first-floor window. He broke his ankle in the fall, but managed to get to a neighbour's house and dial 999.

Chris had eight stitches in his arm wound, and returned to work six weeks later. Although neither Chris nor Phil ever saw the weapon, it was later found to be a bread knife. Although the injury was very painful, no tendons were cut and Chris's arm healed well, albeit with a large purple scar.

Phil's knee recovered within five weeks, but his marriage was almost damaged beyond repair. When he returned home that night he told his wife what had happened, but she had problems dealing with it. She told him she couldn't understand how he could put himself at risk when he had a family at home. Phil tried to explain that it was just part of the job and that events had happened so fast he'd had no real choice, but she couldn't accept it. They eventually worked through their difficulties, but the harm to their relationship was far more painful and enduring than any of his physical injuries.

The arrested man was identified as Leon Smith, who'd only just been released from prison after serving a sentence for another violent attack. Chris and Phil never found out what it was that caused him to have such superhuman strength that night.

The other man who'd been in the house wasn't found.

⟿⟾

Leon Smith had twenty-seven previous convictions – many of them involving violence. He also admitted a separate axe attack on a man the previous year. At his trial, the judge described him as a 'dangerous young man' and jailed him indefinitely for public protection, to serve at least seven and a half years.

Chris Flint and Phil Bainbridge received Chief Constable's Commendations and were nominated for the Police Federation National Bravery Awards. They also received the John Egerton Trophy, named in honour of an officer who was stabbed to death by a burglar and awarded for bravery.

After the trial was over, they received a letter from the woman who lived in the house. In it, she thanked Chris and Phil for risking their lives, and said she was sure they'd saved her life and that of her son.

22

OIL ON THE WATER

'You just needed someone to take action. I didn't want to be in a position where I'm going to look back and regret not getting involved.'

SPC RYAN LAKING

In the mid-twentieth century, Alexandra Dock in Grimsby was at the heart of the self-styled largest fishing port in the world. By the early part of the twenty-first, the fishing fleets were all but gone, and the waters of the docks were becoming silted up and thick with reeds.

Where the River Freshney flows into the southern reach of the dock, bars and shops have replaced fishmongers and warehouses, and canoes and dinghies occupy waters once busy with trawlers and dories.

Gliding along in his kayak, Ryan Laking was well aware that the waters could be treacherous. They weren't deep but could be very cold. Although the quayside was never more than twenty-five yards away, debris and marine plants just below the surface made it necessary to use a technique known as shallow paddling – to ensure the oars don't become snarled up.

After the training session, Ryan and some of his friends from the kayak club went for a drink. The conversation turned to an incident a few days before in which a man had fallen into the water and drowned.

'Police and fire brigade were there,' said one of his friends. 'They were told they couldn't go in. Health and safety.' Ryan knew the emergency services had been much criticised for not entering the water in a rescue attempt. The dead man had been drinking heavily, and had fallen into the water from a low balcony.

'It's winter, though – the water's freezing,' said another friend. Ryan nodded.

'Yeah, but it isn't that deep. I reckon I'd have gone in to get him. Given it a go. At least tried to make a difference,' he said.

'Aye, me too!' agreed the first friend. 'And me!' said the other. The conversation moved on, and all three barely gave it another thought.

By 2008, Ryan was living across the Humber Estuary in Hull and working as an engineer in a factory that made nappies, among other things. He was doing well, and had been given responsibility for the mechanical and electrical engineering requirements of a whole production line.

But though he enjoyed the work, and had earned promotions and pay rises, he felt there was something missing. Engineering work was clear cut: machines either worked, or they did not. The products were either satisfactory or they were not. Ryan wanted a challenge where things weren't quite so black and white, and where identical questions could have very different answers.

At the time, a friend's fiancé was in the police, and Ryan

listened in awe to the stories he told. But he wasn't sure if he was ready for such a drastic career change, and joining the police would mean quite a drop in salary.

'Your job sounds great,' Ryan said, 'but I can't afford to quit at the factory.'

'I'm a special constable,' said the other man. 'I've still got my normal job, but I volunteer. Why not test the water? You'll soon learn if you like it or not.'

Ryan thought about it, and a few weeks later sent in his application to Humberside Police. Special constables are mainly unpaid but have nearly the same powers as regular officers. Specials of some kind or another have been part of British policing since the middle of the nineteenth century. They took on their present form during the First World War, when special constables were asked to take over the duties of the many regular officers who volunteered or were conscripted into the army.

The training lasted six weeks, and Ryan took time off work to get it done as quickly as possible, though others were fitting it around their day jobs. He learned about the law, about what the police could and couldn't do, and took part in numerous training scenarios and role play to teach him how to apply that knowledge. Ryan attested in January 2009, and was out on patrol the next day.

Mick had been drinking for hours. He couldn't remember where he'd started, and couldn't even remember the name of the new friend he'd made earlier that evening. Was it Gareth? Or Gavin? He was a bit confused; earlier the guy had bought him a drink, given him a tenner and said, 'This one's on me.' Now he wanted the money back, and they'd come outside to find a bank.

In Hull city centre, the Thursday night revellers passing by paid little attention to the two drunk men by the cash machine. Mick fumbled to get his bank card out of his wallet. Suddenly, he felt a hand grab his hair and his face was smashed into the glass screen above the machine's keypad. Pain exploded in his nose. His head was pulled back, and smashed into the glass again. Mick slumped to the ground, struggling to defend himself as the other man started punching and kicking him.

'Give me my money,' he shouted, in a drunken rage. 'Give me the fuckin' money back.' Mick tried to defend himself, but he was drunk and half-dazed. Suddenly, the blows stopped and the man laughed.

'Ah, come on,' he said. 'Let's get you on your feet.' Mick looked up. The man reached down to him, and began pulling Mick up. He stood shakily, wondering what had happened.

'You're all right, you're all right,' said the man. Then his face hardened. 'Who the fuck do you think you are? Think you can take the piss out of me?' Suddenly, Mick felt another vicious blow to the side of his head, then another, causing his ears to ring. A hard punch to his midriff knocked the wind out of him and he doubled up, collapsing to the ground again. Blood was streaming from his nose, his mouth, his head. Pathetically, he held up his wallet and mobile phone.

'Take 'em,' he sobbed. 'Just leave me alone.' The blows rained down again and again. As Mick lay curled up on the ground in a world filled with fear and pain, all he could think was please let it end.

Ryan was on patrol with Paul Stanley, a regular officer. It was mid-April, still only four months since he had taken his oath, and he was not yet experienced enough to take to the streets alone. The night was bitterly cold, and it felt as though winter had not yet yielded to the onset of spring. Ryan's hands were particularly cold, and his fingers were turning numb every time he took out his notepad to write. Ryan could have gone off duty at midnight, but was keen to stay on and get in some extra hours.

'Any units Jameson Street? CCTV operators reporting a male outside McDonald's restaurant assaulting another male.' The message came through on the radios of both officers.

'Delta X-ray one one,' replied Paul. 'SPC Laking and I will attend.' Ryan and Paul were outside Pozition, a well-known nightclub at the eastern end of the city. They began making their way west. Jameson Street wasn't far away, and they knew that McDonald's was on the corner of the pedestrianised area in the city centre.

Even though it was after 2 a.m., the streets were fairly busy. As they approached, they saw a man kicking and punching another man who was slumped on the ground. He was clearly begging his assailant to stop, and trying to hand over his mobile phone and wallet. As Ryan and Paul broke into a run, a police car appeared and two other officers got out. They took hold of the attacker.

Ryan went straight to the injured man. He was in his mid-thirties and fairly heavy-set. He had blood down his t-shirt and was slowly getting to his feet.

'Are you all right, mate?' asked Ryan, but before he got a response the man who'd been arrested started shouting and lashing out. Ryan stood up and went to help his colleagues. Eventually the four officers managed to subdue the prisoner, but when Ryan turned back the injured man was gone.

As the other two officers put the attacker in the car to

take him into custody, Ryan contacted the council-operated CCTV control room. He gave them a description of the man, and asked if they could see where he'd gone. Ryan was worried that he'd been hurt during the attack, and felt he ought at least ensure that he was given a medical check-up. He also realised that they'd need to get some kind of statement from him about what had happened for any future court proceedings.

Before long, the CCTV unit told Ryan they'd picked up the wounded man heading towards another well-known bar in a redeveloped dock called Princess Quay. Ryan asked the operator to contact Civic – a council initiative that enabled the police to quickly contact security staff working in the city – and request the bar's doormen stop the man until he and Paul could get there.

But by the time the officers reached the bar, barely two or three minutes later, the man was gone. A bloodied, dazed drunk was hardly good for business, and it didn't surprise Paul that the door staff hadn't tried to keep him there.

The CCTV operator scanned the camera feeds. He radioed through to Ryan and Paul that the man seemed to be approaching the old docks. As the operator watched, he fell over a wall, then staggered across a busy road towards Hull Marina.

'OK, he's crossing the wooden bridge to get into the marina. He's walking along the side, by the water. Hang on, I've lost him again.' The CCTV operator had been following the man from camera to camera, but the one by the marina had a malfunctioning servo and he was struggling to keep it focused.

In Hull, as in many former ports, the old commercial

dock had been reinvented for private leisure use; freighters and barges had given way to much smaller pleasure boats and yachts.

'Got him again. He's moving along the wharf between the boats and the buildings. He's next to a fence.' Listening to the running commentary from the CCTV operator, Ryan and Paul quickened their pace. They knew the man was unsteady on his feet, and there was a chance he might fall into the dock.

'The male's in the water, the male's in the water and hasn't come back up. I can't locate him.' Ryan and Paul ran across the main road and over the wooden footbridge into the marina. The dock was around 200 yards long and 50 yards wide. The CCTV operator directed them to the point where the man had last been seen, near the water's edge. They stood on the wharf, a large warehouse behind them. The still black water reflected the blocks of modern residential flats on the other side.

Ryan and Paul peered over the edge, looking for ripples and listening. There was no moonlight and the waters were dark, cold and forbidding. It was deathly quiet. All they could hear was the gentle creaking of the rigging. The silence was disconcerting. Ryan had felt sure that they would easily find the man, that he'd be splashing around.

Designed for large cutters and freighters, the quayside walls were around eight feet high. Ryan lay face down on the edge to look more closely at the water. There was something odd about it. Reflected in the street lighting, he could see an oily sheen on the surface, but directly below him there was a large round patch that was clear. It dawned on him what he was looking it.

'This is where he's fallen in and broken through the surface.

He went in right here.' But there was no sign of the man resurfacing. Had he been so drunk that the shock of the cold water had sent him into a stupor? Had he already drowned? Ryan's mind was racing. He needed to get closer to the water.

A short gantry led down to rows of floating pontoons that provided berthing for the boats, but it was fenced off. He tried the gate; it was locked.

'I'll contact control to see if they can locate the key-holder,' said Paul. 'There may be an office or a caretaker round here somewhere.'

Ryan nodded. 'We can't just stand here. I'm going to try to climb onto that gantry.' In the water was a floating platform with a long walkway extending from it, parallel to the side of the dock. The walkway was too far to jump to, but the platform was nearer. It was protected by a section of security fencing that projected about six feet out over the water, but Ryan thought he might be able to climb along the fence, then swing down beneath it and onto the platform.

Ryan admitted to himself that there was a good chance he'd slip and fall into the water, especially as his hands were already numb. He unclipped his radio and his utility belt, and took off his fleece and stab vest. Because he'd be hanging by his arms, he wanted to make himself as light as possible.

The metal fence was so cold that he half-expected his palms to freeze and stick to it. He gripped the fence, then lowered himself down, hanging over the water. He moved sideways along the fence, his toes just clear of the water. He could feel the sharp metal of the fence cutting into his fingers. Finally he managed to twist round beneath the fence, so he was hanging from the other side, then pushed back and dropped down onto the platform.

He started running along the floating wooden walkway, looking for any trace of the man. From the quayside above, Paul watched the water.

'There might be something there,' he said, pointing. Ryan ran towards the indicated spot. Nothing.

'Maybe there?' said Paul, pointing again. Ryan ran back and forth along the walkway, and out onto the pontoons that stretched out into the centre of the dock at right angles. There were around half a dozen pleasure-cruisers and yachts moored nearby.

Suddenly, he heard a loud splash and turned round. At the back of a nearby boat he saw a figure emerge, his arms reaching up, gulping in a shuddering gasp of air. The man's skin was pale, and he looked very weak. His t-shirt was stuck to his body and Ryan could see blood on his chest and cuts on his arms. Knowing where he'd fallen into the dock, Ryan guessed he'd drifted beneath the walkway and become stuck, then managed to free himself. The man sank back into the water, just about keeping afloat. He looked as though he had barely any strength remaining.

'Paul!' shouted Ryan. 'I've found him – he's here.' Up on the quayside, Paul nodded and radioed for an ambulance to be sent. Ryan ran along the end of the jetty, as near as he could get to the man.

'Try and get to me, try to reach me,' he called out. The man looked over, and nodded weakly. He was a few feet from an old, slightly tatty, sailing boat, and he grabbed the propeller of a small outboard motor clamped to the stern that was raised out of the water. As he tried to pull himself up, the propeller span round and his hand slid off. He dropped back into the water. He was exhausted. He looked over at Ryan, and then his eyes rolled up into the back of his head and he slipped beneath the water.

Ryan realised that the man wasn't going to come back up; that he had used up his last precious reserves of strength in reaching for the propeller; that he had nothing left. Ryan looked at the water; at the ripples dwindling. This, he thought, was the moment at which a man could lose his life. This is how it can happen, quietly and without fuss.

Ryan remembered his kayaking days in Grimsby long ago, when the man had drowned. He recalled what he'd boasted to his friends: that he'd have tried to make a difference. This was his chance to prove it.

Ryan called to Paul that he was going in, then jumped. As he hit the water, he slapped down hard with his hands to stop his head going under. The shock of the cold stunned him, but he began swimming over to where he'd last seen the man. When he reached the side of the old boat, the man hadn't surfaced again, so Ryan held his breath and dropped down under the water, feeling around. His feet were churning up rubbish and debris, and his fingertips brushed against pieces of tangled wire. Things, he thought, you could easily get snagged up in. He had to find the man quickly.

Ryan dived under again, and this time his fingers brushed against something different, something smooth and soft. With his right hand, he gripped a fold of the man's skin and pulled. The man was surprisingly buoyant and rose back up to the surface. Ryan rolled him into the classic lifesaving position and began to swim for the walkway where he'd jumped in.

The man was delirious, and began groaning and retching. Ryan imagined he'd swallowed a fair amount of the filthy, oily water. He tried slapping the man's cheeks and talking to him, but there was no obvious response.

When they reached the walkway, Ryan tried to push the man up out of the water, but he was far too heavy. Ryan began to worry. The man's skin felt cold and lifeless and was completely white, with no colour at all. He'd been in the water for several minutes, was desperately cold and had been deprived of oxygen. But Ryan wasn't ready to let him die. He pushed again, bracing himself against the man's back and forcing him out of the water. The man began to struggle and kick. Though this was awkward, at least it meant he was still alive.

At this moment, the key-holder arrived on the quayside and unlocked the gate. Paul ran down the jetty to where Ryan was struggling. Ryan looked up with a sigh of relief as Paul grabbed the man's arms and took his weight. The adrenaline had started to wear off, and the paralysing cold of the water was also taking its toll; Ryan was tiring quickly. He clung to the sharp metal edge of the jetty, barely feeling it cutting into his fingers.

Ryan closed his eyes briefly, and suddenly the narrow walkway seemed full of people and the dock bathed in flashing blue light. Two firefighters managed to pull the injured man out of the water and paramedics immediately wrapped a blanket around him. He was lying on his back and his head rolled towards Ryan. He coughed up dark brown water, and he was almost totally limp. There isn't a lot of life left in him, thought Ryan, but there's some, and that's enough . . .

Ryan was taken home quickly to change his clothes. He also vomited up some of the foul, oily dock water he had swallowed. In the police station there was a buzz, but as he walked into the report writing room, his boots squelching, it fell quiet. Then, as one, all his colleagues stood up and applauded. They gathered round to shake his hand or hug him. His supervisor ordered him to go to the hospital for a quick check-up. As Ryan walked in, two green-suited paramedics were leaving. One of them turned to him.

'It was you, wasn't it? You went in the water?' They were the two who'd treated the injured man on the jetty.

'Yes. Yes, I did,' replied Ryan. 'How is he?'

'He's been better, but he'll be all right,' replied the paramedic, then paused and looked Ryan in the eye.

'You saved his life. Come with me.' He led Ryan to the open door of the treatment room. The man was lying on a bed sleeping. Monitors confirmed that his vital signs were strong.

Ryan had made a difference.

❦

The attacker was convicted of assault and given a suspended prison sentence. He was also ordered to pay compensation of £1000, and complete 200 hours of unpaid community work. He breached the terms of his order, was rearrested and served ten months in prison.

'Mick' recovered, but neither he nor his family made any attempt to contact Ryan or thank him.

Ryan received a Chief Constable's Commendation for his actions, and won Humberside Police's Keith Binks Silver Trophy for special constables. His abiding memory of the award ceremony was that he had never seen his father so proud.

23

UNDEAD OR ALIVE?

'She stopped and turned and looked me directly in the eye. But behind those eyes there was nothing. She was totally vacant. Zombiefied.'

PC JACQUI ELLIS

For PC Jacqui Ellis it had been a routine morning, almost bordering on dull. She'd come on at seven o'clock, attended a couple of house burglaries and taken some statements. Now she was back at Boscombe police station, in Dorset, going through her paperwork and thinking about having her lunch.

Then a report came in from an ambulance crew. It had a flash priority: the most urgent, which demanded that any available officer should attend.

'Ambulance crew attending address in Queensland Road but confronted by woman with a knife. Now waiting nearby for police assistance.' Unsurprisingly, when faced with a weapon, the ambulance crew had retreated and called for police back-up. Jacqui knew that such calls often turned out to be false alarms or misunderstandings, but she and her colleagues had to treat each one as a genuine threat until they were sure it was not.

'Bravo Bravo four four attending,' she said into her radio, and went down to the yard. Jacqui hadn't been trained as a response driver, so she wasn't authorised to drive beyond the speed limit. She watched as her colleagues in the incident car, call sign Bravo Bravo four nine, drove out ahead of her and roared off down the street with lights flashing and sirens wailing. Jacqui followed at a more sedate – and legal – thirty miles an hour.

Jacqui had come to the police later than most. She'd grown up in Dorset, but at the age of twenty-two had decided to go travelling. She'd planned to be away for a year, but after being offered a job by a New York art house as an auctioneer she decided to stay. The job took her all the way from Manhattan to Brazil and across the Americas, calling the price of not-quite-priceless artworks.

Her favourite painter was Peter Max, a graphic designer who reinvented himself as an artist and made his name with the 'cosmic' style of bright, primary colours and cartoon-like psychedelic imagery that came to define the late 1960s. Peter Max's ambling figures with their long feet and flared trousers graced bedroom posters and album covers, and he once painted a piano for ex-Beatle Ringo Starr. Never forgetting his commercial roots, Peter Max also designed artwork for a Boeing 777 airliner and a 4000-berth cruise ship. In recent years, his style had become more avowedly patriotic, and he produced numerous paintings after 9/11, featuring brightly coloured renditions of the Stars and Stripes or the Statue of Liberty. On one occasion, Jacqui sold six original paintings by Peter Max to the same woman, an eccentric collector who attended the auction barefoot and, Jacqui was told solemnly, never wore shoes.

301

But after seven entertaining years, Jacqui decided it was time to rediscover her roots, and she returned home to Dorset. She needed a new job, but she had no idea what. Scouring the pages of the local newspaper, she spotted a recruitment advertisement for civilian custody officers with Dorset Police. 'That might be a bit different,' she thought to herself, and almost on a whim she applied.

Four months later, she walked into Bournemouth police station cells in her brand new uniform for her first day as a gaoler. What a shock! In her former life in the world of fine art she'd been used to dealing with people who were rich or cultured or, very occasionally, both. This was very different.

The cell block in Bournemouth at that time was full of character but outdated for modern needs. It made for challenging working conditions at times, but Jacqui loved it. As well as working in Bournemouth, she guarded the prisoners in Weymouth, Poole and Christchurch, and got to know many of the police officers who shared similar shift patterns. Hearing about their work, and seeing the results of it, Jacqui decided after four years in the cells that she wanted to be a police officer too.

Although her application was successful, she had to wait some time for a position to arise but finally, in January 2008, she arrived at Boscombe police station for her first full day. She was usually sent out on her own – single crewed, in police jargon – and to start with always made sure she had a map book with her, as she wasn't that familiar with the area.

But two and a half years later, in August 2010, she didn't need to follow the incident car to find her way to Queensland Road, where the ambulance crew were waiting.

Up ahead she saw her colleagues turn left, and as she approached the T-junction she indicated to do the same. Her lights weren't flashing and the traffic was fairly heavy, so passing motorists saw no reason to let her out. While she was waiting, Jacqui saw a man standing on the pavement on the other side of the road, waving frantically. He seemed to be in his mid-twenties and was wearing a baseball cap. Jacqui's chest was pounding. She was on an emergency call, and the seconds were ticking by! 'Sorry, mate,' she thought, 'but I've got a job to go to here.' Then she looked over to where he was pointing, and her heart almost stopped.

A woman in a bright yellow t-shirt was walking slowly but purposefully in the opposite direction. Jacqui wasn't sure what she spotted first: that her clothing was heavily bloodstained or that she was carrying a large shining kitchen knife.

'Four nine must have driven right past her,' thought Jacqui, and as she pulled out of the junction, turning right, not left, she quickly radioed in.

'Bravo Bravo four four, I've seen a female with a knife on Christchurch Road. I believe she's possibly something to do with this incident.' As she stopped her car and got out, Jacqui looked again at the woman. She was white, a little taller than Jacqui at around five foot six, with shoulder length brown hair. She had blood on her face, her t-shirt and down the legs of her blue jeans. The knife was also heavily bloodstained.

Jacqui looked around. They were next to a school on a busy road, just after lunchtime. There seemed to be pedestrians everywhere. The woman seemed to be walking both purposefully and deliberately but without any clear direction. Jacqui had never seen anything quite like it.

A mother holding hands with two small children was

walking directly towards them. She was talking to the children and not looking where she was going. Oblivious to the danger, she was leading the children right towards the knife-woman.

Jacqui had no choice. She had to distract the woman with the knife – even though it would clearly put her in danger.

'Am going to approach the female now,' said Jacqui into her radio, and took out her Pava incapacitant spray. It wasn't much but it was all she had.

The woman with the children was now just a few feet away. The knife-woman appeared to be walking straight towards them. Jacqui wondered what she could do. The priority seemed simply to be to divert her attention. Jacqui drew herself up to her full five feet four inches, and stepped alongside the woman with the knife.

'Hello!' she said brightly, walking beside her. The knife-woman paid no attention, but the mother with her children looked up and suddenly took in the situation. She looked right at Jacqui and the message in her eyes was clear. 'You're a police officer – what are you going to do about this woman with a knife?'

'Police. You need to stop,' Jacqui said, raising her voice. The knife-woman suddenly stopped and turned to face her. Jacqui looked into her eyes and saw . . . nothing. She was totally vacant. There was no emotion: just blank, lifeless eyes and a slow, dead walk. 'You're like a zombie,' thought Jacqui. 'You look as if you've been zombiefied.'

Then the woman started her slow, deliberate walk straight towards Jacqui. It was unnerving. She seemed more than ever like the living dead. Jacqui could see the knife in her clenched fist. It was so huge! She backed away towards the kerb.

'Put the knife down! Put the knife down!' Jacqui shouted with increasing urgency, but there wasn't a flicker of recognition or acknowledgement from the woman, who kept moving towards her. Not seeing any emotion at all scared Jacqui more than seeing anger or fury or fear. She pressed down hard on the button of her Pava spray canister, and watched as a narrow jet of liquid arced out from the nozzle.

Pava spray is an incapacitant increasingly favoured by UK police forces, as it's considered both safer and more powerful than CS gas. Developed from pepper spray, it uses a chemical irritant that causes the sensation of intense burning in the eyes. The effects are temporary and in outdoor conditions will clear within fifteen to twenty minutes, but Pava only works if it enters the eye.

'Bullseye!' thought Jacqui, as she watched the jet of Pava spray hit the woman right in the eyes. It seemed to have no effect.

'Shit!' thought Jacqui. 'Fucking hell! It's not worked!' Jacqui had been told during training that in extreme circumstances it was possible that individuals could be resistant to Pava, but this was no time to see the theory proved. The woman was still coming forward.

Jacqui had no choice. Her hand flashed out, and she gripped the knife arm with one hand, then grabbed the woman with the other, twisted her round, took hold of the back of her head and pushed her into the brick wall at the back of the pavement. Jacqui heard the knife clatter to the ground, and realised the woman had dropped it almost as soon as she had been grabbed.

Jacqui pressed the woman into the wall to keep her secure, then reached for her radio to alert the rest of the team. The woman was struggling a little, nothing Jacqui couldn't handle but a concern nonetheless. And Jacqui had another worry: where was the knife?

She looked around. There it was: lying on the pavement about four feet away. A couple of people had gathered round it, and it looked as though one helpful soul was about to pick it up and pass it to her. She didn't want anyone touching it for two reasons: first, it was a dangerous weapon, and second, she didn't want the forensic evidence on it contaminated.

'Leave it!' she shouted. 'Leave the knife alone! Don't touch it and don't move it. Leave it on the ground!' The passers-by looked around sharply, and stepped away.

Within seconds, Jacqui's two colleagues from the four nine car, PCs Martin Pace and Mike Stewart, had arrived, and they started securing the area so that forensic work could begin.

Jacqui breathed a sigh of relief, then arrested the woman for attempted murder. She pulled her arms around behind, snapped on the handcuffs and walked her over to a police van that had just pulled up. The woman was calm and made no effort to resist. As they climbed into the van, Jacqui heard her sergeant at the other location radio in to control that the case was now a possible Code 200. Sometimes it was useful to talk in code to avoid bystanders or residents overhearing and immediately overreacting. Jacqui knew that Code 200 meant the victim at the other location had died.

Jacqui searched the woman, then sat her down in the van. Another message came through confirming the Code 200, and advising that the victim was her prisoner's mother. Jacqui looked over at the woman sitting quietly in the van. She'd started to lose her zombie expression but still seemed to be in another world.

Jackie sat next to her, then told her she was being arrested for murder – the murder of her mother. For the first time, Jacqui saw a flicker of emotion cross the woman's face, and heard the faintest of whimpers. Then nothing. The only emotional clue she could see was a slight redness and watering around the eyes, but that, thought Jacqui, was more likely to be the after effects of the Pava spray. Jacqui's own eyes were a little sore: it felt as though some of the chemical had splashed back and hit her. Jacqui didn't rub her eyes but kept them as wide open as she could bear. The fastest route to recovery was, she knew, simply to allow air to dry them out and evaporate any residual irritant.

Despite what had happened, Jacqui felt perfectly calm. Knowing police procedures, she was well aware that her job wasn't over yet. In TV dramas the cops all go for a pint as soon as the van carrying the suspect drives away, but Jacqui knew there'd be plenty more for her to do.

The van was driven down to the custody centre at Bournemouth police station. Jacqui was just about to get out with her prisoner when she was told to wait. Senior officers were trying to decide whether they needed to seize the van as a second crime scene. Jacqui was perplexed, but realised there was nothing she could do but wait. Forty minutes later, she was finally allowed out of the van and asked to bring the woman into the cells.

Because the woman was clearly suffering from mental health problems, it was decided that she should be kept under constant observation. Jacqui was asked to stay with her in the cell.

'Right,' said Jacqui gently. 'You've got me staying with you for the time being. What are we going to talk about then, eh?'

There was no response from the woman, though she'd started rocking back and forth and staring around the room in an unnerving way.

'How are those handcuffs? Are they hurting a bit?' Jacqui knew that after a time the rear handcuff position got very uncomfortable. 'Come on, let's put them round to the front for you.'

The woman was totally passive as Jacqui unlocked the handcuffs, moved them around to the front and reapplied them. Jacqui kept up a stream of conversation, but the woman didn't respond. She kept rocking back and forth, mumbling and staring around the room. There was no other way of putting it: to Jacqui, she looked like a mad person.

Finally, after about four hours, the major crime unit arrived to deal with her and Jacqui was allowed to leave. A mental health expert also came to assess the woman, along with a so-called appropriate adult. All were in their white paper forensic suits to minimise the possibility of DNA cross-contamination. Since Jacqui had been with the woman throughout the entire incident, there was no need for a paper suit for her.

Jacqui wandered back upstairs to the booking-in desk. She lurked around, waiting to get a lift back to Boscombe with a colleague.

'Jacqui!' She turned round as she heard her name – it was one of the custody sergeants hurrying up from the cells.

'We need you downstairs. You've obviously built up a rapport, and no one else can get through to her. Can you please come down and see if you can get her to talk to the mental health people and the psychiatrists?' Jacqui nodded, and went back downstairs.

When she went back into the cell, there was a flicker of recognition from the woman. Jacqui sat next to her again, and began to explain what was going to happen.

'These officers in white suits are going to have to take swabs,' she said. 'They're going to be combing your hair, scraping underneath your nails, that kind of thing. Do you understand?' The woman seemed to acknowledge what Jacqui was saying, though it was clear she was only just taking it in.

'There are also psychiatrists who want to help you,' added Jacqui. Though there was no sign the woman understood, she knew there was little more she could do, and she left.

When Jacqui arrived back at Boscombe, she started to type up her statement.

'There's a debrief downstairs in the canteen in a couple of minutes. You coming?' asked a colleague, putting his head round the door. She nodded.

A few moments later, Jacqui walked through the double doors to the canteen. As she did so, the other officers stood up and gave her a round of applause. She felt a surge of warmth and camaraderie, and smiled, embarrassed. It had been a long and trying day, and while unexpected the gesture was very welcome.

There was more paperwork, and her uniform had to be taken to be used in evidence, but finally it was all done, and around thirteen hours after she came on duty Jacqui walked out of the police station.

As she pedalled home, Jacqui found her mind spinning with the events of the day. One woman had lost her life; another's would never be the same again. A daughter had lost her mother. It all seemed so sad.

It was almost dark, and it's unlikely that any of those out walking that evening paid much attention to the cyclist passing by, or noticed the shining tears streaming down her face.

◈

Ecila Henderson was originally charged with murdering her mother, Rosemary Armstrong, but her plea of guilty to the lesser charge of manslaughter on the grounds of diminished responsibility was accepted. She was given an indefinite hospital order by the judge.

PC Jacqui Ellis received a Chief Constable's Commendation and was nominated to represent Dorset at the National Police Bravery Awards in 2012.

24

THE STRAIGHT AND VERY NARROW

'I knew there was a sheer drop either side, but I wasn't looking at the surroundings. I was looking at him. And concentrating on him.'

PC IAN AINSLEY

On a clear day, twenty-five miles of coastline is visible from the cliffs at Seaham in County Durham: from the Souter Lighthouse at South Shields in the north to the towering blast furnaces of Redcar in the south. But at half past six the sun had not yet risen, and all PC Ian Ainsley could see as he was driving to work was a soft orange glow on the horizon and the outlines of buildings and trees that were no longer dark but not yet light.

Ian lived in the East Shore village – a new housing development built on the site of what was once Vane Tempest colliery, a deep-mine pit that employed 1000 men. The mine workings extended far out beneath the North Sea, 500 feet underground. When the pit closed in 1993, the vertical main shafts were filled in so the houses could be built above, but the tunnels beneath the water remained.

Ian had grown up in Seaham, and it had been expected

that he'd follow his father and his brother down the pit, but when Ian left school he joined Rolls-Royce in Sunderland and worked as an engineer fitting fan blades to the company's successful RB-211 series jet engines. After eight years, he was tired of working in the factory and wanted a change of career. During a visit to Sunderland job centre in the mid-1980s, he noticed that both Bedfordshire Police and the Metropolitan Police were recruiting. He applied, and was offered jobs by both forces; he chose Bedfordshire because it was slightly nearer to home.

Arriving at his new job, Ian was given a bedroom in police flats at Luton and told he needed to specialise. He joined the firearms unit, but by the mid-1990s he wanted to move back up north, so transferred to Durham Police. After a couple of years working the beat, he joined the firearms unit in his new force, and eventually became the oldest firearms officer in the combined Cleveland and Durham traffic and firearms unit.

Ian was also a keen sea fisherman – competing with the British police fishing team – and as he drove along the coast road he noticed something odd: a fisherman standing on a well-known cliff top.

Known as Featherbed Rock, it was a small headland that jutted out into the North Sea from the main cliff face; a narrow ridge stretching over 150 feet into the water with a sheer drop on either side and a craggy point at the tip.

The 100-foot-high cliff edge all around the promontory was notoriously treacherous; like much of the coastline in the north-east of England it was made of crumbly glacial clay deposits and limestone. The unrelenting action of the sea was rapidly eroding it away, and sudden landslips were commonplace. For that reason, fishing there was expressly banned.

As he looked again towards the point, Ian realised the man had disappeared. Where had he gone? Had he jumped?

Ian pulled over and got out of the car. The skies were brightening but it was a bitterly cold morning. On one side of the coast road were the houses and shops forming the edge of Seaham town, the other opening out onto a fifty-yard stretch of grassland leading to the cliffs. The only other person he could see was a woman walking a small Jack Russell terrier.

Ian ran towards the headland. It was fenced off, with a sign warning walkers of the danger.

There was still no sign of the man. Ian knew that if he'd jumped or fallen it was a sheer drop onto the rocks below. He sighed. He'd have to confirm the location of the body and make arrangements for it to be recovered.

He climbed over the fence and started out along the narrow path on the very top of the ridge that stuck out into the sea. It rapidly narrowed to a grass strip roughly five feet wide, with the sheer, red-brown cliffs on either side. Because the area was off limits, the grass had become long and unkempt. It was uneven under foot, and Ian stepped forward slowly and carefully, trying to ignore the drop either side and the strong sea breeze that threatened to lift him up and carry him over the edge.

On one side, Ian could see evidence of a recent landslip; the edge of the path looked as if a bite had been taken out of it, and far below was a fresh pile of powdery clay and rubble.

As Ian approached the tip of the Featherbed Rock, he realised the man had not jumped, nor had he fallen. At the end the path sloped down, and at the very tip there was a narrow ledge that couldn't be seen from further back. The man was on his knees, leaning forward and peering over the edge.

'Hey, mate,' shouted Ian. 'Is everything all right?' There was no response. Ian looked more closely. The man was no fisherman: he had no equipment and was wearing just jeans and a t-shirt. He was shaking violently, either through fear or cold or both.

Ian was worried now. He called to the man again, and again there was no response. Whatever the man's intentions, Ian had a duty of care. 'I'm going to have to get my hands on him and restrain him,' he thought, but that wasn't easy. The man was on the edge of a sheer drop of around ninety feet. Any sudden movement might cause the man to jump or, worse, the cliff edge to crumble. And Ian couldn't approach him too quickly: if he slipped or lost his footing, the combination of the downward slope and his own momentum would probably take them both over the edge. By now, Ian was within ten feet of the man. The narrow ledge was barely three feet wide. Slowly, Ian approached him. The man remained oblivious, and the strong wind hid the sound of his approach. Ian reached forward, and firmly grabbed the man's right shoulder, pulling him round and onto his back, then knelt astride him. The man was still shaking violently, but offered no resistance. Now he was closer, Ian could smell alcohol.

'Have you been drinking or taking drugs?' he asked. The man nodded. Ian decided to be direct.

'I'm a police officer. I need to know: were you going to harm yourself?'

'Yes,' the man replied, speaking for the first time. 'I'm going to kill myself.' He told Ian he'd been on the cliff for several hours, after spending the night drinking in the town centre, and had decided to take his own life.

He explained that he was suffering from Huntington's disease, an incurable condition that was causing muscle spasms. It was inherited: he and his twin brother were both sufferers, and his sister had recently died of the condition. It would also reduce his lifespan and that, more than the symptoms or the side effects, was what he couldn't bear.

Ian knew he had to get the man off the headland and back to safety. He reached for his phone – then realised he'd left it in the car. Stupid! He certainly couldn't leave the man here while he went to fetch it. Then he remembered the woman he'd seen with the dog. He might be able to get her attention – but while he was here on his knees he was hidden by the dip in the rock.

He needed to stand up – but he was on a three-foot ledge, with a 100-foot drop all around and a man at his feet who wanted to kill himself. Ian was considerably taller and heavier than the man, but it wouldn't take that much strength to send them both over the edge – especially if Ian was distracted. Did he have a choice? Ian couldn't think of any other way of summoning help – and he needed to get them both off the cliff as quickly as possible.

He put his feet either side of the man's chest, just beneath his armpits, and stood up. Using his full six foot three inches of height he could just see far enough. The woman was still there! He shouted and waved his arms, and she looked over, startled. Ian didn't want to alarm her, so after identifying himself as a police officer he simply told her to dial 999 and to tell the controller the location, his name, and that urgent assistance was required.

As soon as he was sure she'd understood and was making the call, he crouched down again. It had taken just twenty seconds. Now he turned his attention back to the suicidal man.

Although not trained himself, during his firearms duties Ian had often observed police negotiators in action and understood some of the core principles. He wanted to develop a dialogue with the man.

'Have you got any kids?' he asked. 'Do you want me to let your family know you're OK?'

'Don't worry. My daughter's got her own life and her own family, and me and my wife are separated.' Ian tried again.

'Is there any treatment you need? I can help you.' Ian could tell the man wasn't really listening. Ian tried asking about football – the majority of people in Seaham were Sunderland AFC fans – and about where the man had been the previous evening. It was no good. The man's mind was elsewhere.

It wasn't long before Ian heard the sirens and realised back-up had arrived. Two of his colleagues from the traffic unit – PC Glen Henderson and a young officer whom Ian was tutoring, PC Andrew Guest – were first on the scene. They'd been at the police station waiting to go out on patrol with Ian, and when they heard the call come through – and the mention of Ian's name – they immediately drove down.

'Right, come on,' said Ian to the man underneath him. 'Let's go to the police station and go and have a crack-on – a little chat. You're not under arrest or being detained. Just come back with me and we'll get you sorted out.' The man didn't resist, and Ian helped him to his feet. He put his hands firmly on the man's shoulders, and slowly walked him back along the exposed, narrow path.

His colleagues were waiting – Ian had warned them not to step too far onto the dangerous outcrop – and they all drove to the police station. Ian sat and talked to the man for an hour while they awaited the arrival of a crisis team.

Eventually, the man agreed to be admitted to hospital to be treated for both his illness and his state of mind, and he was taken away.

A week later, Ian was at home when his phone rang. It was a fellow police officer. As usual, news of the rescue had filtered through the station, and most of Ian's colleagues knew what he'd done.

'I thought you ought to know,' he said to Ian. 'That man you got off the cliff – his body's just been found washed up on the beach. It looks as though he threw himself off the pier.'

Ian thanked his colleague for letting him know and sat down. He felt sad, and desperately sorry. He'd hoped perhaps that by saving the man's life once he'd managed to convince him – by word or deed – that it was a life worth saving.

Sadly, he hadn't. The man's overwhelming sense of hopelessness had proved too much, and the grey sea had taken him.

⋘∞⋙

PC Ian Ainsley was awarded a Royal Humane Society Testimonial on Parchment for putting himself in danger to save the man's life.

25

AT THE SHARP END

'The first thing I saw was their balaclavas and their machetes.
And I thought "Oh shit! What am I going to do here?"'

PC SAILESH PATEL

The three-litre V6 Vectra was spotless. PC Sailesh Patel looked on approvingly. It wasn't every day that he took a chief inspector out on duty with him, and he wanted to make the right impression.

Sailesh had loved cars for as long as he could remember. He'd been born in Uganda, where his grandfather owned a large and successful hardware business, but the family had fled with nothing when dictator Idi Amin ordered the expulsion of the country's Asian population in the early 1970s.

Sailesh's parents had settled in Bolton, Lancashire, when he was still a toddler, and he had no recollection of their former life. One of his earliest memories was of a police Ford Capri driving past in Bolton town centre. To the young Sailesh the bright orange and white car seemed impossibly exciting and glamorous, and he vowed one day to drive one.

After leaving school, he took an apprenticeship as a mechanic, but the garage closed down. He applied to join the police but didn't get in, so he found a job as a bus driver to make ends meet and eventually saved enough to buy an off-licence. After five years he realised shop-keeping wasn't for him, and decided to give the police another try. This time he was successful, and he joined as a section officer in Bury. Over the intervening years the cars might have changed but the dream had not, and seven years later, at the age of thirty-nine, Sailesh fulfilled his ambition to become a traffic officer.

On that September morning in 2011, Sailesh had been told that a chief inspector wanted to spend a day with the unit to get an understanding of how they operated. Sailesh agreed to drive from his base at Leigh to Eccles to pick her up at the traffic network centre and take her out on patrol.

After giving the car a thorough clean, he drove out of the compound and turned onto Warrington Road. He planned to drive down to Greyhound Island, a large roundabout south of Leigh, and then join the East Lancs Road, a dual carriageway that would take him virtually straight there.

Just before the roundabout, there was a hump bridge where the road crossed over Glaze Brook, a small waterway that fed into the Manchester Ship Canal. As usual during the morning rush-hour the traffic was fairly heavy, but Sailesh had given himself plenty of time and wasn't in a hurry. As he neared the bridge, a bright yellow Mini bounced over it, coming towards him at high speed in the middle of the road. The Mini was swerving around slower traffic, and as Sailesh slammed on his brakes it cut in front of him, just avoiding a collision.

'Foxtrot Mike, vehicle driving at high speed northbound on Warrington Road, a yellow Mini. Will follow.' Sailesh switched on his lights and sirens and immediately did a three-point turn in the middle of the carriageway while craning his neck to keep an eye on the yellow car.

In the busy traffic it didn't take long for Sailesh to catch up. The Mini was zig-zagging in between other vehicles, and he held back a little to avoid causing an accident or injury to the numerous pedestrians, including schoolchildren, on either side of the road.

He could see there were three figures inside the car, and he called in the registration number, keeping up a running commentary on the pursuit as is standard practice.

'Suspect vehicle slowing, slowing, has turned right into Butts Road.' As he turned in to follow, Sailesh was around two car lengths behind the Mini. It was moving from side to side, almost as if the driver couldn't decide what to do. Sailesh concentrated: he wanted to be ready in case the car suddenly stopped and tried to reverse into him; that would almost certainly damage his radiator or steering and put him out of the chase.

They were now in residential streets, and Sailesh knew they were approaching a dead end. He slowed down, wondering what the Mini driver would do. Was he about to stop the car and run? Would he make a U-turn at the end and attempt to ram the police car? Was he going to try to squeeze into one of the narrow alleys?

The Mini suddenly skidded over to the right and stopped. 'They're going to abandon,' thought Sailesh, and unclipped his seatbelt ready to give chase on foot. He steered his car round to the passenger side, intending to block the passenger in so he could concentrate on arresting the driver. But the passenger door opened just a fraction faster, and Sailesh slammed on the brakes, to avoid hitting the door or crushing the occupant.

Two men got out of the car. Both were wearing balaclavas and carrying long, shining machetes. Wait, what? Sailesh had no time to react. BANG! The first man brought the blade down in a two-handed arc hard onto the windscreen. Amazingly it didn't crack. 'Oh shit,' thought Sailesh, 'what am I going to do here?' BANG! BANG! THUD! CLANG! The men were raining blows onto the car: they were landing on the windscreen, the roof, the bonnet.

'–kin' hell! I'm being attacked!' Sailesh called into his radio, shaken and struggling to believe what was happening. The men were shouting and swearing; the noise was deafening and terrifying. Sailesh was trying hard not to panic, but everything was happening so quickly!

The second man came round to the driver's side and started striking the door window. Sailesh looked up, and all he could see were the man's eyes, radiating fury. Suddenly there was a huge crash as the side window shattered. Sailesh felt his face and upper body showered with glass. He closed his eyes and tried to shake the fragments from his head. Luckily he'd undone his seatbelt, and he leant in towards the centre of the car. He heard a thwack as the machete blade struck the upright of the door frame, and saw the tip of the blade just an inch or two from his face. It seemed to get briefly stuck, and the attacker had to shake the handle to free it.

Sailesh was fumbling for the gearlever but as he leant over it was underneath him and awkward. He pressed his foot hard down on the clutch and finally felt the gearlever slide into first.

He revved the engine and glanced up at the man beside him. All he could see was the menace in his eyes and the blade of machete catching the light as he pulled it up beside his head, ready to stab down into the car; into Sailesh. 'Don't stall, please don't stall,' he thought as he let in the clutch. The wheels spun crazily and the car surged forward. Somehow Sailesh managed to miss the open passenger door of the Mini. He could hear the blades banging on the roof as he sped away.

Sailesh kept looking at his rear-view mirror. What were they going to do? Were they following him? Were they going to drive away? As he watched, the two who'd attacked him, and a third man who'd emerged from inside the car, ran off out of sight down the street.

He pulled over and stopped, then took a deep, shuddering, breath. The intensity of the attack had stunned him. Sailesh had been on many town centre patrols and had encountered many aggressive drunks or abusive suspects, but he'd never been attacked with such single-minded, determined ferocity. Those men had really wanted to kill him, and had come within inches, and seconds, of succeeding. Sailesh was shaking slightly with the adrenaline and felt lucky to be alive, but his panic was starting to metamorphose into a seething rage. Someone had just tried to kill him. And someone was going to pay.

Sailesh turned the car around and drove back to the abandoned Mini. His first thought was to block the Mini in, so that if any of the gang looped back they'd be unable to use it. He looked at the thick black tyre marks on the road surface and smiled to himself. He'd burned a lot of rubber making his escape!

He got out of the car and began running in the same direction as the men. The side street was fairly straight, with semi-detached houses on either side. Most had front lawns and garages, or cars parked in the drive. As he reached a junction, a bystander across the street was pointing up another road. Sailesh ran in that direction, and after a few yards he caught sight of one of the attackers ahead. The man was all in black and still wearing his balaclava. He was running across the middle of an open grassed area in the centre of the housing estate.

It was clear the man was not fit and Sailesh was gaining ground; he was barely 100 yards behind. He couldn't see if the man was still carrying a weapon, but Sailesh was so angry he didn't care. Someone, he thought, is getting it.

On the other side of the road, a jogger had joined in the chase and headed the man off at a T-junction ahead. As Sailesh followed, he could see the man pulling off his balaclava as he ran and throwing it away, then doing the same with his dark top. Beneath he was wearing a pale blue t-shirt. He appeared to be visibly tiring, while Sailesh felt that he had energy to spare. This was partly because he kept himself fit and ran regularly, and partly because he was still brimming with anger and adrenaline.

The man turned into another side street up ahead. When Sailesh reached the corner he paused. There was no sign of him. 'Shit,' thought Sailesh. 'Shit, shit, shit.'

The chase had taken him almost back to the Warrington Road. Would the suspect have headed in that direction, perhaps hoping to make off by bus? Sailesh walked down to the main road and found himself next to an auto parts shop. He looked up and down the street. To his left was another bystander, pointing towards a garden. Sailesh walked around the side of the house and into the back garden, drawing his ASP baton and flicking it out. The telescoping sections locked in place with a reassuring click.

The garden was entirely enclosed by a six foot fence. Sailesh crept forward, looking left and right. The garden was empty, but he could hear the sounds of shrubbery being disturbed. The only way the man could escape was over the fence, or by coming at Sailesh with the machete again. Slowly, Sailesh eased open shed doors, and looked behind bins.

Then there was the crack of a broken twig coming from his right, and Sailesh turned sharply. He walked over to the fence, then climbed up and looked over. The man was almost directly beneath, in the garden next door, looking back at him. He was gasping for breath and perspiring heavily. Sailesh told himself to memorise the man's face.

'Stop, police,' he said. The man's eyes flicked over to the far side of the garden. Sailesh could see he was about to run again, and reached for his CS spray. For some reason, the canister wouldn't come free of its belt fixing. The man took his chance, and climbed onto a glass cold frame before jumping up onto the roof of a shed in the next garden along.

Sailesh put away his baton and climbed the fence. He was starting to feel tired. In his experience, if a suspect wasn't caught in the first 200 yards he was likely to get away, but he was determined to arrest someone.

Somehow the man managed to climb in and out of more gardens, heading back towards the housing estate, with Sailesh in pursuit. Emerging back onto the street, Sailesh saw neighbours gesturing and pointing towards a house in the corner of a small cul-de-sac.

He caught his breath and walked towards the house. Other police cars were arriving, and the streets were crawling with police officers looking for the suspects. They'd all been monitoring Sailesh's radio updates from the attack and the chase, and knew the descriptions of the men they were looking for.

Sailesh made his way into the garden. It was a large corner plot with a lawn and trees and shrubs dotted around. A female police officer was there but she was in plain-clothes, wearing her body armour over jeans and a jumper.

'Seen anything?' asked Sailesh, panting a little.

'No, I only walked in a couple of seconds before you did,' she replied. The garden was bigger than most in the area, probably around 100 square feet, and there were plenty of hiding places. Sailesh started looking in the bins, behind the garage and outbuildings, and combed the shrubbery.

The garden was surrounded by a wooden fence that was hidden here and there by bushes. What was that? Inside one of the bushes he thought he could see three white stripes. He looked again, beckoning over the policewoman. Sure enough, he could see the lower part of one leg of a pair of Adidas tracksuit bottoms. Sailesh took out his baton and spray.

'Come out, come out now,' he called. There was no movement inside the bush.

'Watch yourself,' called Sailesh back over his shoulder to the woman officer. 'He might have a machete on him.'

'Come out! Police,' called Sailesh again. Again, there was no response. 'Perhaps he thinks we can't see him,' he thought. Tired of waiting and still angry, he reached into the bushes, grabbed the suspect's clothing and pulled him out.

'Right, right, all right,' said the man as he emerged. Sailesh looked at him. It wasn't the man he'd been chasing. This one had short dark hair, and was taller and slimmer. As Sailesh threw him down onto the floor, the man caught sight of his baton.

'OK, OK, don't hit me,' he begged, sensing the officer's pent-up fury. Sailesh raised his baton – and paused. He was so pumped up. So angry. This little bastard, or his mates, had just tried to hack his face off with machetes. He wanted to batter him. He really did.

'It's not me, boss. I was just the driver!' he said. Sailesh ignored the confession.

'I don't give a monkey's uncle, mate,' he replied. 'You or your mates just tried to kill me.' Sailesh still had his baton raised, but he knew he couldn't do it. Striking an unresisting man on the ground just wasn't his style. He lowered the baton, knelt on the prisoner's back and put on the handcuffs. As they clicked into place, he felt a wave of euphoria and relief. At least he'd got one of them. He estimated that he'd run around half a mile in his kit, with body armour and boots, and it had been worth it. He reached for his radio.

'Suspect detained,' he said. 'This isn't the suspect I was chasing, and two are still outstanding. Recommend check main road, as he was last seen in that area.'

Sailesh hauled the man to his feet. He was only a young lad, in his early twenties. Now his anger was abating, he was pleased he'd resisted the temptation to lash out. The man would undoubtedly have made a formal complaint, and if he'd suffered serious bruises or broken ribs then Sailesh might well have faced a disciplinary hearing, and even dismissal.

'This was my first job since coming out of jail,' said the lad. Sailesh recorded the incriminating comments in his pocket book, before walking him to a police van that was now parked outside the front of the house.

Once the man was locked away, Sailesh looked around. There were cars, vans, dogs – the whole area was swarming with police. It felt good. Two detectives walked over to him and told him the full story.

The gang had attempted to rob a security van delivering cash to the dispensing machine on the forecourt of the large Greyhound Island service station, but a cashier had spotted them and alerted the guard, who then locked the van. Knowing the police would be on their way, the gang fled empty-handed in their stolen Audi A3.

But a short distance away, possibly panicking, the driver had lost control of the high-performance car and crashed it into a wall.

A passing woman motorist had stopped to see if they were OK, but they dragged her out of her car, a yellow Mini, and then commandeered it to make their getaway. The rest of the story Sailesh knew.

'Can you come with us to walk the route so we can sort out who went where?' asked one of the detectives, and Sailesh nodded.

They walked back to where Sailesh had left his car what seemed like a lifetime ago. White-suited SOCOs (Scene of Crime Officers) were already there starting the forensic work. When Sailesh saw the damage to the car he shuddered.

'This your car?' asked one of the forensic team. 'This cut in the door pillar is two inches deep. Into metal!' Sailesh nodded.

'I should be dead,' he said quietly. In the back of the Mini there was a pickaxe handle, and when they retraced the robbers' route they found discarded balaclavas, gloves and two brand new machetes with the price labels still on them.

Sailesh started to notice his right eye was twitching and painful. He'd been ignoring it, but one of his colleagues suggested he go to hospital, where they removed a fragment of the shattered side window that had lodged in the socket.

Sailesh gave the officers a statement, with a detailed description of the man who'd got away, and was later asked to take part in a Viper ID parade. Viper – Video Identification Parade Electronic Recording – is a computer system that enables witnesses to identify suspects without the difficulties of lining up a traditional ID parade.

Sailesh identified the man without hesitation.

❧

Paul Bentham was arrested at the scene. He'd only been free two months after serving a sentence for a sword attack on another youth. He was given an indefinite sentence after pleading guilty.

Another man, Michael Hayes, admitted robbery in connection with the raid on the Greyhound Island garage.

PC Sailesh Patel received a Chief Constable's Commendation for bravery. His wife called him a stupid idiot, and among his colleagues he's now been given the nickname 'Kinell', a phonetic translation of the comment he radioed back as the attack began.

26

ACE OF HERTS

'It was always at the back of my mind. It was irksome. Some things get under your skin.'

DS SIOBHAN MCCABE

With its two-tone siren wailing, the white Ford Transit ambulance didn't take long to reach the hospital. In the back, the man who'd been shot lay on a stretcher. The blue-shirted ambulance man was giving the kiss of life while the police officer who'd accompanied the victim did all he could to help.

At Hemel Hempstead General Hospital the crash team was ready. The stretcher was wheeled from the ambulance and straight through into the operating theatre. Gunshot injuries were rare, and this one was serious.

The policeman waited outside. A few moments later, a nurse came out and handed him some of the victim's belongings.

'Any news? Is he going to make it?' asked the officer.

'They're doing all they can,' she replied reassuringly, and went back inside.

The policeman looked at the items he'd been given.

Among them was a brass fob with a number stamped onto it: 336. Oh no, he thought. He recognised the fob. Police officers who'd served during the bitter Miners' Strike three years earlier had been given them as mementoes. Quickly, the officer looked through the man's wallet for some means of identification. He pulled out the driving licence, looked at it, then reached for his police radio . . .

In the Hertfordshire police control room, PC Siobhan McCabe was on duty. Normally she worked as a regular beat officer, but she'd recently had an accident while driving a police car and suffered a neck injury. Partly because it was not as physically taxing and partly, she thought, as a penance, she had been assigned to work in control.

Siobhan had always been expected to have a military career. Her father and several other members of her family were in the army, but as a little girl she remembered watching news reports of the Moorgate Underground train crash and accounts of the heroism of policewoman Margaret Liles, who'd been trapped on the train. Inspired by the story, Siobhan decided to join the police cadets at sixteen, and she'd joined up as a constable as soon as she turned eighteen.

At around 10 a.m. the first reports had come in of a robbery in progress at Bank Court in Hemel Hempstead. Bank Court was a small pedestrianised square set back from the main road, so named because of the presence on three sides of branches of Barclays, Lloyds and Midland banks. In the centre was a parking area, and each of the banks had an automated cash machine facing the pavement.

A dark blue Securicor van delivering cash to Barclays had been targeted by an armed gang, and during the robbery a passer-by who'd been walking his dog had tried to intervene. One of the robbers had shot him, and he'd been taken to hospital. Not surprisingly, the robbery was given high urgency and numerous officers were sent.

The call from the officer at the hospital came through on the loudspeaker.

'Bank court robbery victim is an off-duty police officer from Delta Hotel,' he said. The control room fell silent. Siobhan tensed. Delta Hotel was her section: Hemel Hempstead. She would surely know the man. The pause seemed to last for ever.

'It's Frank. Frank Mason's been shot. They're operating on him now.'

Siobhan closed her eyes. Frank was her friend; they'd worked together many times. He'd joined a few months before her, and the same officer had tutored them both. Frank had been a news reporter before joining the police, and Siobhan remembered well his meticulous note-taking and tiny, neat handwriting. She'd been on duty with Frank the night she'd crashed the panda car – it had been the last time they'd worked together.

As colleagues buzzed around her, Siobhan pulled herself together and allowed her training to take over. The control room was at the centre of the hunt for the robbers, and messages and calls were coming in and needed to be relayed or acted upon.

Someone suggested finding out Frank's blood group and asking the hospital if more volunteer donors were needed. The inspector made the call. Then he put down the phone. For a moment, the room fell silent again.

'We won't need any volunteers to give blood,' he said quietly. 'Frank died a few moments ago.'

In the days after the killing, Siobhan was moved by the support from the townspeople. She even remembered some of those whom Frank had arrested coming into the police station to offer their condolences.

Francis John Mason was posthumously awarded the Queen's Gallantry Medal. In Bank Court, a grey stone memorial was erected by the Police Memorial Trust, bearing the inscription 'Here fell PC Frank Mason, 14th April 1988'.

The three robbers were arrested within the hour. The Regional Crime Squad had been watching them, but in 1988 tracking equipment was unreliable and the surveillance team had lost them. As soon as they heard about the shooting, an arrest plan was put into action and the robbers were seized at two locations – a shop and a lock-up garage – in Luton. Numerous weapons, including semi-automatic guns and pipe bombs, were found.

The trial of the three men heard that James Hurley was the getaway driver; the police had been watching him for some time. Charlie McGhee was the other man detectives had intelligence on, and he was described as a 'pathological hater' of the police. Perry Wharrie had not been under surveillance. It was suspected he had been brought up from London for the robbery simply to shore up the numbers.

The court was told that the security van had arrived outside the bank at just after 10 a.m. As one of the guards delivered cash to the bank, the robbers pounced – jabbing handguns into his ribs and threatening to shoot him unless his colleague inside the van passed out more cash bags.

Frank Mason was walking his dog, Scally, when he saw

what was happening. He ran up to one of the robbers and grabbed him, saying, 'You're nicked.'

This distraction allowed the terrified security man to escape, but as Frank attempted to arrest the first robber the second shot him at point blank range in the right shoulder. The bullet passed down through his body, causing massive internal injuries, and lodged in his left thigh.

In 1989, James Hurley, Charlie McGhee and Perry Wharrie were jointly convicted of murder and sentenced to life imprisonment.

The prisoner transfer bus was about a mile and a quarter from its destination. As it passed Wandsworth town railway station, a scuffle broke out, and there was shouting and banging. The bus driver stopped and looked round. One of the prisoners had some kind of improvised blade, and was holding it to the throat of one of the prison guards. Another inmate ran to the front of the vehicle, and demanded the driver open the doors. He did, and the man made off. The date was 16 February 1994. The prisoner who escaped was James Hurley – who'd served just five years of his sentence.

Because he'd disappeared during a prisoner transfer in London, the Metropolitan Police led the hunt for Hurley, though Hertfordshire provided assistance and back-up.

There were some intelligence leads suggesting Hurley might be in Southern Ireland; others that he had fled to Spain. Despite a huge manhunt, no trace of him was found. He seemed to have disappeared.

Eventually, other priorities and commitments intruded, and in Hertfordshire the operation to help find Hurley was shut down.

★

Years went by. Charlie McGhee died of a heart attack in Durham prison in January 1995. By 2000, Siobhan McCabe had joined the newly formed Hertfordshire Constabulary major crime unit working alongside DS Paul Maghie.

Paul was from Enfield in North London. He'd trained as an engineer, then joined the Royal Small Arms Factory and worked for the Ministry of Defence on the design of the then-new SA80 rifle. In 1990, he decided on a career change and joined the police. Because there was a long waiting list at the time for his local force – the Metropolitan Police – he joined neighbouring Hertfordshire.

Siobhan and her colleagues had not forgotten Frank. In 2004, they were approached by Sky News's crime correspondent Martin Brunt. He suggested marking the tenth anniversary of the escape with a fresh appeal for help. Paul and Siobhan thought it was a good idea, and Jill Mason, Frank's widow, flew back from her new home in Spain to take part.

The BBC's *Crimewatch* programme also broadcast an appeal, and for several days the police were inundated with calls and information.

Paul, Siobhan and their colleagues worked through the new leads, checking each one. James Hurley, it seemed, had been spotted everywhere, from shopping in Sainsbury's to living on a boat in Spain.

But within the tidal wave of information were some strong leads. One was particularly promising. The informant knew of a James Hurley living in Puerto Banús on the Costa del Sol. The police hurriedly obtained an extradition warrant and the man was arrested by the Spanish authorities.

But the excitement in Hertfordshire rapidly turned to disappointment. The James Hurley now under arrest in Spain was a different man. He was wanted for questioning in connection with the failed attempt to steal the De Beers diamonds from the Millennium Dome in 2000, not the robbery at Bank Court in 1988. He was later released without charge.

Once again, the trail to Frank Mason's killer seemed to have gone cold.

By 2005, Siobhan was working as an exhibits officer and had become a detective sergeant. But James Hurley's escape was always at the back of her mind. It was irksome; it had got under her skin. She had an idea, and went to see her boss, DI Paul Maghie.

'I want to get all the old evidence gathered by the original investigation team in 1988 sent over,' she told him. 'Forensic techniques have come a long way. Who knows what we might find?' Paul liked it. He was as keen to catch James Hurley as Siobhan. But there was a problem.

'I'm sorry, but the force aren't willing to put resources into this. Budgets are tight and it could be a dead end. But we could go it alone. We've both got day jobs, but if you want to run it as a sort of unofficial enquiry on the side I'll do everything I can to help.'

It would mean a lot of extra work, and long hours, but Siobhan had a gut feeling that it would be worth it. At the time, Siobhan was based at Hoddesdon police station, and the next day she arranged for the exhibits to be sent over.

There were boxes and boxes of them – far more than she'd imagined. She found a storeroom for them, and that weekend she and a colleague, Davinia May, donned white forensic suits and started going through them.

Although in recent times they'd been kept in a secure commercial storage warehouse, that hadn't always been the case – at one point the boxes had been kept in a garage in Hemel Hempstead – and some had deteriorated quite badly.

'We won't know what we've got – and what might be missing – until we've sorted out what there is,' said Siobhan. The original evidence list had been lost, so the first job was to catalogue it all.

It was slow, dusty and in some cases unpleasant work. There were the clothes Frank had been wearing on the day he died, the crash helmets the offenders had used, receipts, disguises and files full of paperwork.

Over the coming weeks, the cramped storeroom started to feel like Siobhan's second home. She and a colleague, DC Trevor Acors, spent hours going through the boxes. Either late at night, after finishing a shift, or early in the morning, before her official duties started, she'd head for the storeroom and look through more of the evidence.

One evening, she came across the file of samples that had been taken at Luton police station on the day the gang had been arrested. Among them was a small sample of hair and a police mugshot. Siobhan froze. The photograph was far better than anything else they'd had previously, and looked different. And the hair meant they could extract a positive sample of DNA. It meant they could positively identify any suspect.

Siobhan took the new items to Paul. Could this be the breakthrough they'd been looking for?

★

At the same time, Siobhan decided to run a computer check on the other robber, Perry Wharrie. He'd served sixteen years of his sentence and been released in April 2005 on licence. One of the conditions was that he had to live at an address in Essex with a woman he'd married while in jail. But, Siobhan explained to Paul, the relationship had broken down, and by January 2006 Wharrie had disappeared.

They decided to contact the Serious Organised Crime Agency (SOCA) for assistance. It was part of SOCA's brief to track criminals thought to be travelling internationally. Members of Wharrie's family had recently moved to Scotland, but investigations there failed to locate him.

All went quiet for a while, then in July 2007 SOCA contacted Paul and Siobhan again. Perry Wharrie had been arrested in south-west Ireland after a bungled attempt to smuggle drugs into the country.

He and three other men had planned to bring in more than £350 million in cocaine. They transferred the drugs into a smaller vessel in Dunlough Bay, off Mizen Head in Cork, but they'd filled their boat's tank with the wrong fuel and the engine cut out. Stranded in the choppy waters, the little boat was so top heavy with drugs that it capsized. The Gardaí recovered sixty-two bales of cocaine from the sea. Wharrie wasn't on board, but was arrested the next day.

'Get the paperwork ready,' said the SOCA officer. 'If he isn't charged, we want to be ready to extradite him straight away.' With the help of the CPS they prepared the documents they needed and travelled to Ireland. Court procedures in Dublin are different to the UK, and Paul Maghie was surprised to see there were no armed officers. When Wharrie arrived, he was brought in the front entrance just like everyone else, and in court Paul and Siobhan found themselves sitting on the same bench, almost next to him.

Wharrie was charged, and after a ten-week trial sentenced to thirty years in prison for what was then the largest ever drugs seizure in the Republic of Ireland.

The extradition papers were served, and after some discussion the court in Dublin ruled that when he had served his sentence in Ireland Wharrie should be immediately extradited to the UK to complete his sentence for the murder of Frank Mason.

By now, Hertfordshire Police had lodged a European Arrest Warrant for James Hurley. This was, at the time, a relatively new piece of legislation that allowed criminals to be transferred between EU member states without the lengthy extradition processes and paperwork that had allowed criminals to hide on the Costa del Sol for many years.

They'd had the photograph of Hurley 'digitally aged' and had sent it to Interpol, immigration and border control departments and to the UK Passport Office.

James Hurley had also been included in a new publicity drive produced by the charity Crimestoppers called Operation Captura, targeting British criminals thought to be hiding abroad.

In 2007, Paul was contacted by the Passport Office. They'd scanned the new photograph of Hurley and come up with a possible match. Paul called Siobhan.

'It's a genuine passport, but it's been fraudulently issued under another name,' he told her. 'To be honest, the photo they've sent looks nothing like the one we have, though they seem confident it's Hurley.'

'But it's a lead, isn't it?' she said. The fake passport gave them a number of new lines to follow: where it had been registered, who'd countersigned the application, and, most importantly, what countries the passport holder had visited.

After so many years of frustratingly slow progress, the detectives were taken aback at the speed with which events started to unfold.

On 20 November 2007, Dutch police, acting on intelligence, raided a house in The Hague. Drugs and a gun were seized, and two men were arrested. One was a scruffy Englishman. Oddly, the name on his passport didn't match their records. They sent a DNA sample back to London. The sample was cross-checked against the UK database and a match came up: James Hurley. The thirteen-year hunt for Frank Mason's killer was over.

James Hurley served a short sentence in the Netherlands for possession of a firearm. In 2011, twenty-three years after Frank Mason was shot dead, he was extradited back to the UK to complete his jail term for murder.

Perry Wharrie is due for release in Ireland in 2030, but will be returned immediately to Britain to complete his sentence after breaking the terms of his parole.

In July 2012, Paul Maghie, Siobhan McCabe and Trevor Acors received Chief Constable's Commendations.

In April 2013, on the twenty-fifth anniversary of his death, Frank Mason's widow Jill presented his Queen's Gallantry Medal to Hertfordshire Constabulary, so it could be put on permanent display at Hemel Hempstead police station. She said:

'I think it's important to remember that Francis did more than try to stop a bank robbery; he saved a life that day by allowing the security guard to get to safety.

'I hope this medal inspires others to do extraordinary things.'

27

TWO LAUREL LEAVES

'I thought, "I've got myself into this, now I've got to get myself out."'

SERGEANT JEFF LOVE

PC Jeff Love looked at the black Lyric message pager again. Still nothing. 'Come on, Jeff,' he thought to himself, 'you know she's still got two weeks until she's due.' Jeff's wife Dawn was eight and a half months pregnant with their second child, and to ensure he didn't miss the birth they'd got the pager for him to carry when he was on duty. He knew she'd activate it if there was anything to report, and they'd tested it and knew it was working, but still . . . he couldn't help looking.

It was evening, and Jeff was patrolling in his marked police Volvo V70. He was based at Warwickshire Police's traffic base at Greys Mallory, just off the M40 motorway south-west of Leamington Spa. He'd been a traffic cop for almost all his police career, although as a boy his ambition had been to fly helicopters for the Fleet Air Arm. That hadn't happened, but a friend's father in Nuneaton was a police inspector, and his job had sounded nearly as exciting – especially as he could ride motorcycles in the police, which were the next best thing to helicopters!

When Jeff first applied to Warwickshire Constabulary, as it was then, he was told he was too young. He went away for a couple of years and worked as a sales rep for a toy firm. He tried again and was accepted – joining in 1982 and based in Leamington. As soon as he was eligible, he requested a move to the traffic unit, with an aim of eventually qualifying as a motorcycle cop.

Jeff's timing was good: The M42 Birmingham orbital motorway had just opened, and Warwickshire Police needed extra staff to police it. Jeff started on the motorway unit in 1986, and had been a traffic officer ever since.

'Robbery in progress at Westbourne Road, Barford. PC Masters in local car requesting urgent back-up.' The call on the radio interrupted Jeff's thoughts. He recognised the name of the beat officer involved – they'd known each other for years. Jeff had a habit of monitoring the local radio channel as well as the main traffic frequency, and called in to say that he was on his way.

Barford was a small village the other side of the M40 motorway, about three miles south of Warwick. It wouldn't take long to get there to give Ian Masters a hand, thought Jeff, and he turned on his blue lights and sirens.

Some officers liked complex high-profile investigations; others preferred neighbourhood policing. Jeff's favourite part of the job had always been arriving at an emergency quickly in a fast car, dealing with the problem, and moving on.

Nearly a decade earlier, in November 1988, he'd been patrolling the M6 on a dank, foggy morning. He and a colleague were in a Range Rover.

The imposing Range Rovers were used as incident vehicles, whereas faster saloons were used for enforcement. When on motorway patrol, the incident cars would set their blue lights to cruise mode, a dull blue glow, so that motorists could see them and, it was hoped, modify their behaviour. In the 1980s, there were considerably fewer cars and commercial vehicles on the roads – which meant traffic tended to go faster.

It was standard practice to patrol at 55 mph. This was the most fuel efficient speed, and meant cars could overtake without bunching up and causing a hazardous tidal wave of braking traffic. It was also slow enough to allow lorries to overtake them, so they could inspect any discs in the window as they passed. Sometimes a patrol officer might feel bullish and cruise at 70 mph, but this wasn't recommended. Jeff knew that a queue of frustrated, tailgating drivers would rapidly build up, and the instant the patrol car peeled off it would be like the Wacky Races.

Jeff and his partner that day, Keith Floyd, were having a hot drink at Corley services when the call came through that there had been an accident on the northbound carriageway at Packington Bank, the long hill where traffic descends into Birmingham. It came as no real surprise to either of them – the fog was so dense that a collision of some sort had seemed inevitable.

Jeff and Keith were there within minutes, the first emergency vehicle to arrive. As they drove cautiously through the fog, more and more pairs of glowing red brake lights emerged from the mist. Normally two police vehicles would respond: one to handle the incident, the other to take up a position 300 yards further back to alert approaching traffic.

They pulled up as close to the front of the accident as they could. Around them they could see damaged cars and lorries, and people milling about, but the fog was so thick they had no real idea how many more vehicles were involved.

'I'll walk forward and find the front of it,' said Keith. Jeff nodded. A couple of motorists were walking towards them.

'There's a lorry driver trapped in his cab over there,' one of them said, pointing.

'OK,' said Jeff, adding to Keith, 'I'll go and check on this.' He pulled on his bright yellow hi-viz coat and followed the two men across the carriageway. Around him he could hear some shouting from other motorists, and the faint whooshing of vehicles on the other carriageway. It was cold, and sounds were far quieter than normal; fog tended to absorb and suppress noise.

As Jeff walked along the carriageway, weaving in between damaged and stationary cars, the dark shape of an articulated lorry appeared out of the mist. It had jack-knifed in the accident, trapping a Vauxhall Carlton saloon against the central reservation and striking a couple of other cars. The cab had ended up at 90 degrees to the flow of traffic. Jeff opened the passenger door, climbed up and entered the cab. The driver was still inside, behind the wheel.

'Hey, are you OK?' asked Jeff.

'I'm fine,' he replied, 'but my left foot's stuck.' Jeff leaned in for a closer look. The lorry's steering column had been bent back in the impact, and was trapping the driver's foot against the gearbox housing. If he hadn't been wearing safety boots it would probably have been crushed; now it was wedged in tight, and the driver was unable to work it free.

'I need to go back to the car to get some gear. I'll be right back. We'll get you out,' said Jeff, and climbed down.

He had a quick look around the lorry. The driver and passengers of the Carlton had climbed out of their windows because the doors were wedged shut. The wing mirrors had been torn off, and the car had damaged the dark green, vertical plastic vanes that were fixed to the central reservation to act as headlight deflectors and stop motorists from inadvertently dazzling each other.

It still felt eerily quiet to Jeff as he made his way back through the thick fog to his patrol car. He reached in to the boot and grabbed the big five-foot wrecking bar they carried as well as a saw. He noticed that a second police team had arrived.

Jeff returned to the truck. The driver told him his name was Mike Bell. Unfortunately Jeff couldn't really get the saw in, but he tried to use the wrecking bar to lever the steering column clear. Even if he couldn't free the boot, it might at least ease the pressure on Mike's foot.

A man's face appeared at the window.

'I'm a firefighter, but off-duty,' he said. 'Why don't you wait for the brigade? They'll have the right tools for this job.' Jeff thought about it. The man was right. Mike wasn't in pain or danger, and Jeff couldn't smell any leaking fuel. There were certainly plenty of other jobs he could be getting on with. He put down the wrecking bar and clambered out of the cab.

By now, it was around nine o'clock in the morning, and Jeff joined the other officers in assessing the crash site. Their first priority was to shepherd everyone away from the road and onto the hard shoulder. Then they started methodically checking each vehicle: making sure no one else was trapped or injured, noting its registration and logging its position.

Keith returned, and reported that ahead of them were a

further four rows of wrecked vehicles – probably sixteen cars in all, and there were many more further back that hadn't yet been counted.

As they chatted, they were approached by another driver, who pointed down the road.

'Have you got a fire extinguisher?' he asked. 'One of the cars down there has just started burning, though there's no one in it.'

In the patrol cars they carried large blue dry-powder fire extinguishers. Jeff and Keith fetched them from both cars and walked forward to the burning vehicle. If it was well ablaze they'd be wasting their time, but luckily the fire was still contained inside the engine compartment, beneath the bonnet. They couldn't open it up as that would allow the flames to fan out, so they popped the bonnet from inside the car as they'd been trained and directed the spray nozzle through the gap. The extinguishers sputtered drily, then nothing. Jeff and Keith looked at each other. Surely both shouldn't fail?

'These are bloody useless,' said Jeff. 'Let's check some of the lorries and see if they've got any that work.'

Checking other vehicles yielded a further half-dozen fire extinguishers. All were of the dry powder type, which was standard at the time for vehicles, and all failed. What they hadn't known was that if the extinguishers weren't shaken at least once a week then the powder tended to settle at the bottom of the canister and set.

Then things started to get serious. Unchecked, the fire in the car had spread to another vehicle, and both were now well ablaze. The fire brigade had already been called, but they were at least eight miles away and would take some minutes to arrive.

The fire spread to a lorry next to the two cars. This was carrying rolls of industrial clingfilm, which burned fiercely, giving off thick black smoke and acrid fumes. It was immediately in front of Mike Bell's truck. Jeff climbed back into Mike's cab. The driver knew the other side of the lorry had caught fire, and he was starting to panic.

'Get me out, get me out,' he pleaded. Jeff climbed behind Mike. There was a small sleeping bunk across the back of the cabin that was getting in the way, so Jeff broke it down. He reached around and grabbed Mike in a bear-hug. Another officer, Kevin Turner, came round to the driver's side door at the front of the truck to try to help. He reached in and pulled at the steering wheel with all his body weight, trying to ease the pressure just enough to release the driver's boot.

Mike was wriggling his foot this way and that, trying to get free. His safety boots wouldn't compress, so his foot was locked in position. Jeff looked out of the cab window. The flames were spreading fast, and he could feel the warmth radiating through the windscreen. Kevin described what was happening outside.

'The flames are coming round the sides and across the rolls of film on top. Now the rolls on this side of the truck are just catching. The flames are almost on top of us.' Kevin kept up a running commentary as Jeff continued to struggle to free Mike Bell.

'Jeff, mate, I'm going to have to go. Burning plastic's dripping on me here, and there's flames around my feet,' said Kevin; and he retreated. Jeff looked up. The windscreen was now just a wall of yellow and orange flame. Nothing else was visible. The glass offered some protection but the heat radiating through was intense. Jeff had avoided thinking about it, but knew that in a few seconds he would face a horrible choice: to stay and perish, or to save himself and leave Mike to be burned to death in his cab. The off-duty fireman was telling Jeff he had to leave now.

'Look, Mike, this is our last chance,' said Jeff, twisting himself round for one final try. 'Come on!'

Jeff grabbed Mike around the waist and heaved, with his feet pushing against the back of the lorry driver's seat. Perhaps it was the slight change of position; perhaps adrenaline and desperation combined to give him an instant of superhuman strength. But without warning Mike's foot came free, and the pair of them flew backwards across the cab.

Jeff scrabbled around and pushed Mike towards the window. The firefighter helped drag him out, and Jeff followed. Once outside, they got to their feet. Mike Bell was limping, so Jeff and Kevin went either side and helped him away. As they reached the back of the trailer unit of Mike's truck, they turned and looked back. The windscreen had shattered and jets of flame were emerging from inside the cab.

The next day Jeff noticed that his face was bright red, with white circles around the eyes. The heat radiating through the lorry's windscreen had been so intense it had caused sunburn. Jeff's face was sore for several days, but this didn't stop his colleagues enjoying a good laugh at his expense.

Later, Jeff was awarded a Queen's Commendation for Bravery, which entitled him to wear a silver laurel leaf on his uniform. He was also invited to the town of Assisi in Italy and awarded the Giancarlo Tofi Trophy – given each year to a European citizen who shows outstanding bravery in rescuing or protecting road crash victims.

And the police replaced all their dry foam fire extinguishers with AFFF (Aqueous Film Forming Foam) types, which are guaranteed to work even if they haven't been shaken.

None of this was on Jeff's mind on a dark January evening nine years later when he approached Barford to provide back-up for his colleague Ian Masters. Ian's panda car was parked outside a house on the High Street. Jeff stopped and climbed out.

'What have we got?' he asked. Ian came over.

'It looks as though two men have broken in, then attacked the residents,' he explained. 'Very aggressive, though unclear why. Young woman slashed across the cheek, her mother stabbed in the eye with some scissors. Nasty. The men are still inside and have a hostage, a young barman.'

Another officer arrived with more information, and between them they pieced together events. One of the intruders, Theodore Kenney, had been in a relationship with Vicky, the daughter. She'd ended it at Christmas, just a few days earlier.

Kenney had come back with an accomplice and entered the house. The intruders had attacked the girl, her mother and her elderly male friend. They'd freed the older couple, who'd gone straight to the village pub, the Granville Arms, and raised the alarm.

At the pub, barman Jeremy Burbill had bravely decided to confront the men and rescue the girl. But what he hadn't known was that as he was walking down the high street to the siege house, the girl had managed to get out of the back of the house and escape through a neighbour's garden. An enraged Kenney and his accomplice then let Burbill in, dragged him into the living room at knifepoint and doused him in lighter fluid. He'd become their replacement hostage.

So, thought Jeff, what the police were facing was a terrified hostage and armed, frustrated and angry men. Not a good mix.

'We need to start talking to them,' said Ian. Jeff agreed. Other police officers had arrived, and as they went quietly round to the back of the house, Ian and Jeff pushed against the front door. It was unlocked and they went in. They found themselves in a small hallway. To the left was an inner door, leading into the living room which stretched the full length of that side of the house. Next to the door was a full height decorative glass panel, giving the officers a blurred view of the room beyond. They could see the yellow flickering glow of an open fire, and in front of it, stretched out, the hostage. He was leaning against Kenney, who was holding a shiny blade of some kind to his throat. The other intruder was out of sight, to the side; it was obvious Kenney was in charge.

Ian began talking to the hostage taker, building up a rapport. Jeff stood to one side with his baton drawn in the textbook position as cover officer.

As he talked, Kenney confirmed much of what the officers knew. The hostage – Jeremy – was so far unhurt.

'I don't want to be trapped in here,' said Kenney. 'I don't want to go back to prison.'

'Well,' said Ian, kindly, 'let Jeremy go and we'll talk about it.'

'I don't want to be trapped in here,' repeated the voice behind the door. 'I want to talk to Vicky.'

'But, Theo, you know there are police all round here now,' said Ian. 'You might as well let him go. He's done you no harm.' There was silence on the other side of the door as the intruder thought it over. But then Ian was asked to go outside and brief a senior officer who'd just arrived to take control of the scene.

Jeff was worried. Ian had done a brilliant job at creating a rapport with the man. Things were at a very delicate stage. In his view, it wasn't a good idea for Ian to break off now. On the other hand, the officer taking charge did need to be briefed and given all the information needed, to take an overview of the situation and make the right strategic decisions. Ian stepped outside and Jeff put down his baton. Another two officers were waiting silently in the hallway.

The hostage taker could tell something was going on.

'What's happening? What are you doing out there? Talk to me!' Jeff was anxious. The man was obviously stressed and highly strung, and an unfamiliar voice might cause him to panic.

'Don't worry. Ian's had to go out for a moment,' said Jeff. 'If you want to talk to anyone I'm here. But if you don't that's fine, because Ian will be back in a minute.' Jeff tried to make it sound reassuring, but he could almost smell the suspicion on the other side of the door. Then he heard scratching and shuffling noises, and suddenly the door was thrown open.

Jeff found himself face to face with the second man. Past him, Jeff could see Kenney on the ground with the hostage, holding scissors to his throat. The man facing him was clearly agitated, hopping from foot to foot and speaking in short, staccato sentences that didn't seem to make any sense. He was holding a kitchen knife. Jeff was sure he was high on drugs.

Over by the fireplace, Kenney was becoming more aggressive.

'Who the fuck are you?' he sneered. 'Where's the other cop? I want to speak to Vicky. Where is she? Get her here.' As he spoke, he kept jabbing the scissors into the neck of the hostage, who was visibly shaking with fear.

Kenney looked up at Jeff. His eyes were shining with fury.

'Come in here. If you don't come into the room, I'm going to kill him.' Jeff looked at the hostage, who stared back at him imploringly.

'Look ...' started Jeff, trying to buy time.

'No, I'm going to kill him. Fucking come into the room.' Kenney's voice was manic, and he was digging his scissors into the neck of the terrified barman. Jeff paused. Knowing his history of violence, Jeff had no doubt he might kill the hostage. Jeff had to go in – didn't he?

Jeff didn't want the intruders getting hold of his baton, CS spray or handcuffs, so as he stepped forward he discreetly unclipped his utility belt. He walked into the room, slightly surprised that he didn't hear the belt hit the floor behind him. It hadn't fallen because one of his colleagues, realising what he was about to do, had tried to stop him by grabbing it. Now he was left standing there, just holding the belt.

As Jeff entered the room, the door was slammed shut behind him by the second man, who then dragged a sideboard across to block it.

'Stand still,' said Kenney; then, to the other man, 'Pat him down.' Jeff stood motionless as he was searched. As well as his usual uniform of boots, trousers, shirt, tie and NATO jumper, he was wearing covert body armour. He was fastidious about this, since he'd been shot at on a previous occasion. He felt the man's hands stop as they touched the edge.

'What's this then?' he said.

'It's a brace. I've got a bad back,' lied Jeff. The man looked at Kenney for guidance.

'Fuck your back – take it off,' Kenney said. 'Take the lot off.' Jeff slowly and carefully removed his jumper, tie and shirt. All were thrown on the open fire behind Kenney. He unfastened the expensive covert armour and handed it over. It too was thrown on the fire. Now bare-chested, Jeff gagged as the putrid, distinctive odour of burning Kevlar filled the room. He also took off his boots, and they too went on the roaring open fire.

The second man pointed to Jeff's waist.

'What's that? A bug?' Jeff's hand instinctively went to the black pager on his belt.

'No, it's just a pager. It can't transmit. It's nothing,' he said quickly. The man prised away Jeff's fingers and removed it from his belt. He handed it to Kenney.

'What do you need a pager for? You've all got walkie-talkies,' Kenney said. Jeff said nothing. He didn't want them to know anything about him: that he had a wife who was heavily pregnant with his second child, and that the pager was his way of knowing when she'd gone into labour.

Kenney threw it on the fire. As he watched the plastic casing bubble and melt in the flames, Jeff felt hot anger welling up inside. He was pushed over to a chaise longue and forced to sit down. Kenney leaned forward with a large tin of lighter fluid and squirted it all over Jeff's feet and up his legs. It ran out before he could spray it on the policeman's bare chest or back. Then Kenney sat back and threw the tin away. He was still pressing the scissors to the barman's throat, but now took a small lighter and began absently clicking the mechanism, threatening to strike the flint.

Jeff started to think that entering the room was not one of his better decisions. He'd had to go in because it was his clear belief the barman's life was in danger. But now he wondered. So far all he'd done was lose his pager and give Kenney and his accomplice another hostage.

A familiar voice came into the room from outside. Ian was back at the door. Kenney looked round, and Jeff relaxed. The tension fell by a few increments. Ian's return took the spotlight off Jeff, and gave him the chance to start weighing up the options for escape.

He could sense officers outside the living room windows. He imagined they were probably armed. Alongside Ian in the hallway, Jeff knew there were two other colleagues, including a huge officer called Norman, and he was sure there'd be more police behind another interior door at the far end of the room.

Suddenly Jeff became aware of a female voice, and realised that Ian had convinced the supervising officer to have Vicky brought down to the house, in an effort to convince Kenney to give up.

It was a good idea, thought Jeff, as Kenney started telling her how much he loved her, how much he wanted to continue to go out with her, and how once the siege was over they could be happy together. Jeff could see that Kenney was calming down as he spoke to her, though he was still absent-mindedly flicking the lighter wheel.

Jeff had realised there was almost nothing in the room that could be used as a weapon. There wasn't a convenient set of pokers next to the fire for him to grab, or a nice heavy glass ashtray he could throw. The room seemed almost to have been designed to be harmless. The only thing that caught his eye was a thick black fireside rug on the ground near Kenney. 'If all else fails,' thought Jeff, 'that might be something I could use.'

The time ticked by; it was now an hour and a half since the barman had been taken hostage. Jeff had zoned out a little from the chatter between Vicky and Kenney, but something struck him as odd. He could tell from a couple of things Kenney said – and the way he said them – that he seemed to have decided to kill himself. This made things much more serious – and much more immediate. Checks had shown that Kenney had a history of violence. Jeff was pretty sure that he wouldn't let the hostages watch him kill himself – that he'd be more likely to kill them first.

Jeff started to worry. 'I've got myself into this,' he thought to himself; 'now I need to get myself out of it.' He was confident his colleagues would come charging in the moment he gave them some kind of signal. Since the girl had arrived the other man seemed to have relaxed too, and had gone down to the far end of the room – though he was still holding the knife.

The most imminent threat was the scissors Kenney was holding to the throat of the barman. They weren't large but had wickedly sharp blades. There was also the danger of fire. Jeff noted that as Kenney was talking to Vicky his occasional hand gestures caused him to inadvertently shift the scissor-tips away from the man's neck. Away . . . and back. Away . . . and back. Away . . .

Without warning, smoothly and quickly, Jeff stood up, grabbed the heavy black rug and threw it onto Kenney and the hostage. Kenney put his hand up to block it, keeping the scissors away from the barman's neck. The rug landed across Kenney's head and body, and Jeff straddled him, landing a hard punch on what he could see of the outline of Kenney's head.

The moment he moved, Jeff had shouted 'Do it now! Do it now!' and as the other man with the knife started crossing the room towards him, all the doors burst open and the room suddenly filled with police officers.

There was an audible swish of batons as the officers came forward, striking the knifeman repeatedly until he dropped the weapon, then handcuffing him. Ian and the others took over subduing Kenney while Jeff helped the barman onto the chaise longue. Jeff's hand throbbed, and he suspected he might have broken it with that first punch; he also had some cuts on his back where Kenney had tried to stab him with the scissors.

Kenney was handcuffed and dragged out, kicking and screaming. An ambulance had been called, and Jeff, Vicky, Vicky's mother and the elderly man were all taken to hospital. Vicky had a nasty cut on her cheek and her mother had been stabbed in the eye, but fortunately the blade went down the outside of the socket and didn't puncture the eyeball itself.

In the back of the ambulance, wrapped in a white NHS blanket and still only wearing his trousers, Jeff started to think about what might have happened if things had gone wrong, and how he might have died without ever meeting his unborn second son. He started to shake a little, partly through shock and relief, and partly as the implications sank in. His colleague Mark Westwood could see he was close to tears. 'Don't you dare!' he said.

Once in the hospital in Warwick, in private, Jeff did shed a few tears. His broken hand was bandaged up and he returned home. The following day was manic. Jeff was visited by his inspector, superintendent and chief superintendent, and the phone didn't stop ringing.

Suddenly, Jeff's wife said she thought she might be feeling contractions. They rushed to hospital and were put in a side room. For two hours there were no phone calls, no distractions, just uninterrupted silence. Dawn and Jeff looked at each other. The contractions were a false alarm, probably brought on by the stress, but the peace and quiet had been just what was needed.

Later, there was a cold debrief. Almost everyone involved, from the call handlers to the incident managers, was present. Discussing the events, one senior officer criticised Jeff for going into the room – saying he should have remained outside. Jeff explained that he'd done it because in his judgement the barman's life was at risk. In measured tones, he agreed that it hadn't, perhaps, been one of his best decisions, but in the circumstances he'd had no choice. The senior officer said nothing. There were mutterings among the others. Then Mark Westwood, the officer who'd told Jeff not to cry, stood up, looked around, and said loudly:

'As far as I'm concerned, Jeff Love has got brass bollocks.'

Some months later, Jeff was awarded a second Queen's Commendation, and now wears two silver laurel leaves on his dress tunic; the only mainland officer to do so.

❧

Theodore Kenney admitted charges of wounding and false imprisonment, and was jailed for twelve years. He had previous convictions for violence and was said to have a psychopathic personality disorder. The judge was told he'd written to his ex-girlfriend while on remand, threatening to cut her throat if she didn't drop charges.

His accomplice had never been in trouble with the police before, and had only met Kenney that day at a pub in Leamington. He was jailed for four years, but became a drug addict and died of an overdose shortly after being released from prison.

Two weeks after the false alarm, Dawn gave birth to Robert, a healthy baby boy and a brother to Mathew, who was then five.

For his fiftieth birthday, Jeff Love got to fly a helicopter.

28

THE WATER BOY

'Sometimes I wish I could arrest people just for being stupid.'

PC JOE KINSELLA

Among police officers in Sheffield, Hammerton Road police station in Hillsborough was nicknamed, perhaps unfairly, Sleepy Hollow. Now earmarked for closure, the red-brick police building with its attendant yard nestled on the hillside among streets of terraced houses. Children from the nearby Sacred Heart Primary School often stood at the fence to snatch a glimpse of the patrol cars and the police officers.

History remembers Hammerton Road as the police station where Yorkshire Ripper Peter Sutcliffe was taken following his arrest in 1981 by two local bobbies who'd spotted him with a prostitute in nearby Melbourne Avenue.

Nearly three decades later, on a bright summer evening in June 2010, PC Joseph Kinsella was just getting changed ready for the start of his nightshift. He was chatting to PC Jenna White who was also putting on her uniform. They were old friends, and were looking forward to working the shift together.

As he was pulling on his stab vest, Joe's radio crackled to life with a message from the call centre.

'Anyone for an immediate job ... Anyone for an immediate job ... A man's fallen into the boating lake at Crookes Valley Park and is in difficulty. There's someone attempting to get him out. Possibly unconscious.' Joe and Jenna looked at each other. The afternoon shift was still on duty, but something about this call was different.

It was odd, but instinctively Joe realised it wasn't a joke call or a well-meaning citizen exaggerating some relatively trivial high jinks. Without a word, he and Jenna ran to their vehicle, a marked Ford Focus patrol car, pulling on their stab vests.

'Have you got your vent-aid?' Joe asked Jenna as they fastened their seatbelts. She nodded in reply.

They both knew the vent-aid units were a lifesaver. Comprising a small plastic mouthpiece with one-way valve and a plastic barrier sheet, they enabled officers to give mouth-to-mouth resuscitation without making direct contact with the casualty. They were issued as standard and were supposed to be in every officer's first-aid kit; the problem was, as Joe knew all too well, such highly valued items had a tendency to get 'lost'. It didn't hurt to check Jenna had hers.

As they pulled out of the police station car park, Joe switched on the siren and blue lights. With 999 calls, the target was to reach the scene within eleven minutes. Given the short distance between Hammerton Road and the Park, Joe was confident the target would not be a problem – but would they be in time to save the drowning man?

The route to the park took them along Walkley Lane, a steep hill, and the 1.6 litre police car struggled to get beyond

50 mph, though under the circumstances to go any faster would've been potentially dangerous.

As Joe drove, Jenna monitored the radio for updates. The reports were conflicting: some callers said the man was conscious and 'splashing around'; others were sure he'd collapsed. Without clear confirmation that all was well, Joe had no choice but to continue as fast as possible.

Joe drove in the crown of the road. Police response drivers were trained to ensure that they could see as far ahead as possible – and to make sure other road users could see them. If it was clear, Joe even drove into the oncoming lane when approaching left-hand bends to maximise his view of the road ahead.

When on an emergency call, the rules for police drivers are different. Joe knew he could treat red traffic lights as 'Give Way' signs, slowing down but not necessarily stopping, and overtaking any backed-up traffic queues.

It took them around four minutes to reach the park, but now Joe had a choice. The lake was set into the side of the hill, with pathways all around, but there was road parking on two sides only. If Joe parked on the wrong side, he would have a long way to run on foot to reach the victim.

Jenna had mentioned that some callers had described the man as drunk. Remembering there was a pub, the Dam House, on the far side of the reservoir, he decided to head that way.

The pub car park was at the far end of a cul-de-sac leading to the reservoir. Because of the hilly terrain, it was considerably higher than the water level, and as he pulled into the car park Joe could see right across the lake.

'Damn, it's all happening on the other side,' he said to

Jenna. He jumped out of the car and ran down the steps towards the water.

As he reached the pathway around the reservoir, Joe could see someone standing in the lake. As he got closer, it became clear that there were actually two people in the water: the standing man was holding another body, at about waist height, and that person looked to be in a bad way. Bizarrely, there were two anglers on the nearer bank who seemed to be oblivious to what was happening and were nonchalantly continuing to fish!

Joe sprinted along the path around the edge of the lake, with Jenna following behind. He could see a few members of the public standing at the side of the lake; one was trying to throw in a lifebelt.

The focus of Joe's attention was now the two men in the lake. It didn't look good. The man who was standing up was clearly drunk and unable to hold the other man's head above the water. This was making him panic and making the whole situation worse.

As he ran around the last corner, Joe began pulling off his stab vest. He kicked off his boots at the edge of the lake and jumped in. The water was only shin deep at the edge, but as he waded towards the men fifteen yards away, the water deepened quickly.

By the time he reached them, it was up to his chest. The water was cold, but in the heat of the moment Joe wasn't aware of it. Beneath his feet, the silty mud of the reservoir bed was interspersed with cold, slimy rocks. It was slippery, and Joe fought to keep his balance.

'Joe's gone in!' Behind him, Joe heard Jenna reporting in to control. A voice ordered him to get out. Joe wasn't sure if it was one of the onlookers on the bank or an instruction via the radio, but he ignored it. Police training tells officers they should not themselves become casualties of a situation, but Joe knew he was the only person there who could possibly save the man – and in his mind he had no choice.

As he reached the two men, Joe tried to take the unconscious man and raise him across his shoulder in a fireman's lift, but the victim's waterlogged clothes made him so heavy that he could only just lift him above the water line. Slowly he carried the man back towards the shore, taking care not to trip or slip.

Jenna was waiting on the bank, having also removed her stab vest. As she reached down, Joe tried to push the man up out of the water and onto the bank, a couple of feet above the water level. But he was too heavy, and they struggled to raise him up.

'Can any of you lot come and help us?' Joe shouted at the bystanders, feeling exasperated that none had stepped forward to assist, and he grabbed one young man – probably a student – and pulled him into the water. Between them they managed to lift the victim out of the lake and lay him down flat on the path at the side.

As Joe climbed from the water, Jenna began checking for signs of life. There were none, so she unwrapped her vent-aid and immediately gave two rescue breaths. Joe then went into the CPR cycle of chest compressions.

The accepted technique was for thirty compressions, followed by two breaths, and repeat. To time his compressions, Joe used a popular children's song, pressing down rhythmically while under his breath he sang, *'NELL-ie the ELE-phant PACK-ed her TRUNK and SAID Good-BYE to the CIR-CUS, OFF she WENT with a TRUMP-ety TRUMP, TRUMP, TRUMP, TRUMP ...'*

It was clear that the man was in a bad way. His face was grey, and his mouth reminded Joe of a well full of water. Each time he did a chest compression water and vomit came out. Jenna's vent-aid ripped and some sick went in her mouth. They also had to remove the victim's false teeth, as they had become dislodged and were a choking hazard.

But this only made Jenna's job worse; with no teeth at the front, his mouth collapsed a little, and she found it almost impossible to make a seal. Nonetheless, as the minutes ticked by the pair continued their CPR efforts.

Soon after, Joe and Jenna heard sirens as other emergency vehicles arrived. Next on the scene were the fire brigade, and Joe felt a strong hand on his back.

'I'll take over now, mate. Don't worry,' said one of the firemen, and Joe sighed in relief.

Administering CPR is tiring, and Joe was glad of the help. He moved away and sat on a nearby bench. Only now, as the adrenaline began to drain away, did he realise how cold and wet he was. Someone handed him a silver thermal blanket, and he was glad to wrap it around himself.

An ambulance had arrived by now, and the paramedics took over. As they stretchered away the victim, they told Joe that there was a faint pulse, and congratulated the two officers on saving the man's life.

As Joe sat there, soaking wet, his sergeant and another colleague arrived, and they drove Joe home to get showered and changed before returning to duty.

A short time later, he and Jenna learned that the man had died. It was, thought Joe, a sad end to a sad life.

In an ironic twist, early the next morning Joe and the rest of the night team were called back to the reservoir after nearby residents reported that there were more people in the lake.

It was just getting light as the officers arrived to find a dozen or so students playing around in the lake following a summer party at the nearby university. Joe and his colleagues told them to get out, and warned them of the dangers that had been demonstrated so tragically just a few hours earlier. Most understood quickly, but some refused to come out until they were warned that if they did not they would be locked up for being drunk and disorderly.

Joe sighed. Sometimes he almost felt as though he ought to arrest people for being stupid.

The victim was fifty-three-year-old Lewis Rose, a street drinker and father of eight who had apparently gone into the lake because he thought his mobile phone was in there. He had died soon after arriving at hospital. The coroner recorded a verdict of accidental death.

In recognition of their efforts in managing to revive Mr Rose until the ambulance arrived, Joe and Jenna received awards from the Royal Humane Society.

At the ceremony was Joe's proud father, Nick. Looking around the room, at all the faces of those being honoured, an idea began to take shape in his mind . . .

A NOTE ON HONOURS

For awards purposes, police officers are normally considered to be civilians. National civilian honours that can be awarded are:

The George Cross

The George Cross is the highest civilian honour, and is awarded only for acts of the greatest heroism or of the most conspicuous courage in circumstances of extreme danger.

It is a silver cross on a dark blue ribbon, and the recipient may use the post-nominal letters GC.

It was instituted during the Second World War to honour the many acts of bravery during the Blitz. There have been just over 400 awarded – most posthumously.

The George Medal

The George Medal is the second highest honour and is awarded for acts of great bravery.

It is a silver disc on a ribbon of red and blue vertical stripes, and the recipient may use the post-nominal letters GM.

It was instituted at the same time as the George Cross.

The Queen's Gallantry Medal

The Queen's Gallantry Medal is the third ranked award and is awarded for exemplary acts of bravery.

It is a silver disc on a ribbon of pale blue, grey and red, and the recipient may use the post-nominal letters QGM.

It was created in 1974 to rationalise and unify a number of other honours previously awarded.

The Queen's Commendation for Bravery

The Queen's Commendation for Bravery is awarded for acts risking life and meriting national recognition.

It is represented by a silver spray of laurel leaves. There is no ribbon, and the recipient may not use post-nominal letters.

Every year, police officers suffer injuries on duty that have a huge impact on their life; in some cases their injuries prevent them from being able to work and support their families. Tragically, some officers lose their lives in the line of duty and for their loved ones life changes in an instant.

The Police Dependants' Trust provides financial support to help ease some of the pressures police families face when an officer has been killed or injured on duty.

Thank you for buying this book; in doing so you have helped to support our work. If you would like to make a further donation or want to find out how you can fundraise for us, please visit our website: www.pdtrust.org